THE ONE THAT GOT AWAY

THE ONE THAT GOT AWAY

KENDAL BURT & JAMES LEASOR

PEN & SWORD MILITARY CLASSICS

First published in Great Britain in 1956 by Collins with Michael Joseph

Published in this format in 2006 by
Pen & Sword Military Classics
An imprint of
Pen & Sword Books Ltd
47 Church Street
Barnsley
South Yorkshire
S70 2AS

ISBN 1 84415 437 8
ISBN 978 1 84415 437 1

A CIP catalogue record for this book is
available from the British Library.

Printed and bound in England
By CPI UK

Pen & Sword Books Ltd incorporates the Imprints of
Pen & Sword Aviation, Pen & Sword Maritime, Pen & Sword Military,
Wharncliffe Local history, Pen & Sword Select,
Pen & Sword Military Classics and Leo Cooper.

For a complete list of Pen & Sword titles please contact
PEN & SWORD BOOKS LIMITED
47 Church Street, Barnsley, South Yorkshire, S70 2AS, England
E-mail: enquiries@pen-and-sword.co.uk
Website: www.pen-and-sword.co.uk

ACKNOWLEDGMENTS

On his return to Germany, Franz von Werra dictated an account of his adventures as a prisoner-of-war. It was never published, for reasons that we explain, and as far as we know, only one complete copy of the typescript survived the war. We found it and obtained permission to make full use of it for the present work. We acknowledge our indebtedness to it, for it is the unique key to von Werra's mind and character. However, his interpretation of events was subjective; by the time the manuscript came into our possession, we had already obtained the British side of the story through contacting most of the people concerned in it, and we have preferred to use their more objective, if less colourful, reminiscences in this book. The help they have given us will be apparent to the reader, and we thank them for the generous way they revealed the part they played, sometimes unwittingly, in the adventures of Franz von Werra. We also gratefully acknowledge the less obvious but not less invaluable help we have received from numerous individuals, libraries and agencies; the Historical Branch of the Air Ministry, particularly its head, Mr. J. C. Nerney, and Mr. L. A. Jackets, Head of the Foreign Documents Section, for their interest and encouragement; the Police, to the detailed nature of whose records we pay a special tribute; the Rolls-Royce Company; the B.B.C. Monitoring Service, and specialist libraries extending from Washington to Vienna.

Except for the Chief of the R.A.F. Interrogation Centre, whose name, " Squadron Leader Hawkes ", and physical description are for obvious reasons fictitious, all the characters in this book appear under their real names, or ranks, or the nicknames by which they were known to German prisoners.

K.B. & J.L.

CONTENTS

CONTENTS

ILLUSTRATIONS

LIST OF MAPS

CHAPTER I

A German Fighter Ace is Captured

The German High Command reckoned that the Luftwaffe would be able to wipe out R.A.F. Fighter Command in the South of England in four days. The task of destroying the R.A.F. entirely, which was regarded as an essential preliminary to the invasion of Britain, was to be fulfilled in four weeks.

On 13 August 1940, known as Adler Tag (*Eagle Day*), *the Luftwaffe launched an all-out offensive against the R.A.F. and the British aircraft industry in Southern England.*

Nearly a month later the Luftwaffe was still struggling to accomplish the first part of its task, which had been scheduled for completion in four days.

The great blitz on London's dockland marked the opening of a new phase in the Battle of Britain: instead of continuing to concentrate on destroying the Royal Air Force, the Luftwaffe switched to mass attacks on London.

But on Thursday, 5 September 1940, two days before the opening of the new phase, inland fighter aerodromes were still being hammered in the last, desperate efforts to smash British air defences.

September 5th was another of the hot, calm and almost cloudless days that provided a backcloth to the drama being staged over the fields of Southern England. At one moment the glorious weather made the life-and-death struggle seem utterly unreal; at the next its very incongruity heightened the dramatic effect. It was impossible to watch the handfuls of Hurricanes and Spitfires climb into the sky to meet the massed formations of enemy aircraft, without feeling a catch at the heart.

It was days like this that gave birth to the expression " real Battle of Britain weather ". The countryside shimmered under an almost liquid haze. Seen from a distance, fields of bleached corn stubble looked like pools of quicksilver.

On the farms of Kent, over which the main engagements of the Battle of Britain were being fought, hop-picking was now well under way, and a start had been made on gathering the main crops of hard fruit.

Despite the battles raging overhead from time to time, families from London's East End worked with their usual cheerfulness and dexterity at stripping the hop vines. Thousands of spent bullets and cannon shell cases were scattered over the fields, giving rise to stories that hop-pickers were being machine-gunned. The children of the East End families collected these cases to take home as souvenirs. Two days later, while they worked and jested in the fields, the homes of hundreds of them were destroyed in the blitz on dockland.

On the morning of September 5th, the Luftwaffe launched an attack on Biggin Hill aerodrome. This was preceded by a feint against Croydon. Its object was to entice British fighters away from Biggin Hill and to give Fighter Command the impression that the whole weight of the German attack was to fall on Croydon aerodrome.

The ruse failed. The R.A.F. stayed its hand until German intentions became clear. Then No. 79 Squadron set upon the main force of bombers as it was going in to attack Biggin Hill, and on this occasion most of the bombs fell wide of the aerodrome.

The formation of bombers that had raided Croydon was on its way home across Kent. Six thousand feet above them weaved their escort, thirty Messerschmitt 109's of No. 2 *Gruppe*, Third Fighter *Geschwader*.

Flying at the head of the Second *Gruppe* was its *Kommandeur*, Hauptmann Erich von Selle. Immediately behind him, to the left and right, flew his two staff officers, Leutnant Heinrich Sanneman, Technical Officer, and Oberleutnant Franz von Werra, Adjutant.

Five minutes after leaving Croydon, the "Tail End Charlie" called urgently over the R/T.

"*Achtung! Achtung!* Four to six Tommies above and behind, coming in to attack!"

The voice of the Commander broke in:

"Stella Leader to everybody. Keep formation! Wait!"

"Stella" was the radio code call-sign of the *Gruppe* for this operation.

As von Selle spoke, three Spitfires, diving almost vertically, flashed ahead of the formation, crashing through the top fighter screen to attack the bombers below.

He spoke again.

"Stella Leader to Fifth and Sixth *Staffeln*. Stay put and watch out! Fourth—attack! Tally-ho."

As the Commander dived to port, the others following, a stream of bullets hit the Adjutant's machine. Three other Spitfires, covering their comrades diving to attack the bombers, had pounced out of the sun.

Three against thirty.

The bullets were probably intended for the Commander in the leading Messerschmitt, but by chance he put its nose down just in time, and von Werra, turning and following, received the burst. His aircraft shuddered. He rolled to starboard away from his comrades and dived steeply. Then he levelled off, glancing behind. The Spitfire was on his tail. He went into a tight defensive turn, hoping to out-turn the British fighter and get it into his gunsight.

His earphones had gone dead. He flicked the transmitting switch. There was no responding click and crackle in his phones. The radio was out of action.

As though gradually, although all this happened in a few seconds, he became aware that the note of his engine had changed. It was no longer "sweet", but off-key. He glanced at the instrument panel, then, eyeing the Spitfire, gingerly opened the throttle a little. The engine responded sluggishly. It was overheating and beginning to labour.

A moment later it spluttered, picked up, spluttered again. Von Werra lost height rapidly. He was completely cut off from his formation. He spiralled down in defensive turns. The Spitfire "sat" on his tail, now and again firing a short burst.

Shortly after ten o'clock, Mr. Donald A. Fairman, a school-master, was standing near the back door of his cottage at Curtisden Green, in the heart of the orchard and hop country south of Maidstone, smoking a cigarette and contemplating his chrysanthemums. He was far from satisfied with their progress and was giving the matter serious thought.

The real trouble was that one could no longer get the proper plant-foods, nor spend much time in the garden, owing to the war.

" Blast the Germans ! "

This thought recalled to him the noise of distant air battles—a noise to which he had grown accustomed in the past few weeks. He looked up.

Behind the trees to the north, heavy anti-aircraft batteries along the Thames were putting up a terrific barrage. With all the noise in the sky it was frustrating not to be able to make out what was happening. Then his eye caught the silver flash of sunlight on weaving fighters. As he watched, his eyes focused unexpectedly on the ghostly outline of a bomber ; the haze and the pale blue background made it appear transparent. Then he saw another bomber close to the first, and then another. Three . . . six . . . nine . . . twelve . . .

Suddenly, above the pulsating drone of the engines came the rising howl of diving fighters, followed by bursts of cannon and machine-gun fire. Confused dog-fights developed all over Mr. Fairman's personal patch of sky. As the formation passed overhead he saw two fast machines spiralling down, the leading one clearly in trouble. Its engine spluttered and banged, now and again leaving a puff of black smoke behind. When the following aircraft fired a short burst, the other waggled its wings violently. They came lower and lower and then passed out of view behind the trees. A plane suddenly skimmed over the trees round the garden, the engine making a series of bangs. In the split second it was overhead, Mr. Fairman clearly saw a black and white cross on the fuselage and a swastika on the fin. As it disappeared he heard a long burst of machine-gun fire, which he identified as coming from a search-light battery just down the road on Mannington's Farm. A moment later there was a loud bump, followed by a tearing sound, and Mr. Fairman knew that the plane had crashed only a few hundred yards away, probably on one of the big fields on the east side of Winchet Hill. He hurried into the house and changed into his Home Guard uniform.

His car was parked outside the cottage, but petrol was rationed and scarce. He had a nice sense of values. He slung his rifle over his shoulder and set off on a bicycle. However, by the time he arrived at the scene of the crash, the pilot, Oberleutnant Franz von

Werra, who was uninjured, had already been taken prisoner by members of the searchlight battery.

The stories von Werra told later of how he was shot down varied widely, and all of them differed from the foregoing account based on official records and the testimony of eye-witnesses. Sometimes he is quoted as claiming to have shot down three British planes that morning (*The Times*, 27. 1. 41.) before " colliding with another Messerschmitt and being forced down " (*New York Herald Tribune*, 25. 1. 41.). To the New York correspondent of the *Daily Express* he claimed to have destroyed only the fighter that attacked him. But he was consistent on some points: he always maintained that his Messerschmitt caught fire when it crashed, and was burned out, he himself being miraculously thrown clear of the wreckage and knocked unconscious.

He also told various tales about the manner of his arrest after crashing, without, apparently, ever remembering the right one. He usually said that members of the Home Guard with old-fashioned shotguns advanced upon him in the field from several directions. Some would creep forward cautiously while others knelt down and drew a bead on him. Then those kneeling down would get up and advance a few paces while the others covered him. Finally, he said, they all rushed at him. The German aviation magazine *Der Adler*, in an article dealing with von Werra's exploits illustrated by an " artist's impressions ", shows him being led away from the burning Messerschmitt by two sour-looking Tommies in full battle order, including steel helmets and fixed bayonets.

The truth of the matter was that von Werra was captured by the hatless, collarless, shirt-sleeved and unarmed cook of the searchlight battery, who dashed out of the cookhouse as soon as the plane crashed and was first on the scene.

As the illustration of the crashed plane shows, it was untouched by fire.

The actual crash was witnessed by several men loading boxes of fruit on to a lorry in the yard of Love's Farm. They had been startled out of their workaday unconcern by a long burst of Lewis-gun fire from the nearby searchlight battery. Then a plane just cleared the trees on Winchet Hill and swooped over the farm buildings in a right-hand turn. It disappeared momentarily behind the orchard a little higher up on the other side of the road, and came into view again just as it was about to land, its wheels retracted, in a field a quarter of a mile away. It bounced off the ground a few feet, then ploughed up the stubble for thirty yards or so before coming to rest in a cloud of dust.

For a few tense seconds nothing happened. Then the hinged hood of the cockpit opened and the head and shoulders of the pilot appeared. He pulled off his leather helmet and looked around him slowly, then hoisted himself out of the cockpit and jumped off a wing on to the ground.

He stood looking at the aircraft. Meanwhile soldiers from the searchlight battery were hurrying across the long fields in ones and twos.

As soon as he noticed the soldiers entering the field, the pilot seemed to pull himself together, and looked quickly in every direction, as though he were about to run away. If that was his idea, he thought the better of it. Instead, he took some papers from the breast pockets of his uniform jacket, replaced something or other, then squatted down. The men by the lorry saw a flicker of flame and a wisp of smoke on the ground in front of him. The leading soldier evidently thought the German was trying to set fire to the aircraft, for he shouted and started running. The pilot glanced up and unfolded the papers to make them burn more quickly. They were effectively destroyed.

The first to reach him was the unarmed cook. Hard on his heels came several of his fellow gunners, carrying rifles. Von Werra was thoroughly searched. Everything found in his pockets, together with his identity disc and wrist watch, was placed in his helmet and carried by one of the soldiers. Two men were detailed to guard the aircraft, and the remainder of the party set off across the field in the direction of the searchlight battery. The prisoner walked a few paces ahead, covered by the soldiers' rifles. He walked slowly, with studied nonchalance, one hand in his trouser pocket. No attempt was made to hurry him.

They passed from the field on to a path through an orchard. At the first low bough he came to the prisoner shot up one hand and grabbed an apple. He took a great bite out of it without a backward glance. The soldiers looked at one another but said nothing. Von Werra was about to reach up at the next low bough, but this time the muzzle of a rifle was jabbed in the small of his back.

" Keep moving! "

He moved slowly, munching thoughtfully.

High above, he could hear the Heinkels, Dorniers and Junkers flying home with their Me. escorts. In little more than half an hour the pilots would be pulling off their helmets, lighting cigarettes, and strolling towards the huts and tents on the advanced airfields in the Pas de Calais.

While he, Franz von Werra, was being led along a cinder track towards the huts of a British searchlight battery. It was absurd.

The searchlight men were very pleased with themselves for they thought that it was their Lewis gun that had shot down the Messerschmitt. They were even more gratified when they saw the thirteen notches painted below the swastika on the fin of the plane, for they obviously represented victories claimed by the pilot.

There were free rounds in the Woolsack Inn at the top of Winchet Hill that night, and the next issues of local papers gave the searchlight men credit for having brought down " a leading Nazi fighter ace ".

In both respects, the newspapers were quite wrong.

In contrast to von Werra's stories, the combat report of the Spitfire pilot who shot him down was brief and to the point. He simply said he attacked a formation of enemy fighters and fired a good burst from 48 degrees astern into one Messerschmitt, which then rolled over and crashed near Maidstone.

He was Flight Lieutenant John Terrence Webster, of No. 41 Squadron, based at Hornchurch. He had just been awarded the D.F.C. for gallantry in leading his flight during the Dunkirk operations and in the intensive air fighting over the English Channel. At the time of the award he had personally destroyed seven enemy aircraft and assisted in the destruction of two others. That score had been doubled during the next two weeks of the Battle of Britain.

After shooting down von Werra on the morning of 5 September, Flight Lieutenant Webster went into action again in the afternoon and was killed.

Von Werra was taken under armed escort by Army vehicle to

Headquarters, Kent County Constabulary, Maidstone. Pending the arrival of an R.A.F. field interrogation officer, he was placed in a cell under the charge of Police Sergeant W. Harrington.

Sergeant Harrington's house adjoined Headquarters and his wife was responsible for feeding German prisoners passing through the station. Sometimes there were as many as a dozen Nazi airmen to be catered for at a time. This presented Mrs. Harrington with a difficult problem, what with rationing and the fact that the official allowance per head for prisoners' meals was very small. Despite the difficulties, she made it a point of honour to give the Germans at least one good meal while they were at Headquarters; she felt it would show them that the British were neither half-starved nor inhuman, and provide a little object lesson on the duplicity of German propaganda.

Sergeant Harrington, who has since retired from the Force to become landlord of a public house in Whitstable, remembers von Werra well.

"I saw hundreds of German airmen during those days," he says. "Some were tough and arrogant, others completely deflated by the shock of being taken prisoner. Von Werra was neither one thing nor the other. He was quiet, polite and correct and very much master of himself. He spoke English quite well.

"He struck me as being a bit conceited, though. When I asked him his rank he clicked his heels together and said he was an Oberleutnant and a Baron. As though to prove he was an aristocrat, he showed me the big signet ring he was wearing, bearing some sort of crest and a coronet. He also said he was of Swiss origin, and that his father had owned several castles in Switzerland.

"He told me the German Air Force was having a wonderful time in France, and said with a laugh that the R.A.F. had prevented him from keeping an important dinner engagement that night.

"Von Werra impressed me more than most of the other Germans I saw. He was confident, alert and highly intelligent. I was glad he would not be my responsibility for long. I wasn't surprised when I heard several months later that he had escaped and got back to Germany."

Sergeant Harrington's son was then eleven years old and a keen collector of autographs. When he learned that a German fighter ace was in the cells, he made his way unobtrusively into Head-quarters on the pretext of taking a message to his father. He found von Werra's cell and handed him an autograph book and a pen through the bars, making signs that he should write his name in it. The entry (reproduced facing page 17) was made in the comedians' section of the book : on adjacent pages are the signatures of Tommy Handley and Tommy Trinder.

Although von Werra had talked freely to Sergeant Harrington he refused to give any information other than his name, rank and number to the R.A.F. interrogation officer. That evening he was handed over to the Army and taken to Maidstone Barracks, where he spent the night in a detention cell.

The next morning an officer and two armed guards called for him and he was bundled into the back of an Army truck. It had a canvas hood, but the back was open and he was also able to look out ahead through the windshield.

He had recovered quickly from the initial shock of being taken prisoner. His morale had been only temporarily affected and was now high. But the ride from Maidstone to London did much to undermine his confidence. Neither the guards nor the driver spoke a word the whole way, and the officer, sitting in front, gave only one or two expressionless orders regarding direction.

Von Werra smiled at each of the guards in turn, but they looked straight through him. He would have felt better if they had betrayed hostility. Their aloofness was unnerving.

He was curious, even apprehensive, about where he was being taken and what was going to happen to him, but he sensed that it was useless to ask and that his question would be taken as a sign of weakness. So he held his tongue and tried to appear as dignified and unconcerned as the swaying and bumping of the truck would allow. He concentrated on the road, looking either ahead or behind, trying to guess the direction and watching for traces of bomb damage.

All signposts seemed to have been removed and milestones had been painted over or otherwise obliterated. Tall, stout poles had been erected in rows on open fields as anti-glider obstructions. There were also anti-tank ditches stretching away into the distance. At nearly every bend of the road there were camouflaged pill-boxes, and what at first sight appeared to be a derelict roadside café proved at a second glance to be a concrete block-house. The truck was frequently held up and checked by soldiers or police at road blocks and bridges.

Von Werra had made about ten operational flights over England before he was shot down, and he had seen the anti-tank ditches from the air. But the extent and thoroughness of British anti-invasion measures were a revelation to him. Camouflage netting was strung up on poles along hundreds of yards of the concrete road at one point. On the grass verges below the netting was an unbroken line of heavy tanks, armoured cars and Bren-gun carriers.

They passed a small airfield. It seemed to be untouched by bombing, but in one corner there was a huge heap of wrecked German aircraft. They passed through several large towns but von Werra saw scarcely a trace of bomb damage.

They were entering London now. Von Werra was surprised and disappointed to find the shop windows full of goods. Perhaps they were all dummies. He was tremendously impressed by the piles of colonial fruits in greengrocers' shops—oranges, grapefruit, bananas and pineapples. (It was not until the following year that imported fruits disappeared from the shops.) The pineapples, a luxury in Germany at the best of times, impressed him almost as much as the anti-invasion measures. Occasionally, when the truck slowed down, he was recognised by children. They shouted and whistled and gave him exaggerated Nazi salutes. The guards took no notice.

Eventually they came to a large park and drove through a gateway into a quiet, tree-lined, private road. The truck turned into the gateway of the second house on the left. Two Military Policemen were on guard on either side of the gate. The gate itself was surmounted by strands of barbed wire, and there were black, billowing coils of it rising twelve feet high above the garden walls.

The Military Police saluted smartly. One examined the officer's pass, the other looked into the truck. The M.P.s saluted again and the truck moved forward as they opened the gate, which closed as soon as it had passed through. The process was like clockwork. Not a second or a movement wasted.

The truck stopped in front of a drab, unfriendly-looking house. The guards dropped the tailboard.

" *Aussteigen !* " (" Get out ! ") commanded the officer.

Oberleutnant Franz von Werra had arrived at London District Prisoner-of-war Cage.[1]   And, as had perhaps been intended, he arrived in a chastened frame of mind.

The serious part of his interrogation was about to begin.

[1]In Kensington Palace Gardens

CHAPTER II

Interrogation in the London "Cage"

At that stage of the war nearly all Germans thought that total victory was not only assured, but at hand.

It was symptomatic of the optimism and success-mentality obtaining at the outset of the Battle of Britain that the Supreme Command of the Luftwaffe did not envisage large numbers of their airmen being killed or captured in the offensive against Britain. However, losses proved to be high from the beginning and mounted steadily as the offensive gathered momentum. The Luftwaffe showed acute sensitivity to the large proportion of aircrew who failed to return. Such casualty lists as were published in the German press in those days not only gave an entirely false picture of the extent of the losses, but failed to mention the names of men who had been captured. Perhaps Goering felt that live prisoners made more of a mockery of his boasts than dead heroes.

The fact is that security briefing was negligible. The Luftwaffe may have thought it would be bad for morale to draw the attention of aircrew to the possibility of capture. They may have thought it superfluous, since it was taken for granted that captives would soon be liberated.

The blind confidence and optimism with which the Luftwaffe began the Battle of Britain had many repercussions. Not the least of these was on British Intelligence: owing to the inadequacy of their security training, captured German airmen were often found to be carrying all manner of secret documents—maps, strength returns, target material, orders relating to attacks, and tactics, technical data, etc.—in addition to personal papers—diaries, address books, letters, photographs and bills. Just how important such material was to British Intelligence may be judged from the fact that it was sometimes possible to deduce, for example, the location of a particular Luftwaffe unit from a tattered bus ticket, or half a cinema ticket, bearing the name of a town, or a crumpled, forgotten receipt slip from a shop, found in the corner of a prisoner's pocket. And such was the arrogant confidence of the majority of the airmen captured that, unlike von Werra, they made no attempt to destroy secret and personal papers immediately they landed. The average German prisoner's attitude seemed to be that the odd bits of paper he happened to be carrying when captured would not enable the British to win the war, which would be over in a few weeks anyway, so why worry?

Von Werra was ushered into a small office off the vestibule and handed a form printed in English and German to fill in. Like a guest at a hotel, he thought wryly. He read the form carefully and filled in his name, rank and number. The other spaces, requiring information such as his home address, his unit and Army Post Office numbers and the nature of his mission when captured, he left blank. He wondered how many of the dimmer wits of the Luftwaffe fell for this simple trick to obtain information from the unsuspecting.

Meanwhile, the officer who had brought him from Maidstone handed two sealed, buff envelopes to the M.P. sergeant on duty. One of them was bulky, and von Werra guessed it contained his personal possessions. The other envelope, he thought, probably contained reports from the police and from Maidstone Barracks.

The officer obtained receipts for the two envelopes and for von Werra's "body", and then left with the two guards from Maidstone.

The prisoner returned the form to the sergeant who glanced at it, then handed it back.

"That's no good," he said. "You speak English?"

"Yes."

"Well, fill the form in properly, then. You left half the spaces blank."

"I know. It is not permitted that I write more."

The sergeant glanced at him, then turned to two soldiers who were standing by to act as escort, and said crisply:

"Take him to Number Thirteen."

Von Werra was taken up two flights of steps and along several corridors. There were Military Police everywhere, erect, motionless, expressionless, all Blanco and shining brass buttons.

The party halted at a door numbered " 13 ". The leading guard unlocked it and the prisoner entered. The lock clicked behind him. He stood listening. Only one pair of footsteps receded down the corridor : one guard had remained outside the door.

The room was fairly large, dimly lit by a small, closed window. A threadbare rug, a deal table, one chair. An unshaded, fly-spotted light bulb hanging from the centre of the cracked, grey, stuccoed ceiling. And that was all, apart from stuffiness and the dry, resinous smell of old timber.

Von Werra's mind seethed with questions :

" What happens next ? What do they want from me ? When am I going to meet other prisoners ? When am I going to be sent to a permanent prisoner-of-war camp ? "

He racked his brains trying to remember what had been said at the one security lecture that had been given to his unit just before *Adler Tag*. It had been delivered by the unit intelligence officer in a half-hearted manner, almost apologetically—" a routine matter, gentlemen : the British are unlikely to take many prisoners ! "

Von Werra had remembered that a prisoner could not be compelled to reveal more than his name, rank and number ; now he recalled vaguely that prisoners were paid according to their rank, that officers were not made to work, and that the maximum punishment that could be inflicted for attempting to escape was thirty days' solitary confinement. The only thing he remembered that seemed to have any bearing on his present position was that permanent prisoner-of-war camps were supposed to be situated in areas remote from fighting zones. Since London was a target area, this place must be a transit camp. This seemed to be borne out by its small size and the large number of guards. But why so many guards—not ordinary soldiers but Military Police ? And why had he been turned over to the Army and not to the R.A.F. ?

There had been stories of German prisoners being maltreated, tortured even, by the British. Supposing they were true ? Supposing, because of the bombing, Britain no longer honoured the Geneva Convention. Supposing he had been brought here for trial. *That* would explain the presence of all the Military Police and the fact that he was in the Army's hands.

His comrades did not know what happened to him when he

was shot down. Since he had been captured he had not seen another German prisoner. If the British chose to pretend he had been killed in the crash, who was there to disprove it?

He suddenly felt very alone. Out of the window beyond the coils of barbed wire on top of the wall, he could see a woman pushing a pram. She was leaning forward over the handle, smiling and shaking some sort of toy.

If only he had someone to talk to. He thought of the airfield on the cliff top in the Pas de Calais. The pilots would be sitting in deck chairs, sun-bathing, while ground crew in their black denims serviced the Messerschmitts. Simba, von Werra's pet lion cub, famous now in the Luftwaffe, thanks to the pictures in newspapers and magazines, would be padding from one chair to the next. Sanni, the technical officer, his great friend, would wind up the gramophone and play that tango for the tenth time.

Oberleutnant von Werra and Leutnant Sanneman. They had been known as Max and Moritz, the Clowns of Lützow's Flying Circus.

Well, there was one good thing about his having been taken prisoner: it was certain that the court-martial proceedings against Max and Moritz would now be dropped. During the lull between the fall of France and the beginning of the Battle of Britain, they had once spent a mildly diverting afternoon in their Me.'s buzzing cars along the main roads in the Pas de Calais. Just as the sport was beginning to pall, they came upon a solitary German staff car. It was just the thing to pep up the proceedings. They subjected the car to one mock low-level attack after another. The Colonel riding in the back had been most alarmed and annoyed. He had made a note of the Messerschmitt's markings and forwarded a lengthy report to the proper authorities.

Von Werra remembered the kit and personal possessions he had left lying about in the tent he shared with Sanni. The thought of the packets of cigarettes, the pipes and the tobacco haunted him. What wouldn't he give for a smoke . . . Then there was the just-opened bottle of Cognac. A stiff peg of that wouldn't come amiss just now.

No more jawing over an illicit nightcap after lights-out. No more going to sleep with the smell of trampled grass and water-proofed canvas in his nostrils, and the distant swish of the sea on the sand in his ears.

His reverie was interrupted by the sight of some words scratched on the paint of the window ledge. Bending closer he read :

IHR WERDET LACHEN, TOMMIES, ABER DEN KRIEG VERLIERT IHR DOCH !—Leutnant Manhard. (You can laugh, Tommies, but still you'll lose the war !)

Below, an Oberleutnant Müller had added his signature to the inscription.

His spirits rose at once. It was not for nothing that his friends called him *Sonny*, used in the sense of the English nickname *Sunny Jim*.[1] He was an extrovert ; he liked always to be surrounded by people, whether friends or strangers, whom he could impress and dominate. He required an audience.

Other German prisoners had passed this way. It was comforting to note from the way Manhard's message was worded that he, too, had been depressed when he occupied the room. But no doubt he had survived. Perhaps he had already been sent to a permanent prisoner-of-war camp and was even now planning to escape. . . .

Escape ! The more he thought about it, the more the idea excited him. He began to pace the room. This need not mean the end of his war, but a second beginning. A fight with wits rather than with weapons, but nevertheless a fight.

Until a few weeks previously, von Werra had shared the belief that Britain would be defeated and the war in the West concluded by the beginning of the winter. He no longer thought this likely. In contrast to the previous German campaigns, the assault on Britain had not proved to be a walk-over. The high technical standards, the fighting qualities and the flexibility revealed by the R.A.F. when the Luftwaffe came to close grips with it, had been a most unpleasant surprise. In the few weeks since *Adler Tag*, No. 3 Fighter *Geschwader* alone had lost nearly fifteen pilots, killed or captured, among them many of the Old Guard, like von Werra, who had been with it since its formation at Bernberg in 1939.

Von Werra had also witnessed the rout of the Junkers 87 Stukas (dive-bombers) over England. Acclaimed as the wonder planes of the Luftwaffe, hitherto they had had things all their own way and had been highly effective. But within a few weeks in operations

---

[1] He made the same impression on members of the British public whom he encountered later. He is variously described as " perky ", " cheeky ", " cheerful in spite of everything ", and " a delightful personality with a twinkle in his eye."

over England, the Spitfires and Hurricanes had found the dive-bombers' vulnerable moments—when climbing after dive attacks—and had then proceeded to swat them out of the sky like flies. It had been found necessary to assign single-engined fighters to dive with the Stukas to protect them during their subsequent climb. Von Werra had been on missions of this kind and knew all about it.

No, whatever else the Englishman might be, he was not effete. Britain showed no signs of going to pieces as France had done.

Von Werra thought about the invasion of Britain. It might well prove a difficult and costly undertaking.[1] He had been impressed and discouraged by what he had seen in England since he had been captured. The war might not end this year. It might not be possible to launch the invasion until next spring or summer.

There was a shout up the stairs. The guard outside the door replied. The lock clicked, the door opened and the guard called :
" Come with me, Mister Werra ! "

In the twenty-four hours since he had left Maidstone Police Station, von Werra had spoken scarcely half a dozen sentences.

There was nothing fortuitous about his isolation. It was deliberate. It formed part of a carefully contrived plan applied to all newly-captured German airmen. Von Werra, of course, had not the slightest suspicion that such a plan existed.

If his tongue had been still, his mind had been feverishly active. He had been stewing in his own juice. He had thought himself into, then out of, one bout of depression after another. The more he mused and the longer he waited, the more his loneliness, exasperation and apprehension had increased. His desire to talk and to hear other human voices had become urgent.

He was, in fact, like a fruit being ripened quickly by artificial means. He was being made ready for plucking. In the majority of cases the artificial ripening process was so effective, that at the appropriate moment a hand had only to be stretched out for the mature fruit to fall into it.

[1]The fact that von Werra wasted no time in attempting to escape tends to confirm that he was sceptical about being set free as a result of a successful invasion. On the other hand, the fact that the majority of Luftwaffe prisoners sat tight and waited confidently for the arrival of German troops would seem to be proved by the figures for attempted escapes : it was not until after the invasion of Russia, which ruled out the possibility of an early invasion of Britain, that escape activity developed on any appreciable scale at internment camps for war prisoners in the United Kingdom, Canada and Australia.

And the hand the fruit fell into was that of a British interrogator.

Von Werra entered the interrogator's office prepared for anything, but determined to stick to the name, rank and number formula. He was prepared for everything—except for what actually happened.

In the course of the long interview—with an Army officer—he was astonished not to be asked a single question that seemed in any way connected with secret military matters. After the apprehension of Room 13, the interrogation came as an anti-climax. He had expected to be asked all manner of questions on technical, tactical, supply, strength and other matters relating to the German Air Force. But the officer did not appear to have the slightest interest in these things. He did not seem to be aware of von Werra's status. He did not seem to realise that, if he had the mind to do so, the prisoner could disclose much vital information. Von Werra might have been any common German soldier or civilian the British had picked up.

The Englishman did not even ask von Werra what unit he belonged to and where it was based. He was friendly, sympathetic, anxious to know whether the prisoner had been properly treated, whether he needed medical attention. He immediately produced a packet of cigarettes and matches, and allowed von Werra to enjoy the first few long, soothing draws of smoke in silence.

As though to put the prisoner still more at his ease, after chatting for a minute the Englishman went to the door of the room, outside which the guard who had brought von Werra to the interview was now stationed.

" It's all right, corporal," the officer said. " You can go now. I'll ring for you later."

During the first part of the interview the officer did not sit at his desk, but moved about the room informally, now standing with one elbow on the mantelpiece and the other hand in his trouser pocket, now lolling against the desk, now leaning against the window ledge with his arms folded across his chest.

He wore a captain's " stars ". At a later stage of his captivity, comparing notes with other German prisoners, von Werra discovered that British interrogators changed their names, ranks and even uniforms to suit the particular prisoner being interviewed. But whatever changes were rung, the interrogator's rank was always one higher than that of the prisoner being interviewed.

The Captain was a dapper man with iron-grey hair, a veteran of the First World War. He was amiable, but his friendliness never appeared forced or excessive. It was tempered with a respectfulness that increased as the interview proceeded. He might have been von Werra's family doctor or solicitor. He spoke German fluently, with hardly a trace of accent, yet he somehow retained his essentially English identity and character : even if he had been dressed in German uniform he still would have been an Englishman. Now and again he fumbled for the right word or expression, and it was only natural that von Werra should help him out by supplying it. However, when the prisoner refrained from suggesting the desired word or expression, the Captain quickly thought of it of his own accord, or expressed himself equally clearly some other way. For, if the purpose of this interview was to be achieved, it was essential to make it absolutely clear to the prisoner, and subtly to remind him of the fact from time to time, that he was dealing with a true-blue Englishman. Had it appeared that the Captain might be a renegade German, the prisoner would have been ill at ease, resentful and would not have emerged from his shell.

The Captain never alluded to military matters. All he was interested in was politics, particularly von Werra's politics. What did he think about the origins of the war ? How had he reacted to the signing of the Russo-German Non-Aggression Pact ?

Von Werra felt on safe ground. There could be no possible objection to his answering such questions. In fact, they gave him a welcome opportunity to demonstrate his unshakable convictions and loyalties. He glibly gave the stock answers.

The Captain seemed visibly impressed by the replies. His interest appeared to quicken. He became confidential, almost conspiratorial. His attitude suggested that he ought not to be wasting time on such questions, but that he had a keen personal interest in Nazi politics, and having at last met someone capable of giving him clear, concise and knowledgeable replies to his doubts and queries, he was going to exploit the opportunity to the full, even to the extent of ignoring the questions he ought to ask.

In a very short time, von Werra's inner tension and defensive crispness completely vanished. He became relaxed, expansive, natural. How pleasant it was to be able to talk again and to watch the blue smoke curling upwards ! What an agreeable surprise to find an Englishman, especially under such circumstances, who was the antithesis of the *Engländer* of German propaganda! Neither effete nor snobbish, neither bullying nor insulting, neither stupid nor narrow-minded, but correct, friendly, almost deferential—a thoroughly decent sort. Except for his inquiry as to how the prisoner had been treated, the Captain made no allusion to their respective roles of captor and captive.

The subject of politics seemed to fascinate the Englishman. It was almost as though he secretly admired National Socialism and realised that Britain had little chance of winning the war. He posed question after question, seemingly groping for the truth.

Once, when the prisoner was in the middle of a lengthy explanation of the German claims to its former colonies, the Captain, who seemed absorbed, abruptly intervened:

" And since you come from that part of the world yourself, Oberleutnant, do you think the German-speaking part of Switzerland should be incorporated into the Reich ? "

The suddenness of the interruption, its unexpectedness, cut von Werra off in the middle of a sentence.

How in God's name did the Captain know he was of Swiss origin?

But the Englishman appeared not to notice the prisoner's discomfiture, or completely to misunderstand its cause. He smiled disarmingly:

" You look perplexed ! Sorry, I was being too clever by half : I thought perhaps from your intonation and some of the expressions you use that you had lived some time in Southern Germany, near the Swiss border. But perhaps you are Austrian ? . . . However, you were saying about Africa . . .? "

It was with relief, even eagerness, that von Werra resumed his explanation of German claims to its former colonies.

He had only one other bad moment, but it passed off as smoothly as the first.

The prisoner was smoking his third cigarette when the Captain fired a series of questions at him requiring simple " Yes " or " No " answers.

" I should like," he began, " to make sure that I have fully understood your viewpoint on the various matters we have been discussing. You say the Treaty of Versailles was grossly unfair to Germany ? "—" Yes."

" That she was right to rearm ? "—" Yes."

" That the reoccupation of the Rhineland was justified ? "—
" Yes."

" That the Austrians did not oppose the incorporation of their country into the Reich ? "—" Yes."

" That Hitler was right to help Franco ? "—" Yes."

" That the attack on Poland was justified ? "—" Yes."

" And the attack on the Low Countries and France ? "—
" Yes."

" That the attack on Britain is different ? "—" Yes, well, that is to say, it was fully justified of course, and there can be no doubt about the outcome, but from a military point of view it is a different kind of attack."

The Captain appeared to reflect, and von Werra continued :

" In any case, we had not previously discussed the attack on Britain, and I had not said that it *was* different."

The Englishman was unabashed.

" No ? My mistake, then. Now, I'm rather puzzled by National Socialist views on the role of women in Germany. Perhaps you would be good enough to explain them ? "

And so it went on. If the Captain had noticed that his question about the attack on Britain had caught von Werra on one foot, he certainly made no attempt to take advantage of it.

The Captain seemed gradually to lose heart. The last part of the interview dealt mainly with the morale of the German people. As von Werra boasted of their solidarity, their complete faith in Hitler, their eagerness to work and sacrifice for victory, the Captain looked more and more discouraged. Von Werra seemed to swell and the Captain to shrink.

At last the Englishman said :

" Well, Oberleutnant, we've had a most interesting talk. You've made a great many things clear to me." He pressed a bell-push on his desk, and stood up. He seemed slightly embarrassed, almost apologetic, because it was necessary for him to ring for an escort.

" Do have another cigarette before you go," he said.

" Thank you, sir," von Werra replied. " I have answered all your questions to the best of my ability, may I now be permitted to ask a question, Herr Hauptmann? "

" Yes, of course, what is it, Oberleutnant ? "

" When shall I get my personal belongings back and when am I going to be sent to a proper prisoner-of-war camp ? "

The Captain pursed his lips and looked at him with a very perceptible twinkle in his eye.

" Supposing you make it one question instead of two ! "

" Well, then, when am I going to be sent to a proper prison camp ? "

" H'm. Interesting that you should select that as the more important question. I should think, though I don't know, that the answer to both questions is ' Fairly soon.' "

There was a knock on the door.

" Come in !—Right, corporal, take Herr von Werra back to his room."

Von Werra left the interview in high spirits. The strain he had been under since being captured had evaporated in the friendly, smoky atmosphere of the Captain's office. He supposed that his interrogation was now over and that he would soon find himself among comrades in a permanent prisoner-of-war camp. And then . . . *escape !*

It was not until much later, when he was able to see the interview in perspective, relating it to what happened to him subsequently, that von Werra realised just how clever the Captain had been. His interest in politics had not been as simple as it appeared. No doubt he knew more about the subject than von Werra was ever likely to know, and there was nothing the prisoner could tell him about it that he had not heard a hundred times before.

The Englishman's interest was in von Werra himself. He wanted to assess his character, intelligence and morale, to discover his weaknesses and the limits of his intellect and education. He wanted to decide which technique was likely to yield the best results in the main interrogations, which were yet to come.

To be able to do this it was necessary to get the prisoner to talk freely and at length. In most cases politics, especially Nazi politics, did the trick. In the first place, the prisoner was usually so surprised and relieved to find he was not required to discuss military secrets, that he completely forgot his iron resolve to say nothing. Grateful for a " safe " subject of conversation, he went to the opposite extreme and became garrulous. Whenever there was a pause, the interrogator had only to wait, or to pretend to consult his notes, and the prisoner, fearing a change of subject, would quickly start talking politics again of his own accord. Secondly, even the keenest supporters of Nazism seemed continually to need to convince not only disbelievers but themselves, that it was a great and noble system; they enjoyed instructing the interrogator, demonstrating their loyalty and airing what they thought to be their political wisdom.

And while he listened for the umpteenth time to the gush of clichés and parrot-cries, the mild-mannered interrogator missed nothing of the prisoner's gradual unfolding of his personality. Did the prisoner really believe what he was saying? A few trick questions, like the one about the attack on Britain which the Captain put to von Werra, soon determined whether he swallowed all that he was told, or whether he preserved any power to think for himself.

Thus, the Captain had lulled von Werra's fears and fostered in him a false sense of superiority and security. All this prepared the way for the next moves, which were to send his mind reeling.

A few months later, when von Werra was able to look back calmly and see the whole picture of British interrogation methods in perspective, he suddenly recalled that momentary twinkle in the Captain's eye. The recollection afforded him rueful amusement. The Captain knew exactly what was going on in his mind! He knew, for instance, that when von Werra had asked how soon he would be sent to a proper prisoner-of-war camp, the thought that had prompted the question was—escape!

CHAPTER III

The Significance of Simba

VON WERRA was returned to Room 13, elated by the ease with which he handled the so-called interrogation. He had not divulged one scrap of military information, but he had given the interrogator an object lesson in the loyalty and soldierly qualities of the Luftwaffe. He had made it quite clear that being taken prisoner had not shaken his beliefs nor impaired his morale. The Captain had manifested by his increasing glumness that he derived no grain of comfort from the interview.

The German leaders were right : the British *were* stupid ! Here he was, the Adjutant of a *Gruppe* of the famous " Udet " Fighter *Geschwader*, a not altogether insignificant or ill-informed member of the most powerful, the most revolutionary and technically the most advanced Air Force in the world. Having had the good luck to capture him, did the British confront him with, say, a young, quick-witted, knowledgeable R.A.F. fighter pilot, who would know the sort of questions to ask ? They did not ! They took him to a veteran of the Great War, a thoroughly decent old English gentleman, who was content to chat about politics, an Army man, who probably couldn't tell a Junkers 52 from a Messerschmitt ! The Captain had probably been so impressed by the prisoner's bearing and morale that he had seen it would be futile to try to get military information out of him.

It was not until much later that von Werra appreciated the art of interrogation and realised that the prisoner who left an interview feeling he had been very clever was most likely to have revealed the information the interrogator wanted to get from him.

Von Werra glowed with satisfaction. Having refused to give information to the R.A.F. interrogator at Maidstone, and having side-tracked the Army interrogator, von Werra felt that if there was any more questioning to come, he was well able to cope with it. It was only the unknown that was unnerving. Now he knew the sort of thing to expect.

Half an hour after his return to Room 13, there was another shout up the stairs. Again the guard replied, unlocked the door, looked in and called :

" Come with me, Mister ! "

He was escorted downstairs to the little office off the vestibule. A lieutenant and two M.P.s were waiting for him. The officer was holding two large buff envelopes, one of them bulky. *His envelopes !*

Von Werra at once came to the conclusion that he was about to be taken to a permanent prisoner-of-war camp. His spirits soared. His interrogation was over.

" Fall in, the escort ! " the Lieutenant commanded. The two M.P's jumped to attention, one on either side of the prisoner.

" Follow me ! " The officer led the way to a small truck parked in the drive. He was bundled into it between the two guards, the officer climbed in beside the driver, and they moved off.

The guards on duty at the gate checked the officer's papers, identified von Werra's escort, then closed and fixed the back-flap of the canvas hood. This time the prisoner was unable to look out rearward, but could see ahead through the windscreen.

The guards saluted. The truck emerged into the quiet road, then turned right along the side of Hyde Park.

It was late afternoon. After many twists and turns and halts at traffic lights, they came on to a busy main road leading out of town. Von Werra judged by the position of the sun that they were travelling in a northerly direction. Nobody spoke, but he didn't care.

Some time later the officer looked back over his shoulder. He did not speak. His face was straight but there was a suggestion of amusement in his eyes. Then von Werra realised he had been whistling, softly, cheerfully, as was habitual with him when he was in a good mood. The officer exchanged glances with the driver. The prisoner looked quickly at the two M.P.s. It was gloomy in the back of the truck and their eyes were shaded by their peaked caps but he thought he detected a flicker of a smile passing between them.

What was so funny? Damn them for their coldness, anyway. He resumed his whistling.

They passed through the northern outskirts of London, and then turned off on to a side road. Presently they halted at some lodge gates, set in a high wall. A tall, burly man in civilian clothes examined the officer's papers, there was a murmured exchange of passwords, and the truck moved off along the drive of a huge park.

They passed through a wood and soon afterwards halted at a gate in a high barbed-wire fence. A little farther on there was another gate in a similar fence. Sentries patrolled the strip between the two securing rings. The sides of the drive between the two gates were blocked by barbed wire, so that the space thus enclosed formed a sort of lock. There was an exchange of passwords at the first gate. The guards checked papers, lifted the back-flap of the hood and looked inside, made entries on a form clipped on a board. The vehicle was then allowed to enter the lock. It halted at the second gate but the guard standing there at the door of a hut made no move, either to open the gate or to examine passes. He just stood there. The officer did not seem a bit put out. Then a telephone bell tinkled in the hut and another guard apparently answered it, for a second later someone called out: " O.K." The soldier moved from the doorway at once and opened the gate.

" My God!" thought Werra. " They're certainly not taking any chances!"

The vehicle proceeded a little farther and then stopped. Von Werra was ordered to get out. He saw that they were at one end of a huge mansion built round three sides of a square.

Von Werra heard later that it was " Cook Foster ", and that is how the name appears in his autobiography and in the official reports he eventually came to write. It was, in fact, Trent Park, Cockfosters, nowadays a teachers' training college run by Middlesex County Council.

As the party dismounted, a sergeant hurried out of a side door putting on a red cap. The Lieutenant returned his salute and said:

" One Boche, delivered. Sign here, Sergeant!"

The two envelopes were handed over, the formalities completed, and the sergeant led von Werra through the side door and down a flight of steps into the basement. He was marched down a long, low corridor, the roof of which was covered with lagged hot-water pipes. There was a bizarre mixture of smells—the stoke-hole smell

36

of coke and warm ashes, and another that recalled hospitals—was it ether, or surgical spirit? The sound of nailed boots on the concrete floor reverberated hollowly along the dimly-lit passage.

Von Werra felt strangely uneasy. There was something odd about this place. He had expected to see prisoners walking about in the grounds, or playing football. But he had not seen any, either in the grounds or at the windows of the house. It looked as though prisoners were not allowed to leave the building. Another thing that struck him was the hush-hush air of the place: the plain-clothes man at the lodge, the whispered passwords, the formidable double ring of barbed-wire entanglements and the telephoning between gates. Why was he being taken into the cellar, and what was the significance of this hospital smell? The sergeant knocked on a door, then opened it.

Von Werra found himself blinking on the threshold of a small brilliantly-lit room, all white paint, starched white overalls, white enamel dishes and the glitter of surgical instruments in a glass cabinet. A bald-headed man was seated at a desk, writing. He glanced up.

" Right, Sergeant. Wait outside ! "

The sergeant's heels clicked. " Yessir ! "

" Von Werra ? Speak English ? " The man had a loud barking voice.

" Yes, sir."

" Good ! Go in there and strip."

" Please, sir ? "

" Strip—take all your clothes off. *Verstanden* ? "

" *Jawohl, Herr Doktor !* "

Another, younger man, also in white, appeared at an open doorway on the other side of the room.

" Usual thing, Corporal."

" Very good, sir—This way."

Von Werra remembered rumours of what went on in the basement of Gestapo Headquarters, in Berlin. He also recalled the tales of German airmen being tortured in England. As he passed into the adjoining room, his glance fell on a trolley on which, among other things, there was a hypodermic syringe in a kidney-shaped dish, and behind it, an enamel jug containing a coiled length of rubber tubing.

Von Werra stripped. His body was deeply tanned by the sun

and sea-water of the coastal airfield in the Pas de Calais. The orderly weighed him, measured his height, took his temperature and pulse, handed him a bottle and motioned with his head—" Through there."

After a few minutes the doctor came in briskly. As he advanced he noted the prisoner's perfect physique, small but broad-shouldered, narrow-waisted, tough, muscular, lithe. Quadriceps and biceps of an athlete. Clear skin, no adipose tissue. (They were nearly all the same, these German prisoners—so much for the tales of malnutrition in the German Armed Forces !) Poised, intelligent-looking, clear eyed, wary as a cat. Slightly scared, but determined not to show it—as though freezing the facial muscles into that " Do-your-damnedest, you-can't-frighten-me " look could conceal the slightly moist skin, the high rate of respiration, the visibly pounding heart !

" Slip your pants on and sit down over here," the doctor barked. " Open your mouth. Ready, Corporal ? "

" Yes, sir." The corporal's pen was poised half-way down a large, closely-printed form, over a diagram of a full set of teeth.

Nothing worse was going to happen to Oberleutnant von Werra than a thorough medical examination. The R.A.F. was very interested in the physical condition of captured enemy air crew.

The following entries on von Werra's medical form were later to be widely circularised by the police, and broadcast by the B.B.C :

Age : 26.
Height : 5 ft. 7 in.
Weight : 10 st.
Physical appearance : Sturdy build. Fair, wavy hair. Blue eyes. Sound white, even teeth. Fresh complexion. Clean shaven.
Distinguishing marks : Stiff, straight, scarred forefinger, right hand. Has no lobes to his ears.

After the medical examination, the guard sergeant took the prisoner to the Supply Room, where he was issued with a collarless flannel shirt, long woollen underwear, a pair of thick woollen socks, toilet articles and a civilian gas mask. It was explained to him that as a prisoner-of-war with the rank of Oberleutnant (equivalent to R.A.F. Flying Officer), he was entitled under international agreements to receive three pounds pocket money per month (paid in tokens or credits). The cost of the articles issued would be deducted from his first month's pay.

He was then escorted along corridors, through hallways, up flights of stairs, his heart sinking lower with every step. There were armed guards on duty everywhere. Dozens of them. Several times he and the sergeant had to halt at an iron grille at the junction of two corridors, while the guard on the other side unlocked the iron gate and let them through. Escape under such conditions seemed utterly impossible. And why was there no sign of other German prisoners ? Either the British had an exaggerated idea of what a few unarmed prisoners could do, or . . . or *this was not a permanent prisoner-of-war camp at all !*

His hopes were dashed. He felt weary and defeated. These frequent fluctuations between anxiety and depression, on the one hand, and confidence and hope, on the other, were beginning to wear him out. Were the British playing some sort of game with him ? Whatever it was they were going to do with him, why didn't they do it and get it over ?

The British did not let you see what they were thinking and feeling. They were inscrutable and infuriating.

At last the sergeant halted at a door in a corridor on the third and top floor. There was a key in the lock with a brass disc hanging from it.

" This is your room," he said. " Food will be brought to you. Later."

He went out, locked the door and von Werra heard him remove the key. After a few moments the footsteps died away.

Silence. A room large and high, gloomy in the gathering dusk. Four iron bedsteads, each with three mattress " biscuits " and several neatly folded khaki blankets in a pile at the foot. Table, lockers, chairs of grubby, unpainted deal. Strips of coconut matting on the board floor. No sign that the room was being used by other prisoners. Von Werra let the supplies he had drawn fall on to the table, and went to the window. It was open at the top, but barred on the outside. He could see the double ring of barbed-wire entanglements, sentries patrolling in between. Beyond was a wide sweep of parkland, with here and there an enormous shadowy oak or beech. A scarf of mist hovering above a large ornamental lake, and white blobs, probably swans, on the steel-grey water. Distant woods. On the horizon, above the tree tops, a rash of black dots in the paling sky : barrage balloons over London.

Night fell. Von Werra lay on one of the beds in the dark. There was a bulb hanging from the ceiling, but he could find no switch. Not that it mattered very much. He lay listening. He seemed to be entirely alone in this part of the building. There were no sounds in the adjacent rooms or in the corridor outside.

Eventually he heard approaching footsteps. The door was unlocked, flung open violently. The beam of a torch stabbed into the room, swept over the bed, rested on von Werra. He sat up.

" Stay where you are ! "

" What happens ? "

A man moved to the table and set something down, pushing the prisoner's kit on to the floor. The torch remained pointed from the doorway. There was a fumbling and a banging near the window. A shutter was placed over it, blocking out the starlight. The torch was switched off. Blackness. Footsteps moved away from the window. A switch clicked in the corridor outside and the room was flooded with dazzling light from the powerful bulb hanging from the ceiling.

Von Werra blinked at the sergeant and another soldier standing by the door. They were impassive.

" Your supper," said the sergeant.

Von Werra saw the tray on the table. A mug of cocoa, a plate with three thick slices of bread, margarine and a scraping of marmalade.

The men went out.

" Don't try to touch the blackout shutter," said the sergeant before closing and locking the door.

It was several minutes before von Werra felt able to eat. He sipped the cocoa suspiciously. It seemed to be all right.

He did not get much sleep. It was some time before a guard came and took away the tray and switched off the bright light. Thereafter the prisoner was woken up at intervals by the sound of approaching footsteps, the light was switched on, a guard looked in, then locked the door again and went away.

Von Werra was kept in isolation twenty-four hours. He was unable to sleep much during the next day, for there were frequent checks on him. He had nothing to read, nothing to smoke, nothing to do but wait and think. His only diversion was a heavy raid on London during the afternoon. He had three days' growth of beard and he needed a bath. The guards would not be drawn into conversation. He protested about his treatment to the sergeant when he came and was told that his complaint would be passed on.

Von Werra later discovered that the sergeant was known to prisoners as *Feldwebel Später* (Sergeant Later), because of his habit of replying : " Later " to all their requests:

" May I have a wash and shave? "—" Later."

" May I have something to read ? "—Later."

" I need to go to the W.C."—" Later."

" I demand to see the Commanding Officer."—" Later."

" I demand to be sent to a proper prisoner-of-war camp."—" Later."

By evening von Werra's morale had reached a new low point. Then, at dusk on the evening of Saturday 7 September, he was marched downstairs between two guards, one in front, one behind. They went through a different part of the building from that through which he had previously passed. The tapping of typewriters, the ringing of telephone bells and the buzz of conversation came from behind some of the doors. Finally, the leading guard knocked at a varnished door, which bore neither number nor sign. There was a moment's pause, and a cheerful voice called " Come in ! "

Von Werra was ushered into a pleasantly furnished office. The walls were panelled, the floor carpeted and there were several leather-upholstered arm-chairs. Blackout curtains were drawn across the windows. Contrasting with the soft illumination of the ceiling, a powerful reading-lamp cast a circle of harsh light on the top of a massive mahogany desk, at which an R.A.F. officer was seated, writing. The circle of light ended on the top of his bowed head. His hair was thin and receding at the temples, but jet-black and gleaming.

Von Werra took in the buttons on the uniform jacket, the pilot's wings, the two rows of medal ribbons ; the cigarette box with a model Spitfire on the lid, all in silver ; the cut-glass ash-tray ; what appeared to be the heavy silver knob of a walking-stick propped against the desk. The stick reminded him of the foppish British officer of German newspaper cartoons.

The escort marched him up to the desk.

" Well ? " inquired the officer casually, without looking up.

" Corporal Bates reporting with Prisoner von Werra, sir," said one of the guards.

" Right-ho, Corporal. Mount guard outside. You may go."

As the door closed the officer at last glanced up. He had a thin, lined face, bushy upswept eyebrows and an upward-curling black moustache. His eyes, small and sunken, shone like black beads.

Speaking in facile but slightly accented German, he said :

" I am Squadron Leader Hawkes. Sit down, Oberleutnant von Werra."

The prisoner clicked his heels together, bowed stiffly, and then sat down in a low, leather-covered chair a little to one side of the desk.

The Squadron Leader continued writing for at least two minutes. Then he closed his file, tossed it into a basket on the desk and pressed a button nearby.

Almost immediately a side door opened and a flight lieutenant entered carrying several folders, which he placed on the desk beside the Squadron Leader. Then he went out, switching off the ceiling light before closing the door. Now the only illumination was from the desk lamp.

Squadron Leader Hawkes reached for the silver cigarette box, opened it and held it out to the prisoner.

" Thank you, Herr Major ! "[1] said von Werra. He sucked the smoke deep into his lungs. The satisfaction of his craving for nicotine made him feel a little dizzy.

The Squadron Leader leaned back in his swivel chair, out of the circle of light. Von Werra could see him only dimly.

" Thirteen aircraft shot down in combat, and half a dozen others destroyed on the ground, is quite a respectable score, Oberleutnant," the Englishman drawled :

There was a cold mockery in the words.

" As one of the very minor aces of the First World War," the Squadron Leader continued, " I am especially thrilled and privileged to meet one of the major aces of the Second ! "

Was it his imagination, or did the Englishman's words have a hidden meaning ? Was it bluff, or did the Squadron Leader know just where to attack him ?

[1]R.A.F. Squadron Leader=Luftwaffe Major.

Von Werra felt his fear and fury rising. He must at all costs retain control. Perhaps he was being deliberately provoked. He must assert himself quickly, and try to turn the tables on the Englishman.

"It was kind of you, Herr Major," he began, mimicking the other's casual drawl, "to give me a much needed cigarette. But, intrigued as I am to meet an ace of the Royal Flying Corps—all the more so since I have not seen your name nor read of your exploits in the course of studying the Corps' fascinating history, my sense of obligation is not going to make me reveal any military information. Not even the name and number of my unit. Not even my Army Post Office number. *Nichts* ! "

Another thought struck him :

"But how stupid of me, Herr Major ! No doubt it was you who shot me down the other day ! " There could be no mistaking his sneering insolence.

"If that doesn't make him raving mad," thought von Werra, " nothing will."

The Squadron Leader said nothing.

The ensuing silence lasted so long that von Werra felt more and more of a fool. He was saved by the distant wail of an air-raid siren. Another siren began, and then another, and then one close by. In a few seconds the wailing cacophony had spread right across the London area. Von Werra settled back in his chair, as though making himself comfortable at the beginning of a theatrical performance. He smirked.

The Squadron Leader suddenly seemed to come to a decision. He gripped the arms of his chair and stood up.

Quite unexpectedly, he leaned over the desk and pressed the white button in the base of the reading-lamp. The room was in total darkness.

As the left hand moved towards the button, von Werra saw the right hand close over the silver knob of the walking-stick.

He sat rigid, holding his breath. The Englishman was moving across the floor, away from the desk. Despite the wailing of the sirens, he could hear that the Squadron Leader limped heavily, and that one of his boots squeaked. Then the significance of the squeak—and of the walking-stick—struck him ; his interrogator was wearing an artificial limb.

"Forgive me, Herr Major. I'm terribly sorry. I had no idea——"

There was no reply. There was only darkness and the wailing of the sirens.

There was a sudden rasping sound on the other side of the room. A blackout curtain had been drawn back. Von Werra saw a square of pale sky, the faint glimmer of a star and the silhouetted head and shoulders of the Squadron Leader.

Siren by siren the wailing died. The blackout curtain was closed, and the squeak began again, approaching the desk. It stopped close to the prisoner in the chair.

Click !

The light on the desk came on again. Its reflector had been tipped up, and von Werra was now in a circle of harsh light. His eyes glittered and blinked, his brow glistened.

The Squadron Leader was silently holding out an ash-tray. The prisoner glanced down and saw that there was a long ash on his cigarette and that he was in danger of burning his fingers. He squeezed the stub into the side of the ash-tray.

" Thank you, Herr Major ! " he whispered.

The Squadron Leader replaced the ash-tray. Then he leaned back, half sitting on the edge of the desk. He folded his arms and looked down at the prisoner, only a few feet away from him.

" You mentioned something about your unit a few minutes ago, Oberleutnant," he said casually.

Von Werra banged an arm of his chair in agitation.

" *I tell you I can't reveal——* " he began.

"—And that set me wondering," the Englishman continued, " which of your friends in the Headquarters *Staffel* of the Second *Gruppe* of Number Three Fighter *Geschwader* will look after Simba, your lion cub, now that your deathless exploits with that unit have come to an end—' Sanni ' perhaps ? "

Von Werra's mouth opened, and stayed open. His mind reeled.

But that was only the beginning of what was probably the most devastating experience of his life.

Von Werra was dumbfounded. He had consistently refused to give the British authorities any information about himself other than his name, rank and number. He had made it clear that nothing would induce him to reveal military secrets. He would not even say to which unit he belonged.

And now, here was a British interrogator showing that he

44

already knew not only to which section of which unit he belonged, but also the name of his pet lion cub and the nickname of his best friend.

It was incredible and uncanny. But by far the most unnerving thing was the certainty that this drawling, imperturbable Squadron Leader had not been bluffing earlier when he had implied that he knew certain things which the prisoner had imagined no one knew but himself, things that not even his closest comrades suspected. His innermost secrets were laid bare to a total stranger, an enemy in a foreign land.

The only thing was to say nothing. Though he looked and felt an utter fool, he must say nothing. It would be futile and dangerous to deny ; to affirm would be an admission and a retreat. If he admitted one fact, it would be difficult for him not to admit others. Before he knew where he was he would be led into confirming or denying facts which the enemy did not know for certain, but only guessed.

" The Great War gave us the fighter ace Manfred, Freiherr von Richthofen," the Englishman said at length. " And now, to carry on the noble tradition, this war has given us Franz, ' Freiherr '—or, should I say ' Baron ' ?—von Werra." There was no mistaking the sarcasm in his voice.

" Franz ' Freiherr ' von Werra, the Luftwaffe fighter ace," the Squadron Leader repeated, with relish. " Yes, I congratulate you, it really has the authentic ring."

His tone changed.

" However, since you are of Swiss origin, and the democratic Swiss have no titles of nobility, I don't quite see how you——"

Stung to the quick and flushed with rage, von Werra interrupted.

"—Since you know so much about me, I'm surprised that you seem to be unaware that in 1806 the Emperor Francis of Austria conferred the title of Freiherr on my ancestor, Ferdinand de Werra, of the then Republic of Valais."[1]

" Indeed ! Then at least you admit to your Swiss origin ? "

Von Werra did not reply. He was furious with himself for having fallen into the trap.

" You really should send a stiff letter to the editors of the *Almanach de Gotha*, you know. They have consistently omitted your name from their lists of the European nobility. But after all,

[1] See Appendix I.

whether you are, or are not, an upstart and an impostor, is a small matter, since there can be no doubt whatsoever that you have to your credit the noble deeds that go with a noble name ! Is that not so, Oberleutnant ?

" Another thing I must congratulate you on, Oberleutnant, is your flair for publicity, especially when competition for the lime-light is so keen among fighter pilots of the Luftwaffe ! From an unknown Leutnant to cover boy of the picture magazines in a few weeks—now, that's what I call *Draufgängertum !* (go-getting). And how is it done ? Childishly simple ! Other pilots with pet dogs, pigs or falcons get their pictures in the papers, so you outdo the lot and acquire a pet lion cub, and presto ! you and the cub jump straight on to the front page. ' One of our dashing young fighter pilots with Simba, his pet lion cub.' And I see you've gone one better than the pilot who always wears a Tyrolean hat on operations: you are reported to wear a red jerkin, and are billed as ' The Red Devil—the Terror of the British Air Force.' Yes, you have the flair, Oberleutnant ! "

As the Englishman was speaking, the first bombs fell on London. The explosions were a long way off, but they caused the windows in the room to rattle in their frames.

These noises off put new life into the prisoner, and gave him a moment to think. Obviously the British Intelligence Service went through the German Press with a fine-tooth-comb, extracting every scrap of military information. That explained why the Squadron Leader knew so much about him. And although his name had not appeared, for security reasons, under the pictures of himself and Simba, no doubt other prisoners had identified him under interrogation.

If others had talked, why shouldn't he ? He could save himself so much unpleasantness if he did—for he had a shrewd idea of what was still to come.

No, he could not possibly do it. Whatever happened, whatever others said, *he* could not give away military information.

The unmistakable, pulsating growl of a stray German bomber overhead broke through his thoughts. Quick-witted and resilient as ever, an idea struck him for turning the situation to his own advantage.

" When there are so many German pilots still free to roam at will over Britain," he said, " the preoccupation of the Royal Air

Force with the pet animal of one captured pilot seems rather odd. Touching, but odd. However, what's a little thing like a war to a nation of animal-lovers! First things first . . . About these magazine pictures, I take it the captions give my unit and number, as well as my name, so I don't see what it is you want me to tell you!"

Squadron Leader Hawkes leaned back over the desk and picked up a file. From it he took a popular German radio magazine, *Hör mit mir*. It was dated 24 August 1940. On its front cover was a picture of a Luftwaffe Leutnant leaning against the wing of a Messerschmitt 109 fighter, and holding a snarling lion cub in his arms. The Squadron Leader read the caption aloud.

"This is the *Staffel* lion, Simba, taking the place of the British Lion, who seldom shows himself in the vicinity of German fighter pilots!"

Von Werra laughed scornfully.

"And you really think that looks like me? Nonsense, Herr Major! There must be dozens of men in the Luftwaffe who look more like this man than I do. And I'm sure you will have noticed that he is a Leutnant, while I am an Oberleutnant!"

"Care to tell me when you received your promotion—or shall I tell you when it was?"

Von Werra shrugged his shoulders.

The Squadron Leader handed him a picture cut from another magazine.

"If you feel that the first one doesn't do you justice, what about this one?"

"Really, Herr Major," the prisoner scoffed. "Isn't this a bit too thin? After all, it's impossible to see the features of the man on this one. The whole of the upper part of his face is hidden by the barrel—of a cannon." His voice faltered and trailed off. He had spotted a significant detail on the picture that he had never noticed before.

"Exactly, Oberleutnant!" said the Squadron Leader with amusement. "The man's right hand rests on the wing of a Me. 109. An interesting hand! On the third finger is a massive signet ring set with a square stone engraved with a crest. Do you know, it's remarkably similar to the one you are wearing on that finger at this moment! But that is not all! In the picture the forefinger sticks out straight, as though the man were unable to bend the knuckle.

I noted when you were smoking just now—and I see the fact is mentioned in your medical report—that the forefinger of *your* right hand is stiff and straight ! "

Von Werra was silent. He could not but admire the skill with which the British Intelligence Service built up the mosaic. And it was the Germans who were supposed to be thorough !

"Tell me, Oberleutnant," the Englishman went on, " what has happened to your friend, War Correspondent Doctor Erhardt Eckert ?[1] Have you lost touch with him lately ? After the thrilling stories he wrote of how you shot down two French bombers— Potez 63's, weren't they?—and then six British bombers, I should have thought you would have gone out of your way to cultivate him. He did much to promote your career and put you in the public eye, didn't he ? "

Von Werra said nothing.

The Squadron Leader bent forward over the prisoner, and when he spoke, it was not with his usual drawl, but with a sharp, stinging spitefulness.

"That yarn about the two Potez," he said. " Do you mean to tell me that you can get away with such transparent falsehoods ? Do you mean to tell me that the German public swallows such journalistic muck ? "

Von Werra half rose out of his chair, livid with rage.

"Herr Major," he shouted, " I am an officer of the German Armed Forces. I demand to be treated with proper respect. *I will not be insulted !* "

"Well, well ! So at least that particular exploit was true ! Congratulations, Oberleutnant ! "

"I have admitted nothing," von Werra said quickly.

"No ? There is no one more indignant than the habitual liar

---

[1] An account of von Werra's exploit appeared in a number of German and Austrian newspapers in the middle of June 1940. It was headed :

DESTROYED TWO POTEZ BOMBERS
ON ONE SORTIE!
Leutnant von Werra's Big Day
by Dr. Erhardt Eckert

A long and flowery description of von Werra's destruction of the two French aircraft is not without humour. Referring to his return to base, the learned Doctor writes : " The Leutnant flies accurately by the compass, but not too high, as he does not have his parachute with him." He concludes his report : " Leutnant von Werra laughs joyfully when he tells the story of his great day. And with reason, for it earned him the Iron Cross 11 Class."

who is disbelieved on the rare occasion that he tells the truth!"

Von Werra's voice trembled. "Are you suggesting that——"

The interrogator interrupted and asked coldly:

"—Yes? Suggesting what, Oberleutnant?"

"That—that I am a habitual liar?"

"Stripped of all your humbug—what else are you?"

"Herr Major," said the prisoner, as evenly and quietly as he could, "I am your prisoner. I am in your power. You can do and say to me what you will. But though you insult me for weeks on end, you will not succeed in getting any military information out of me. I protest most emphatically against the way I am being treated. Why am I not sent to a proper prison camp?"

"Another cigarette?"

"Thank you. No!"

"We have touched lightly on the two stripes for French bombers, and the six stripes for British bombers painted on the tail of your aircraft."

The Squadron Leader paused.

"And that brings us, does it not, to the remaining five stripes for British fighters shot down in combat . . . Are you sure you won't have another cigarette?"

The prisoner shook his head stubbornly.

"It also brings us to another of your War Correspondent friends, Harry Gehm, and to the broadcast you made over the Deutschland-sender, at 18.00 hours a week ago yesterday."

Von Werra's morale slumped and reached bottom. This was it. He had long known it was coming, but he had under-estimated the extent of the Englishman's knowledge. It was hopeless—the man knew everything, everything.

With an effort, he focussed his eyes on the silver box which was being held open in front of him.

He took a cigarette unthinkingly.

CHAPTER IV

" The Greatest Fighter Exploit
of the War "

---

*That night, Saturday, 7 September 1940, marked the beginning of mass
night raids on London. German bombers were overhead from 8 p.m. until
4 a.m. the next morning. Guided by the great fires started by the afternoon
attacks, they dropped another 300 tons of high explosive and 13,000
incendiaries on the dock areas and the East End.*

The air raid had intensified. Explosion followed explosion,
and the windows of the room rattled in the frames.

Invisible in the shadows beyond the ring of light cast by the
reading-lamp, Squadron Leader Hawkes leaned casually against
the desk. His purpose and tactics were now clear to von Werra.
Everything that had happened to him since his capture had been in
preparation for this interrogation. Step by step the Englishman
had tried to break down his self-respect ; now he was about to give
the screw the final turn.

" I'll be damned if I let him do it to me ! " thought von Werra.
" He can spread the sarcasm as thick as he likes, but I will not let
him break me. I'll deny the whole thing, and keep on denying it.
What can he do ? Jeer at me, show his contempt for me—so what ? "

" I don't know what on earth you are talking about, Herr
Major," he said.

" I'm talking about your friend War Reporter Harry Gehm,
and the broadcast you made over Deutschlandsender at 18.00 hours
on Friday, 30 August—just eight short days ago. Shall I refresh
your memory still further ? "

The Squadron Leader picked up the file again and took from
it several pages of typescript, which he handed to the prisoner.

" That is the text of your broadcast. If you like, you shall hear the actual recording."

Von Werra took the sheets. Following is a translation of what he read :

Deutschlandsender : 1571 *metres. In German for Germany*
Time : 18.00 hours B.S.T.   Date : 30. 8. 40
Title of Programme : *Frontbericht* (front report)
Excerpt from above

An Airman's Feat

A famous fighter squadron has returned from operations over England. Its orders were to carry out a free-lance sweep between Dover and London.

In the course of the patrol, heavy losses were inflicted on the R.A.F. Leutnant von Werrer (sic), in particular, distinguished himself in the operation. The exploit he is going to describe is the greatest we have so far heard of to be carried out by a fighter pilot.

Leutnant von Werrer : As soon as we reached England we encountered a formation of British fighters, which we immediately engaged. A tremendous battle ensued. I was on the tail of a Hawker Hurricane, in a favourable position, when I noticed at the last minute that I myself was being tailed by a Spitfire. Its first burst of fire put my radio out of action. However, I managed to out-manœuvre the Spitfire, and finally got into position to attack it.

After a few bursts of machine-gun fire—I wanted to save my cannon ammunition—the Spitfire tried to break off the engagement and went down in a steep dive. I followed, firing whenever I could get it in my sights.

After a few seconds I began to feel uneasy, and flattened out. The Englishman continued diving and I saw him strike the ground. He had evidently been seriously wounded in the combat and had passed out. I was now so low that I could not attempt to climb without attracting violent A.A. fire. Moreover, I was separated from my formation and could not call them up as my radio was out of action. I decided to hedge-hop to the Thames, follow it to the estuary, and then strike out across the Channel.

While I was hedge-hopping towards the estuary I suddenly

noticed, about 300 metres ahead of me and to the left, six fighters in close formation circling a field with their undercarriages down. I looked intently at the field and saw dust swirling up. Aircraft that had just landed were evidently taxiing across the field ; those still airborne must be the second half of a fighter squadron returning from patrol.

It then occurred to me to pretend to be part of the British squadron. Accordingly, I lowered my undercarriage and attached myself as seventh to the line of fighters. We circled the field waiting for permission to land, and I was therefore able to study the lay-out of the aerodrome.

My moment came after the first three of the six aircraft had touched down. I retracted my undercarriage and opened the throttle. When I was almost within ramming distance of the last plane of the remaining three airborne, I fired a short burst. The plane crashed in flames. I repeated this with the next. I caught the third just as its wheels touched the ground. However, it did not catch fire and I do not know what happened to it ; later, I saw the burning wreckage of only two planes on this part of the airfield. The British pilots could not have known what hit them, because when you are landing, you cannot let your attention wander.

Then I flew across the aerodrome towards a little wood. I had previously seen aircraft taxiing to the edge of it. They had not yet been put under cover, so that they provided a good target. Three aircraft were parked beside a tent used for camouflage purposes. A mobile petrol tanker stood nearby, so I shot it up as well. I hit it with fire from my machine-guns and two cannons. It went up in flames. Soon, lakes of burning fuel spread under the three aircraft, which also caught fire.

I followed up this success with three more low-level attacks and destroyed one more aircraft on the ground. Meanwhile, machine-guns round the field had been manned and were firing wildly at me. However, my high speed gave me a distinct advantage in the duel, for, of course, I returned their fire. Finally, my position became uncomfortable when a curtain of tracer bullets was drawn in front of me. I turned back and made off.

Interviewer : Down below everything was burning. How many aircraft did you shoot down ?

Werrer : I shot down three with absolute certainty, but most probably four.

Interviewer : And how many did you destroy on the ground ?

Werrer : Five on the ground ; two of them in their dispersal bays and three in front of the tent, which also went up in flames. Of course, I don't know what was in the tent.

Lack of fuel compelled me to make an emergency landing as soon as I reached the French coast. I arrived back at my base two hours overdue. Of course, I was glad to get back and report my success.

Interviewer : Success, indeed—the greatest fighter exploit we have heard of in the present war.

Franz von Werra was normally the most unselfconscious of men. His embarrassment as he read the script was all the more acute for being unfamiliar.

The story had sounded so simple and plausible when he had recorded the interview in a camouflaged hut at the cliff-top airfield in the Pas de Calais. He had spoken partly extempore and partly from a hurriedly pencilled script. The recording had been flown to Berlin and broadcast two days later. He had supposed it would be heard in German homes, marvelled at, and then forgotten as far as the details were concerned. All that would be remembered was that a fighter pilot named von Werra had made a daring single-handed attack on a British airfield and had destroyed a large number of enemy fighters. And that was all he wanted to be remembered. It would serve its purpose and give him added prestige, both with the German public and in the Luftwaffe.

It had never occurred to him that the broadcast would be listened to in England, much less that a recording would be made of it. In print it looked horribly and completely false. The spuriousness of the story was manifest in every sentence. It was as though the unguarded confidences whispered in the early morning hours in a dim corner of a night-club had been taken down and turned into a legal document.

Von Werra handed the sheets back to the Squadron Leader, and said :

" A remarkable story, Herr Major. But what has it to do with me ? "

" *Remarkable ?* As the interviewer says, it's ' the greatest fighter exploit of the war '—and you call it remarkable? Come, my dear Oberleutnant, this access of modesty is quite unlike you! You're not going to pretend that because your rank is given as Leutnant and, through a perfectly natural error in transcribing the spoken word, your name is wrongly spelt, that it was not you who made the broadcast? Perhaps you would be not able to recognise your own voice if I played the recording, either?"

"I know nothing whatever about it," the prisoner replied.

"You mean you're ashamed to admit that 'the greatest fighter exploit of the war' is fictitious from beginning to end—that it is a typical piece of von Werra romancing!"

"I have nothing to say."

Squadron Leader Hawkes began to show signs of impatience.

"The trouble with you, von Werra, is that you can't keep a story straight. In the broadcast you said one thing, and in the story you told War Correspondent Harry Gehm, which was published in some of the Berlin newspapers[1] the day before you were taken prisoner, you said something quite different. I doubt whether you have seen the published version yet, so I will tell you that Harry Gehm has taken into account your recent promotion and refers to you as Oberleutnant!"

The Squadron Leader took a newspaper clipping from the file and glanced through it.

"He also states that your great exploit took place on 28 August, that you are the Adjutant of the Second *Gruppe*, and that, when the other aircraft had returned from the mission without you—I quote —'Even Simba, the lion cub, seemed aware that his master was missing and slunk snarling under the H.Q. staff car!" The Englishman leaned forward and added angrily.

"Are you still going to make out that this has nothing to do with you?"

"I have nothing to say."

"Do you realise you are the laughing-stock of every Mess in Fighter Command?—'The Red Devil' Strikes Again! The bold baron who all alone wiped out nine Hurricanes—a flight, near enough—in five minutes.

"How very fortunate that you *were* alone—there was no other German pilot within miles to disprove your story. You could say what you liked, and the fact that you were alone added to your

[1] See Appendix II.

glory. What a line-shooter! I can understand the German public swallowing this yarn—it will swallow anything—but what nerve it must have taken to pitch it to your Commanding Officer, Oberstleutnant Brieger!"

Von Werra's spirits rose. He thought: "Ah! He doesn't know everything. He doesn't know that Major Lützow replaced Oberstleutnant Brieger a couple of months ago!" It was a trivial enough point, but in von Werra's present distress of mind, the fact that there was something he knew which the Squadron Leader did not, gave him some comfort.

Squadron Leader Hawkes went on relentlessly.

"Your comrades, at least, must know something of the realities of the fighting; did they believe your story? Or were they only mad because they didn't think of something like it before you did?"

Von Werra was silent.

"Are you going to tell me that in the heat of a dog-fight, when it's your enemy's life or your own, you, von Werra—you, of all people—are deliberately going to conserve your cannon ammunition and use only your machine-guns? When one little squirt of cannon fire might make all the difference? Why should you *want* to save your cannon ammunition under such circumstances? Did you know beforehand that you would come across the formation of Hurricanes? The truth is, you only put in that bit about conserving your cannon ammunition in order to make your story of the shooting up of the airfield sound more plausible.

"And what about the six Hurricanes you tagged on to, with your cannon ammunition providentially intact? What of the Tail End Charlie, who would be keeping a particularly close watch behind in these vulnerable moments? Do you really imagine he could mistake a Messerschmitt for another Hurricane? And what of the other five pilots? Wouldn't they have rear-view mirrors, too? And since they were making slow circuits while waiting for permission to land, they must have been in radio contact with Control. Supposing, by some miracle, you were not spotted by the pilots themselves—don't you think you would have been seen from the ground? Don't you think that a Messerschmitt, with its black-and-white cross and its swastika, its smaller size and different silhouette, would have stuck out like a sore thumb behind a flight of Hurricanes?—Von Werra, you're a fool!

"Then there are the discrepancies between the broadcast and

published versions ! On the air you said you made a forced landing on the French coast. There you presumably refuelled, for you say you arrived back at your base two hours overdue. But the base from which II/JG 3 operates *is* on the French coast, is it not ? And why, if you refuelled, does Harry Gehm say *twice* that you arrived back on the last drops of fuel in your tanks ?[1] And since the maximum time that a Messerschmitt 109 can remain airborne, assuming it takes off with full tanks, is 105 minutes, how do you account for the fact that, according to the published story, you must have been up at least three hours ? "

The prisoner was silent.

" Where was this British airfield at which you wrought such havoc ? It must have been somewhere in Kent or Essex." The Squadron Leader bent over the prisoner and barked :

" Where ? "

The prisoner was silent.

" Where ? " insisted the interrogator.

" I have nothing to say. I don't know what you are talking about."

" You will note that I am not asking you to tell me the location of a German airfield—but of a British one ! Come, now, where was it ? If you don't know the name, where was it approximately ? "

The prisoner was silent.

" The loss of nine Hurricanes at the present time would be a serious matter to the Royal Air Force. If it had occurred in five minutes at one airfield in the manner you alleged, I feel pretty certain somebody would have noticed it. Who knows, some awkward questions might have been asked." The interrogator bent over the prisoner again, and when he spoke his voice was icy.

" You know as well as I do, don't you, Oberleutnant ' Baron ' von Werra, ' The Red Devil ', ' The Terror of the R.A.F.', that there was no incident even remotely resembling your alleged exploit at any airfield in England on 28 August, or on any other date. There is absolutely nothing in squadron records that bears out your tale : not one fighter, whether Hurricane or Spitfire, lost in the way you claim ; no instance of a Messerschmitt tagging on to a flight of fighters ; no low-level attack by a single enemy fighter. So what remains, Oberleutnant ' Baron ' von Werra, of ' The Greatest Fighter Exploit of the War ' ! "

[1] See Appendix II.

The prisoner remained silent.

" Still, your story served its purpose, did it not ? The Luftwaffe took your word for it. But since your score up to 28 August was eight[1] victories, and when you were shot down you had thirteen chalked up, it would seem that they took your word for only five of the nine Hurricanes you said you had destroyed, which was very naughty of them. Still, you can't complain : nine ghostly Hurricanes became another five substantial notches painted on the tail fin of your Messerschmitt, and you jumped from seventh on the list of German fighter aces to fourth, equal with Joppien. A few more such exploits and you would have surpassed even Mölders and Galland !

" Mölders, Galland, your old friend Balthasar, and one or two others, are men apart, aren't they ? They are above suspicion, their achievements are incontestable. What would chaps like that think of you, von Werra, if they knew what you and I know ? "

The prisoner said nothing.

" Oberleutnant von Werra, in due course you will be sent to a permanent prison camp. There you will find many of your *Geschwader* comrades who have passed this way before you. The war will probably last a long, long time. You will spend every minute of your captivity in the pockets, so to speak, of your comrades—day in, day out, month in, month out, probably for years on end. Supposing your fellow-prisoners, especially your *Geschwader* friends, some of whom are in this building, got to know what you and I know about your famous exploit with the Hurricanes —what sort of life do you think you would lead ? "

Von Werra smiled. It was a weak smile, but a smile nevertheless. Exhausted though he was, he knew that Squadron Leader Hawkes had fired the last shot in his locker. When he spoke, his voice was a little unsteady, but it gathered firmness and strength as he proceeded.

" Herr Major," he said, " do you know what I would say if I were in the position of this Leutnant von Werrer—the one who made

---

[1]The German High Command war communiqué for 28 August 1940 listed the accredited air victories of the leading Luftwaffe fighter aces up to that date : Maj. Mölders 29 ; Maj. Galland 24 ; Oblt. Schöpfel 14 ; Oblt. Joppien 13 ; Lt. Manhard 9 ; Oblt. Klaus, Oblt. von Werra 8 ; Oblt. Schnell, Fw. Behr 7 ; Oblte. Stange, Schultze and Blanck 6.

Curiously enough, the third most successful fighter pilot, Hauptmann Balthasar, with about 20 accredited air victories, was not mentioned.

the broadcast? I should tell you to go right ahead and tell them! For if the R.A.F. *had* lost nine Hurricanes to one German fighter, do you think the loss would be admitted? I think it would be kept very dark! That is a fact which would be obvious to any German airman. So, how would you set about proving to Leutnant von Werr*er*'s fellow prisoners that his claims were false?"

The interrogator was silent.

"It would be the word of this Leutnant von Werr*er*, a German officer, a comrade and a fellow prisoner, against your word as an enemy interrogator. Whom do you think his friends would believe, you or him? You said not long ago that Germans will swallow anything, but I don't think these particular Germans would swallow your particular story, even if it were true!

"Those are the first things I should think of if I were this unfortunate Leutnant von Werr*er*. Then I should consider what price you were likely to ask for keeping quiet; the answer is easy to guess—military information. Of course, I cannot answer for von Werr*er*. But if I were in his place, even if I knew you could *prove* to my friends that my claims were false, I would still say: ' Nothing doing, Herr Major!' "

Von Werra paused, then added in a hard, determined voice:

"Even if this Leutnant von Werr*er* and myself, Oberleutnant von Wer*ra*, were one and the same person, I should still say: ' Nothing doing, Herr Major!' For though you might be able to make it impossible for me to live with my comrades, the alternative, telling you whatever it is you want to know, would be infinitely worse—I should never be able to live with myself."

There was long pause, broken only by the rattling of the windows and the sound of distant explosions. Then the interrogator's voice came flatly from the shadows.

"You have a most extraordinary code of ethics, Oberleutnant."

"Herr Major, as I see it, what you say this Leutnant von Werrer did is one thing; the deliberate betrayal of military secrets to the enemy is another."

Squadron Leader Hawkes reached for his silver-knobbed walking stick, limped over to the side door, and switched on the main light. He returned and sat down at his desk. Without a word he offered von Werra another cigarette.

"Well, Oberleutnant, you received the Iron Cross Second Class for shooting down the two French bombers; your claims to have destroyed six British bombers earned you the Iron Cross First Class. No doubt, in due course, you will be awarded the Knight's Cross of the Iron Cross for destroying nine phantom Hurricanes over a non-existent British airfield. However, there will be nothing insubstantial about the prison camp in which you will have to celebrate the award. Corporal Bates!"

The two men who had been mounting guard outside the door entered and saluted.

"Escort the prisoner to his room, Corporal."

Von Werra stood up.

"Herr Major," he said, "whether I get the Knight's Cross or not remains to be seen. But I'll wager a magnum of champagne to ten cigarettes that I escape within six months!"

Squadron Leader Hawkes, writing at the desk, did not bother to look up.

"Remove him, Corporal," he said wearily.

Perhaps it was as well he did not accept the wager.

He would have lost.

CHAPTER V

Walls have Ears

VON WERRA was taken back to the room at the top of the house. He flopped on to his bed and fell asleep at once. He was left in peace; the guards switched on the light and looked into the room only once during the remainder of the night. And in the morning he was allowed to wash and shave.

But the R.A.F. Intelligence Branch had not finished with him yet. Not by any means. Because he had successfully withstood one kind of interrogation—the gruelling frontal assault using the sledge-hammer technique—did not necessarily mean that he was proof against all forms of attack. He remained at Cockfosters for two weeks, during which he was interrogated repeatedly at all hours of the day and night by half a dozen different German-speaking British officers, working separately and in collaboration. Between them they tried every trick and technique in " the business " to get him to talk, but he refused to be drawn into any discussion. He had learnt his lesson.

He was cajoled, flattered, tempted and provoked. It was suggested that it might be possible to arrange for him to visit the West End—discreetly escorted, naturally, and in civilian clothes; everything would be laid on for him—dinner, a show, a visit to a night-club. He declined the offer. The guards took him to one interrogation which turned out to be " a friendly chat between flying types " with a bottle of whisky (" Help yourself, old man ") and a box of cigars on the table. And to another which turned out to be " a bit of a party while the Old Man's away. We thought you might like to join us."

Von Werra would play none of these dangerous games. He had no illusions about their purpose. He would not talk.

He was kept in solitary confinement for several more days. He was ineffably bored, but now that he had guessed some of the reasons why the British kept him and all newly-captured prisoners in isolation, it no longer preyed on his mind. He ceased to alternate between unwarranted gloom and unfounded hope ; he knew now that his interrogation must run its course and that however long it took, the only thing for him to do was to " sweat it out ". Only thus could he hope to beat the interrogators at their own game. His natural optimism marked time on the certainty that he would eventually be sent to a permanent prisoner-of-war camp, from where he would get a chance to escape.

When, one morning, an interrogator, breezily affable for a change, asked him whether he would like to be moved into a room with other prisoners, von Werra showed no enthusiasm.

" No doubt you will do as you think fit," he said.

As usual, he was sitting in a low chair facing the tall windows, while the interrogator stood with his back to the light, looking down at him.

" I'm going to read out a list of prisoners," the interrogator said. " If you will simply nod your head whenever I mention someone whom you know personally, I will see that you are moved in with any man on the list you care to choose. That's a fair bargain, isn't it ? Note that I'm not asking you to *say* anything. You see that, don't you ?—I'm not asking you to *say* anything. Simply to nod your head ! "

What was the hidden purpose of this new game ? There were a dozen possibilities. Perhaps there were one or two prisoners whom the British had been unable to identify as belonging to any particular unit ; if von Werra indicated that he knew them, it would suggest that they belonged to his *Geschwader*. Perhaps some prisoner had lied, and said he belonged to von Werra's unit when he didn't. Perhaps any prisoners with whom he acknowledged acquaintance would subsequently be interrogated about him. But interrogations, von Werra had learned, were never what they seemed. There was only one golden rule : say nothing.

Listening to the names being read out was a minor ordeal, for he was facing the light and he knew that the interrogator was watching him closely. The list was read with a deliberate, maddening slowness. It contained the names of a dozen men he knew, many of them *Geschwader* comrades. But he did not nod his head and he did not attempt to mislead the interrogator. He sat immobile. The interrogator then read out the names of some of his *Geschwader* comrades again, but the prisoner refused to commit himself to any preference.

The interrogator was much less affable at the end of the interview than he had been at the beginning. Von Werra was given to understand that he was stupid and unreasonable. Finally, the interrogator said :

" Although you have not kept your part of the bargain, I shall keep mine. Whom do you wish to be moved in with ? "

Von Werra did not fall into the trap of denying he had ever made a bargain, thereby becoming involved in an argument. He said :

" I have no preference. Any German will do."

" Right," said the interrogator shortly, " I shall put you in with Leutnant ——. Poor fellow's a little queer in the head. I think you'll very soon adopt a more reasonable attitude. Come with me ! "

He called in the guards and together they went upstairs to a different part of the house from that where von Werra had been confined hitherto. The officer detailed one of the guards to fetch the prisoner's belongings from his old room. Half-way down a corridor the interrogator halted the remaining guard and the prisoner, and went ahead a few paces by himself. He took a key from a hook beside a door, unlocked it and went in, leaving it open. Almost immediately he called out :

" Right, Corporal. Bring him in."

The Englishman was standing near the open window, from where he could observe von Werra's reactions and those of the other occupant of the room. This prisoner was not the expected Leutnant ——, but Oberleutnant Carl Westerhoff, an old and close friend of von Werra, and one of his *Geschwader* comrades. His name had been on the list the interrogator had read out, and had von Werra chosen to share a room with anyone, it would certainly have been Westerhoff. And here he was ! But there was obviously some catch in it.

Quick in the uptake, as usual, von Werra clicked his heels, saluted, and introduced himself as though Westerhoff was a complete stranger.

" Heil Hitler ! Oberleutnant von Werra, fighter pilot."

But Westerhoff was unable to conceal his surprise and pleasure. He, too, had been expecting someone quite different. He gasped.

" Sonny ! *You* here ? " he cried.

The interrogator turned on his heel and walked to the door, shepherding the guard out. Before closing and locking the door behind him, he said with a chuckle :

" Well, so long, *Sonny !* I'll leave you two *Geschwader* comrades together."

Westerhoff said later that the British had evidently not been able to find out for certain to which unit he belonged. He had refused to give any information on this point, and after crash-landing his Messerschmitt he had set fire to it and burned all his papers.

Von Werra had refused to " betray " Westerhoff with a nod ; Westerhoff had given himself away by a gasp. The British, von Werra thought ruefully, killed their cats in a variety of ways.

When the interrogator and the guard had gone, the two prisoners greeted one another with more warmth, and Westerhoff plied his friend with questions.

" How and when were you shot down ? How long have you been here ? Were you at the Hyde Park camp ? Have you seen Squadron Leader Hawkes yet ? "

Von Werra answered briefly, guardedly. He glanced continually round the room, at the walls and the ceiling, and especially in a dark corner, where there was a little ventilator grille. Finally, he interrupted Westerhoff's eager chattering and whispered :

" How long have you been in this room ? "

" They brought me here first thing this morning. I've been alone all the time. You're the first——"

" Ah ! " said von Werra. He put a finger to his lips and whispered :

" There's bound to be a microphone in this room somewhere ! Let's look for it. That ventilator grille in the corner, first. I'll climb up on to your shoulders and have a look. Don't say anything ! "

Westerhoff looked incredulous, but did as he was asked. When von Werra got down off his shoulders he pulled him away from the corner before whispering :

" That's where it is ! Can't see very well, but there's definitely a black thing in there and some wires. And you can see that the face-plate has been removed recently. Let's lean out of the window and talk. We'll be safe there."

" What made you suspect . . . ? "

" Obvious. The British didn't put us together for nothing. We'll have another look at the ventilator to-night, when the light's switched on—be able to see better then."

The presence of a microphone in the ventilator was confirmed by a further inspection after the light had been switched on that night. As far as possible, they avoided dangerous topics of conversation while the window was closed at night and the blackout shutter in position. If they wanted to say something and not be overheard, they moved to a corner remote from the ventilator and spoke in whispers. At first it was a strain remembering to keep a curb on their tongues, but they kept watch on each other and so avoided making any serious blunders. Then von Werra thought of an amusing way of passing the time. He talked loudly for the benefit of the microphone, about imaginary characters, giving them nicknames, describing their appearance, their hobbies, their girl-friends, their exploits, and assigning them to imaginary units. Westerhoff joined in the game, but was no match for von Werra at this sort of thing.

During the day they could lean side by side out of the window, and provided they talked quietly, feel safe from being overheard.

Von Werra kept thinking about the microphone. It irritated him. There was something about it that was not quite right. But however much he thought about it, he could not figure out what it was.

Then, on the morning following his third night in the room, he woke up to find Westerhoff had already removed the blackout shutter and was leaning out of the window. He sat up in bed as though a pin had been stuck into him.

" God, what a fool I've been ! " he cried. " What an utter fool ! "

The ventilator was the most *obvious* place in the room to put a microphone. It was the sort of place that Germans might have chosen, but not the subtle British ! *They had put it there intending it to be found !*

" Hey, Carlchen, could you open the window of the last room you were in ? "

" No. It was fixed. Screwed, I think. Anti-escape measure, I suppose. Why ? What's all the excitement ? "

" Yes, and an anti-suicide measure, too, maybe . . . Carlchen, you poor mutt, we've been done. We've been had. The Tommies have diddled us properly ! "

" What are you blathering about ? Go back to sleep and wake up coherent."

Von Werra groaned. " God, when I think of all we've talked about . . ." He leapt out of bed and went to the window.

" Get your great fanny out of the way, Carlchen, and help me to look for the microphone hidden round this window somewhere ! "

" You're crazy. What microphone ? What *are* you . . ."

" Look," said von Werra seriously, " the window of your last room was fixed, so you couldn't open it. So was mine. So are those of all the other rooms on this side of the house. That's why we've never seen anybody leaning out. The Tommies deliberately left this window in working order so as to entice——"

" But what about the mike in the ventilator ? "

" Probably a dummy—a blind, anyhow. Don't you get it ? Eight chaps out of ten would look for a microphone as soon as they were moved into the room, and find it, as we did, in the first half an hour. Having found it, they would feel so pleased with their cleverness that it would never occur to them, as it has only occurred to me when it's too late, that they were being deliberately tricked into talking into another properly concealed mike, outside the window ! "

But although they closely examined every inch of the window framework, and the wall surrounding it, both inside and outside, and although they tapped the window-ledge and looked underneath the window-sill, they found no trace of a concealed microphone.

While they were making their inspection, von Werra gave a running commentary in a loud clear voice :

" Hallo, R.A.F. Intelligence. Oberleutnant von Werra calling R.A.F. Intelligence. I'm trying to find a microphone concealed near the window of my room. I am now tapping the hollow sash-board on the left-hand side. Are you receiving me ? Oberleutnant von Werra calling and testing . . ."

It may have been pure coincidence, but that same morning both Westerhoff and von Werra were moved out of the room.

Von Werra was moved into a room with five other Luftwaffe officers. There now occurred what German ex-prisoners still talk about when they get together—*Fall Fünfundachtzig*, which may be freely translated as The Eighty-fives Scare. The interrogators suddenly switched from more subtle techniques to an all-out frontal attack against the prisoners. The purpose of the campaign was to obtain information about the Eighty-fives (*die Fünfundachtziger*). One by one, in endless rotation, von Werra and his companions were taken away and asked : " What are the Eighty-fives ? " No sooner had they returned to their room than they were hauled away again : " What are the Eighty-fives ? " No other subjects were discussed. Only this one question : " What are the Eighty-fives ? " Were they a new type of aircraft, a new bomb, a new gun, a new tank, a secret weapon, a radar set—what were they ?

Even if von Werra had been willing to help, he could not have done so, for neither he nor the other prisoners in the room knew what the Eighty-fives were.

The campaign lasted several days and nights. Then, abruptly as it had started, it stopped. The interrogators never referred to the Eighty-fives again.

Next, von Werra was moved into yet another, smaller room. The only other occupant was a German Air Force Leutnant, who was standing at a corner wash-basin washing a pair of socks.

The man introduced himself as Leutnant Kleinert, pilot of the " Schlageter " fighter *Geschwader*. He was an Austrian, very talkative and friendly, but oppressed by a great sense of grievance against the world. He said he had been an aeronautical engineer up to a few months previously. He claimed to have been an assistant of Professor Willi Messerschmitt, and to have met all the important people in the Luftwaffe and German Air Ministry connected with the arms programme. In order to get first-hand experience of Messerschmitt aircraft under combat conditions, he had been temporarily " loaned " to the Luftwaffe, and on his first operational flight had been shot down and taken prisoner.

" Naturally," he went on, " I'm especially interested in technical matters relating to Messerschmitts. For instance, we had endless trouble in designing the bomb-racks and release mechanism for the 109's. Have you had any experience with——"

" Shut up ! " said von Werra coldly. " Walls have ears."

Leutnant Kleinert looked pained and puzzled.

" I don't quite understand you, Oberleutnant. You mean, there might be concealed microphones ? Ah, that's a lot of nonsense ! "

"Possibly," said von Werra, "but there's always the risk. We shall not, therefore, discuss service matters of any kind."

"On the other hand," he added, looking Kleinert straight in the eye, "concealed mikes might be superfluous in this particular room."

"W-what *do* you mean?"

"I mean that as you have never seen me before in your life, I might be a stool-pigeon. And if I were, concealed microphones wouldn't be necessary, would they?"

Kleinert laughed uneasily.

"What a terrific imagination you have, Oberleutnant!" he said.

Shortly afterwards, the Austrian was taken away, "for interrogation," and did not return. Von Werra remained alone in the room for a couple of days, then he, too, was moved again.

After two weeks at Cockfosters, von Werra was returned to London District Cage, Kensington Palace Gardens, where he was interrogated for another four days.

He now learned what it was like to be on the receiving end of a German bombing raid, for he passed the nights with other prisoners in an attic room, with bombs falling nearby and anti-aircraft guns in Hyde Park blazing away uninterruptedly. Added to the external din of the raid there was intermittent stamping of feet, beating of fists on doors, prisoners demanding to be taken to an air raid shelter, other prisoners shouting at them to shut up, and guards bawling the lot down to restore order. Von Werra's sleep was fitful.

The menagerie in the "Cage" just then included some odd characters. One of the prisoners, a bomber pilot, was in full service evening dress. He had been invited to a party, which he was reluctant to miss altogether, on the night of his final flight, and had worn evening dress under his flying kit in order to save changing time when he arrived back at his French base. He arrived at London District Cage instead. Another prisoner had been roped in to make up a deficient crew a few minutes before take-off, when he was on the point of setting off for Germany on leave. He arrived at the "Cage" with a suitcase packed with wine, Cognac and French farm butter. No doubt, it was just these little attentions that the interrogators appreciated.

Another prisoner looked more Chinese than a Chinaman. Large patches of his uniform, his hands, face and hair were a brilliant yellow. German airmen had recently been issued with small containers filled with a special dye. If they had the misfortune to come down in " the drink ", they could release the dye as a marker for Air-Sea Rescue. This particular pilot had somehow released the stopper of his dye container as he baled out. The rush of air had done the rest. He was only a youngster, cheerful, no whit the worse for his experience and sublimely indifferent about his fantastic and frightening appearance. He told von Werra the Luftwaffe made an indelible impression on the farm hand who found him in a field of kale.

Late on the fourth night, at the end of a long and acrimonious interrogation, von Werra was told he would be sent to a permanent prison camp for officers the next morning. The interrogators had finished with him at last. They had worked on him for three weeks. During that time he had not knowingly given away any military information whatsoever.

But the British had given von Werra a great deal of information : in the process of questioning him they had unavoidably provided him with an almost complete picture of their interrogation methods and techniques. And thanks to his shrewdness, he had gained an insight into other work of the R.A.F. Intelligence organisation.

It was to transpire that the information the British gave von Werra was of far greater importance than anything he could have told them—if he had been willing to do so.

He subsequently went to great lengths to amplify the knowledge he had gained at Cockfosters and London District P.O.W. Cage. He did this by gathering impressions and information about their interrogation experiences from other prisoners. He discussed the matter fully with several German Staff Officers who had been captured. They, too, had been strongly impressed and slightly awed by British interrogation methods, and agreed with von Werra that the German High Command probably had no conception of the menace these methods were to German security. The Staff Officers were especially concerned about German prisoners' lack of " security consciousness ", and were aghast at the number of prisoners who had been carrying documents, maps, diaries, letters, etc., when captured.

No doubt, the number of Germans who knowingly betrayed military secrets was negligible ; but such was the inadequacy of their security training that the majority of prisoners gave away information without ever realising that they had done so. Von Werra felt that most Germans underrated the importance of interrogation and the skill of the interrogators, whom they dismissed as " old women " and " desk warriors ". Few of them understood what " information useful to the enemy " meant, nor how wide a field it covered. To them, betraying secrets meant giving away names, strengths and locations of units, drawing maps of airfields and revealing technical data. As long as they were not asked to do any of these things, they seemed to be quite willing—and even eager —to gossip about generalities with the British, for they felt that they were thereby keeping the conversation off dangerous topics. Von Werra had had first-hand experience of the use to which all this " harmless " talk could be put, and he knew that there was no scrap of apparently trivial and irrelevant information that the R.A.F. Intelligence Branch did not record and eventually fit into the picture.

In the end, there was at that time no German better informed about British interrogation methods than Oberleutnant Franz von Werra. This fact was to acquire an immense significance and to have far-reaching consequences for both the Royal Air Force and the Luftwaffe.

CHAPTER VI

Escape in the Lake District

VON WERRA arrived at Officers' P.O.W. Camp No. 1, Grizedale Hall, in the Lake District, towards the end of September 1940. At that time it was the only camp in the country for captured officers. None of the other camps set up later matched the setting of Camp No. 1, and until Cockfosters became an internment camp for captured generals in 1944, none could compare with it for excellence of accommodation. Nevertheless, judged by the standards set later by Canadian and American prison camps, Grizedale Hall was dreadfully primitive. For example, Bowmanville Camp on Lake Ontario, was described, somewhat plaintively (because German prisoners persisted in escaping from it), by editorials in Canadian newspapers as "the most luxurious prison camp in the world." It contained an indoor swimming bath, a theatre-cum-cinema, a large library building, a gymnasium and a covered tennis court. There was nothing like that at Grizedale Hall.

Grizedale is in Lancashire, three miles south of Hawkshead, a mile north of the hamlet of Satterthwaite, and midway between Windermere and Coniston Water. On the Coniston side of Grizedale the wild moorland country begins, extending almost without a break for twenty miles to the Irish Sea.

The Hall was once one of the stately homes of England, a gaunt, stone mansion containing thirty to forty rooms. The nearest shops are in Hawkshead, three miles away over a desolate moorland road ; the nearest town approachable by road (Bowness and Windermere are on the other side of the Lake) is Ambleside, fourteen miles away ; except in the tourist season, no buses pass through Grizedale. After standing empty for some years, the house had been turned into a holiday camp, and then in 1940 the War Office took it over for use as a prison camp. Its isolation made it ideal for the purpose.

In the early part of the war it came to be known locally as ' U-boat Hotel '; then later, when it was used as a special centre for top-ranking German officers, including Field Marshal von Rundstedt, it was rechristened ' Hush-Hush Hall '.

It stands empty again to-day, though the Forestry Commission work the estate for its timber. The army huts and the complicated system of barbed-wire fences have long since been removed, but there are still traces of its wartime role. The imposing, studded main door opens into a gloomy hall lit by stained-glass windows incorporating the armorial bearings of the last private owner. Here in one corner is a built-in clothes cupboard, which is a memorial to German military discipline and orderliness. The cupboard is shelved from top to bottom, and on the edge of each shelf is glued a strip of paper bearing in neat italic lettering the rank of officers to which it was allocated. The shelves were allocated on the basis of convenience. Thus, the shelf at shoulder level for a man of average height is labelled *Obersten* (Colonels), the one immediately below it *Oberstleutnante* (Lieutenant Colonels), then, at the bottom, *Majore*. It was evidently decided that it was less inconvenient to stoop down to a shelf than to stand on a chair to reach one, and the top three shelves are labelled *Leutnante* (second Lieutenants) *Oberleutnante* (Lieutenants) and *Hauptleute* (Captains) in that order.

The large, panelled library, with its handsome fireplace and wide windows overlooking the valley and the road winding down towards Satterthwaite, was used by the prisoners as a common room. The walls of the best bedrooms, used, no doubt, by Colonels, are covered with material, possibly silk, bearing hand-painted floral designs. There are no signs of vandalism, and though the walls of some of the rooms used by German O.R's, assigned to the camp as batmen and orderlies, are scribbled on, the oak panelling was respected and is unscratched. Round the walls of one of the servants' rooms there is a striking frieze bearing an elaborate, repetitive floral pattern. On close examination it can be seen to be painted in water colour on toilet paper. It must have taken months to complete.

The British military authorities converted part of the basement into cells for prisoners sentenced to disciplinary punishment. The walls are covered with pencilled drawings of U-boats and sinking ships, and of German bombers and fighters shooting down Hurricanes and Spitfires.

The senior German officer was responsible to the Camp Commandant for the prisoners' discipline. He and the officers next in seniority formed the *Ältestenrat* (literally, ' council of the eldest ' of the camp—a sort of governing body. Its overt functions were to maintain discipline in the camp, to look after the welfare of prisoners and to act as their representatives in dealings with the British military authorities. Theoretically, no power whatsoever was vested in the *Ältestenrat*; punishment for infractions of discipline, for instance, was determined and carried out by the British. But in practice, it wielded immense power. It acted as the Escape Committee for the camp, censored mail, and sat as a secret court to try prisoners suspected of having anti-Nazi views or of having betrayed military secrets to their captors. There were several cases at camps in this country of prisoners being secretly condemned to death and executed, and many more in camps in the U.S.A. It is certain that members of a later, different *Ältestenrat* at Grizedale Hall were implicated in an incident in 1941—a year after von Werra was there—in which an officer, "convicted" of having betrayed his trust, was compelled to attempt to escape with fatal results.[1]

At the time Franz von Werra arrived at Grizedale Hall, the *Ältestenrat* comprised two Luftwaffe General Staff Officers, Major Willibald Fanelsa and Hauptmann Helmut Pohle, and a U-boat commander, Kapitänleutnant Werner Lott. Fanelsa had arrived at the camp only a few days before von Werra. He had been shot down while trying out a new German aid to target location in a small raid on Coventry.

Pohle was one of the R.A.F.'s first victims of the war. A personal friend of Goering, he had demanded on capture that Berlin be telephoned and asked to send a Red Cross plane to pick him up Instead, he was sent to the Tower of London, which at that time was an interrogation centre.

Lott had made the first attempt to escape from Grizedale Hall.

[1]Leutnant Bernhard Berndt, a U-boat captain, surrendered his ship on its maiden voyage in 1941 to a Hudson aircraft.

German officers at Grizedale Hall, especially other U-boat commanders, made his life unbearable. He was finally told there was " no longer any room " for him at the camp. He must escape that night, or take the consequences.

He managed to get out of camp, but guards noticed his absence immediately. The next morning members of the Home Guard found Berndt under a tarpaulin in a shed two miles from the camp. He was glad to be captured, thinking he would be taken to another camp. When his captors made it clear they were returning him to Grizedale Hall, Berndt broke away and dashed across a field. The Home Guards fired warning shots over his head. He continued running. The Home Guards fired again. Berndt stumbled and fell. He died a few minutes later.

Somehow or another he acquired several pounds of English money (prisoners were paid in token money valid only in the camp canteen), an identity card (faked) and civilian clothing, but he did not succeed in getting beyond the inner ring of barbed-wire entanglements surrounding the camp.

The arrival of a new batch of prisoners was always a great event at prison camps. In accordance with custom, von Werra and the other newcomers in his group were invited by the *Ältestenrat* to relate their experiences to a meeting of prisoners held in the panelled common room. Von Werra described how he was shot down and captured, and some of his experiences at the interrogation centres. When he mentioned Leutnant Kleinert, the Austrian engineer who had been shot down on his first operational flight, he noticed that many of the men in his audience smiled and nudged one another.

" When I was taken into the room," von Werra continued, " Kleinert was——"

"—standing at the wash-basin, washing his socks ! " chanted his listeners in unison.

Von Werra had to shout to make himself heard above the general laughter :

" You may laugh, but I'm convinced that Kleinert was never in the Luftwaffe, but is a——"

"—British spy ! " the prisoners cried in chorus.

When the laughter subsided, Major Fanelsa explained to von Werra that most of the prisoners had come into contact with this " Leutnant Kleinert ", in one guise or another. But whether he was posing as a fighter pilot or a member of a bomber or U-boat crew, he was always found in the act of washing his socks, as though he were a prisoner of long standing. Prisoners who failed to mention an encounter with " Leutnant Kleinert " in one of his guises, were suspected of having been taken in by the stool-pigeon and would subsequently be more closely questioned by members of the *Ältestenrat*.

In the evenings prisoners gathered in the common room where a log fire was burning. There was a piano and sometimes there were concerts and sing-songs. Some played chess, draughts or a card game called *Skat*, others stood in groups, talking. On his first evening von Werra was standing in an animated group of fighter pilots, when he chanced to overhear a German naval officer in a neighbouring group say :

" Just you chaps wait till the Eighty-fives arrive . . ."

Von Werra grabbed the naval officer's arm.

" Did I hear you say ' the Eighty-fives ' ? " he cried.

" Yes," laughed the sailor, " Why ? "

" Quick—for heaven's sake tell me what they are ! The interrogators drove us nearly mad asking about them."

The naval officer explained that they were the men of the 85th Marine Infantry Regiment, and that it was a current joke in the German Navy, when things went awry, to say " Wait till the Eighty-fives get here ! "

Apparently R.A.F. Intelligence had heard the phrase—perhaps it had been picked up by a concealed microphone—and had concluded that the Eighty-fives were some new German secret weapon.

Within ten days of arriving at Grizedale Hall Camp, von Werra had devised a plan for a solo escape.

He worked out the details and completed the preparations as far as he could, and then asked the senior German officer, Major Fanelsa, for permission to submit the scheme to the *Ältestenrat* for " official " approval.

He was told to report to the senior officer's room that evening. On his way there he noted that two prisoners were on sentry duty in the corridor outside the room. The three members of the *Ältestenrat*, Major Fanelsa, Hauptmann Pohle and Kapitänleutnant Lott, were already present.

" Take a seat, Werra," said Major Fanelsa. " First of all we should tell you that in our opinion there is little possibility of a successful escape at the present time. I don't know how much you have heard of Kapitänleutnant Lott's attempt to escape. It was made at a time when conditions were very much more favourable and had been prepared down to the last detail. Since then the guard has been doubled and all kinds of new security measures have been introduced—for instance, the barbed-wire fences are now floodlit at night. There are other, even more serious drawbacks to attempting to escape at the present time. When Kapitänleutnant Lott made his attempt it was reasonable to assume that the attitude of the British authorities, and of the British public, towards an escaper would be fair and sportsmanlike. Since then, Britain has been bombed on a large scale. The chances are that a prisoner who escaped at this time would be shot, deliberately or ' accidentally ', or at least severely beaten up, if he were recaptured.

" Kapitänleutnant Lott, together with Hauptmann Pohle and other officers, have tried constantly to devise some new means of escape. Dozens of plans have been submitted to them and they have all had to be rejected outright as hare-brained and impracticable, or shelved until a more favourable moment arrives to put them into practice. Now you, Werra, who have been here barely a week, report that you have worked out a feasible scheme for a solo attempt !

" The last thing we want to do is to discourage men with the will to escape. If you have a sound scheme we will do everything in our power to help you—otherwise, we can give you neither help nor permission to proceed."

" If you will permit me, sir," said von Werra, " I should like to explain my plan."

" Right, go ahead."

" As you know, gentlemen, three or four times a week— usually every other day—a party of twenty-four prisoners, escorted by four armed guards at the front, four at the rear, a sergeant on horseback and one officer on foot in charge, is taken out of the camp at 10.30 a.m. for exercise along the road. The road runs practically north and south, and the party never knows beforehand whether it will be marched to the north, uphill and over a bleak moor, or to the south, downhill and through a little village. The decision regarding the direction to be taken seems to depend on the whim of the mounted sergeant at the moment the party arrives at the gateway of the camp. Sometimes the party is taken in the same direction on two consecutive outings.

" Whether the northern or the southern route is taken, the procedure followed is the same. The prisoners are marched at a smart pace for about three kilometres to a selected bend in the road, where they are halted and rested for ten minutes, before being marched back to the camp. In either case the halt is made at a bend in the road because that makes it easier to keep an eye on the party during the rest period.

" I have been on all the marches, both to the north and the south, since I have been here. Discipline and surveillance during the march is strict. The prisoners march in eight ranks of three abreast. The mounted sergeant rides continually up and down and round the column. However, it is possible for a prisoner to move from one rank to the next without being spotted—the outside man on the left of one rank moves up to the next, and the man on the outside right in that rank moves back to take the first man's place. In that way I have moved from near the back of the column to its head and back again without being noticed.

" There is a wire fence on the bend of the road where the halt is made on the northern route, and there is no cover of any kind. But I believe the point where the halt is made on the southern route offers a great opportunity for one man to escape during the rest period. Hauptmann Pohle and Kapitänleutnant Lott both know the place.

" Soon after passing through the little village one comes to a wood that rises steeply off the right-hand side of the road. On the left is flat meadowland. After passing along the edge of the wood for a couple of hundred metres, there is a sharp right-hand turn in the road. In the angle of the turn there is a five-barred gate. A wall of the kind you see everywhere in this district begins at the gateway and stretches southwards into the distance along the road. The wall is breast high on the road side, and is made of flat stones laid one on top of the other. It is finished off with a row of stones placed on end, so that the top is jagged. The level of the meadow is somewhat lower than the level of the road.

" As soon as the party reaches this bend in the road, the mounted sergeant shouts ' Halt ! ' The prisoners then move over to the wall to rest. Some lean against it and those who have coats lay them on the jagged stones and sit on top.

" Immediately the party is halted, the four guards at either end of the column move across to the opposite side of the road, from where it is easier for them to keep the whole group of prisoners under observation. There is a huge boulder in the angle of the road on the wooded side opposite the spot where the party rests. The mounted sergeant takes up a position in front of this boulder, or near it, so that he, too, can keep an eye on the prisoners.

" Thus, all the guards are on one side of the road, and the prisoners on the other. *The rear of the party—the meadow side of the wall—is not covered by the guards !*

" Although a long stretch of the road can be seen to the south from the bend, only one of the two sets of four guards can see it. Moreover, it has a blind spot. About fifty metres south from the bend, the road dips and twists at the same point. You will see what I am getting at, gentlemen. If a man could drop unseen from the wall into the meadow, he could run along behind the wall to the blind spot in the road, climb over into the road again, and cross into the woods opposite without coming once into the guards' field of view !

" Can this be done ? Gentlemen, I'm sure it can—and I have already tried it out to the point of lying out flat on top of the wall without being spotted !

" This is my plan : as soon as the party is halted, two men drape their coats side by side on the top of the wall so that they partly overlap. I am already at this spot and am immediately surrounded by eight of the tallest and heaviest prisoners who completely screen me from the guards, who are in the process of taking up their positions on the opposite side of the road. Keeping as low as possible, I climb on to the wall and lie out flat on the coats. They are necessary as they prevent the loose stones from being dislodged. One of the eight men will give me a dig with his elbow as soon as the guards' attention has been momentarily distracted by four other prisoners. This will be the signal for me to drop into the meadow. I shall wait at the base of the wall for a moment in case any of the guards have spotted me. If everything appears to be normal, I shall be given a verbal signal to proceed. I shall then run crouching along the wall to the dip in the road, climb back over the wall and cross the road into the wood on the other side. I shall penetrate as far into the wood as possible as quickly as I can without making a noise.

" As soon as I have dropped into the meadow the eight prisoners who have been screening me must spread out a little, but not obviously, so that the guards can see gaps between them and part of the coats. If this is done adroitly, there is no reason why they should suspect anything.

" The operation must be carried out as quickly as possible after the arrival of the party at the bend, preferably immediately, while the guards are taking up their positions.

" As far as the actual operation of getting over the wall into the meadow is concerned, there is only one source of danger, and that is the mounted sergeant, who will probably be directly opposite me on the other side of the road. Being on horseback, he might be able to detect some movement over the shoulders of the men screening me at the moment when I am getting on to the wall. Several of the prisoners are in the habit of admiring and patting the sergeant's horse before the party leaves the camp, and again after we get back. One, in particular, is known to the sergeant as a keen horseman. To-day, to test the sergeant's reactions, I got this prisoner to cross the road to pat the horse immediately the halt was called. This had never happened before, but the sergeant let the prisoner make a fuss of the animal for about a minute before telling him to go across to the other side of the road. Meanwhile, the rider's attention was distracted from the prisoners. There is no reason why this should not happen again.

" There is one other danger : the telephone box on the roadside as you enter the village from the camp end. No roster of prisoners taking part in walks is prepared and there is no roll call during the rest period. Only numerical checks are made. The prisoners are counted before leaving the camp and again on their return. The sergeant makes two further checks while they are marching, once on the outward trip and once coming back. .The check on the inward march usually takes place as the party is moving off after the rest period, or at the latest, before it passes back through the village. The danger is that the sergeant will discover that one prisoner is missing, ride ahead to the telephone box and warn the camp. This would result in the mobile search party being sent out and the anti-escape machinery set in motion long before the party of prisoners gets back to the camp. It is therefore essential for the prisoners to try to confuse the counting for as long as possible after the return journey has been started. This can be done by the continual movement of men from one rank of three to the next, in the manner I mentioned earlier. If the discovery that a prisoner is missing can be delayed until the party has passed beyond the telephone box, it should give me a better chance of getting out of the wood and away before the mobile search party arrives on the scene.

" Under the circumstances, it is not possible for me to carry any kind of rucksack. What little I can take with me I shall have to carry in my pockets. I propose to take with me only shaving kit, so as not to present a scruffy and suspicious appearance if I succeed in reaching a West Coast port. My object is to stow away on a neutral ship, or to get to Ireland. I shall also carry soap, towel, and a pair of socks. Food is the principal difficulty. I have saved my chocolate to carry as iron rations. For the rest I shall have to rely on my wits and the little English money I have managed to acquire. Though rainfall is heavy here at this time of year, as I must travel quickly, I believe any kind of greatcoat or raincoat would be more of a hindrance than a help. I have acquired a small, home-made compass and one of the prisoners, Oberleutnant Perchermeier, who was a draughtsman in civilian life, has drawn me a map of the area and part of Northern Ireland. I don't suppose it is accurate, but it is the best I can do and it embodies everything that men in the camp remember of the area. Perchermeier has made a copy of it for possible future use.

" I realise that the country round here is very rough, but I have trained as unobtrusively as possible since my arrival, particularly by joining the men who run round the little exercise ground in the evenings.

" One other thing, gentlemen. I should like to take with me some notes, written in miniature, of the information which I have picked up since I was taken prisoner."

There was a moment's silence as von Werra finished speaking. The three members of the *Ältestenrat* looked at one another. Then Major Fanelsa said :

" I see you have given the matter very careful thought, Werra. I give you full marks for that. And equally important, you have no illusions about the difficulties. The way you presented it, the plan sounds feasible enough, but I do not know the place. Lott, you know it—what are your views ? "

" I have no hesitation in saying that Werra's plan is by far the best that has so far been laid before us, but I'm not sure that he realises what he's up against once he gets away. I am wholeheartedly in favour of giving him permission to make the attempt the next time the exercise party is marched south. As the Herr Major knows, my most secret and valuable possession is a large-scale British map of the area. I suggest this be made available to Werra to study and have copied."

Major Fanelsa turned to the other member of the *Ältestenrat*.

" I agree with Lott," Hauptmann Pohle said. " I'm in favour of letting von Werra try, and I think we should give him all the help we can.

" The first thing you must understand, Werra," said Pohle, " is that if you do manage to reach the coast, you will not find any seaworthy small craft that you can ' hire ' or steal. Owing to the threat of invasion, owners of small craft have been ordered to immobilise them. Your only hope is to get to a port and stow away on a neutral vessel."

"The country between here and the coast is extremely hard going," said Lott. "It's a switchback of hills and dales the whole way. The hills are high and bleak, and your only cover will be the stone walls, which you will find everywhere. You will have to climb over hundreds of them! The sides of some of the valleys are strewn with rocks and boulders. You will also have to walk through stretches of swampy land and to wade or swim across rivers. In addition, the chances are that at least half the time it will be raining—the cold, driving penetrating rain that no greatcoat or raincoat can keep out—I think you are wise not to bother with one. The wear and tear on your clothing is going to be very heavy. "By the time you reach the coast your appearance might easily give you away. It is therefore essential that you wear the toughest possible clothing. There is a U-boat officer in the camp who has a pair of long leather trousers hidden away. I think we could arrange to let you have them—they would be ideal for your purpose—and perhaps also a leather jerkin and a pair of sea boots."

"I should be most grateful for the trousers and jerkin," von Werra said, "but my own jackboots are almost new—nicely worn in. I don't think I could do better than wear them on the trip."

"I think it's time to tell you about some of the other things you will be up against," said Major Fanelsa. "It seems that the British think we shall drop paratroops in this area in the event of an invasion. We understand that there is one battalion of troops in Windermere and another at Ulverston some twenty kilometres south of here. So you will see that apart from guards from the camp, the police and the Home Guard, there are large numbers of troops at hand to join in the hunt for you! It is likely that the British authorities will use your escape as a means of testing and exercising their anti-paratroop defences in the area."

Lott got up and went to the panelled wall of the room. He took a table knife from his pocket and carefully removed with it, first the beading round the panel, and then the panel itself. The parts came away quite easily, as though they had often been removed before. From the cache behind the panel, Lott took a folded map.

Von Werra was delighted by the cleverly concealed cache but

the map was a disappointment. It was a tattered negative photostatic copy, and was very faint.

" You don't know the worst yet, Werra," said Lott, as he spread the map over the table. " In the event of an escape a mobile search party of at least fifty men can be sent out at once. They will throw a cordon round the whole area. The fact that we are in between two long parallel lakes, Coniston Water and Windermere, running north to south, makes the task of encirclement much easier. A river runs south from both lakes, and these rivers converge on the coast, so that, to all intents and purposes, we are on a peninsular.

" The mobile guards from the camp patrol the roads on the neck of the peninsular, that is, between the northern ends of the two lakes, and cover the bridges over the rivers to the south. Within half an hour, all strategic points will have been occupied. In order to discourage escape attempts, the Camp Commandant has let it be known that, as soon as an escape is reported, police in launches will clear the two lakes of all other boats, which will be guarded or immobilised as long as the emergency lasts, so that the prisoner cannot break through the cordon by rowing from one bank to the other. The police will patrol the lakes in case he should attempt to swim across.

" Your best plan, Werra," Major Fanelsa said, " is to break through the ring at an isolated spot by crossing the river running south from Coniston Water during your first night of freedom. From then on you must, as it were, disappear off the face of the earth. Keep to the hills and avoid villages and farm houses like the plague. Rest during the day and travel at night."

Two days later, on Monday 7 October 1940, Franz von Werra and twenty-three other German officers, led by Hauptmann Pohle, set out on a route march from Grizedale Hall, at 2 p.m. In the meantime Major Fanelsa had asked the Camp Commandant to change the time of the walks from 10.30 a.m. to 2 p.m. as the morning walks interfered with the educational classes at the camp. The real reason was that by escaping in the afternoon instead of the morning, von Werra would only have three, instead of seven hours to wait for nightfall, when he could move with greater security. There would also be less time for the hunt to get under way before darkness fell.

The prisoners were escorted by one British officer, two N.C.O.s

—one of them mounted—and seven men. They carried side arms or rifles. Later, the camp authorities were unable to find out who had given the order for the party to turn southwards at the camp gates. The mounted sergeant, who was usually in charge of the party, said he did not give the order, as on this occasion an officer was taking part in the walk. The officer said he hadn't. In point of fact, the order was given, according to a prearranged plan, by Hauptmann Pohle. The leading guards never suspected that a German had given the order, and obediently wheeled to the left.

The party passed through the village of Satterthwaite, and ten minutes later approached High Bowkerstead corner, where the halt was always made. As soon as von Werra turned the bend and looked southwards down the road, his heart fell. The unforeseen had happened. On all the previous outings he had made from the camp, he had seen only a few people and hardly ever a car or lorry. But now, about a quarter of a mile away, coming towards them, was a man with a horse and cart.

The party halted. The guards took up their positions, the prisoners moved across to the wall, the sergeant halted his horse in front of the big boulder on the opposite side of the road, and the officer stood nearby. He instantly ordered back the prisoner detailed to distract the sergeant's attention by moving across the road to pat the horse.

Von Werra dared not move because the man with the horse and cart would have seen him on the meadow side of the wall. However, he got into position and waited, sick with suspense and frustration. The minutes of the rest period ticked by. The horse and cart approached the bend with maddening slowness.

As the cart drew nearer, von Werra saw that it was loaded with fruit and vegetables. The driver was the local greengrocer. Instead of ruining von Werra's plan, he proved to be its saviour, for when he reached the party he provided the perfect distraction. As the cart drew level von Werra hoisted himself on to the wall, keeping as low as possible, and stretching himself out on his back on the coats covering the loose, jagged stones. He was completely hidden behind his carefully grouped companions. After a moment an elbow nudged him urgently. Simultaneously, he rolled over and dropped into the meadow, landing neatly on his hands and toes. It worked perfectly. No sound was heard above the loud chattering of the prisoners. Not a stone was dislodged.

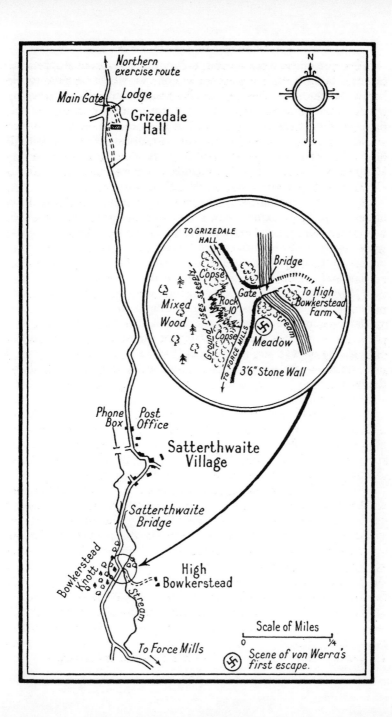

Northern
exercise route

Main Gate   Lodge
Grizedale
Hall

TO GRIZEDALE
HALL
Copse   Bridge
Gate   To High
Bowkerstead
Mixed   Rock   Farm
Wood   10'   Stream
Copse   Meadow
TO FORCE MILLS
3'6" Stone Wall

Ground rises steeply

Phone   Post
Box   Office

Satterthwaite
Village

Satterthwaite
Bridge

Bowkerstead Knott
High
Bowkerstead

Stream

To Force Mills

Scale of Miles
0   ¼

Scene of von Werra's
first escape.

With the officer's permission, the mounted sergeant stopped the cart and bought some eating apples, one of which he gave to his horse. Some of the other guards also bought fruit. By the time the transactions were completed and the greengrocer had moved off, there were only about two of the ten minutes rest period left.

The sergeant ordered the column to re-form. The guards took up their positions at the head and rear. As the order to march was about to be given, there were sounds of cries coming from a long way down the road to the south. Nearly half a mile away two women were running along the road, shouting and waving their handkerchiefs. Looking back, the guards and prisoners could see only the heads and waving handkerchiefs of the women above the wall. With great presence of mind, Hauptmann Pohle started waving in reply, and other prisoners followed suit.

The officer and the sergeant immediately ordered them to stop it. Muttering darkly about women who waved to German prisoners, the sergeant ordered the column to march, and it disappeared round the corner on the way back to the camp.

The two women were not waving to the prisoners, but to the guards. They were trying to draw their attention to the escaped prisoner who was running bent double along the meadow side of the wall.

CHAPTER VII

Mystery on Hesk Fell

AFTER DROPPING off the wall into the meadow, von Werra waited for a moment until he received the prearranged verbal signal from one of his comrades. He then ran crouching along the wall to the spot where he was to climb back into the road and cross to the wood on the other side. He faintly heard the cries of the women, but he did not see them immediately as only their heads were showing above the wall. When he spotted the waving handkerchiefs, he realised that the women were trying to give him away to the guards.

It was a horrible moment. He crouched down waiting for the rifle bullet. He had to fight back an urge to stand up and raise his arms in surrender. He very nearly did so when the prisoners started shouting and whistling, as this was not at all according to plan, and for a moment he thought they must be signalling that the game was up and that he should surrender to save himself from being shot. But if that were the case, he reasoned, they would call him by name. So he shrank to the smallest possible size, held his breath, and waited.

The sergeant shouted an order. There was a sound of shuffling feet, the grinding of nailed boots on the gritty road.

They were moving off!

In a flash von Werra realised that the prisoners, all of whom had played a part in the plan and knew that he had escaped, had saved the situation by shouting, whistling, and no doubt waving, to the women. A feeling of gratitude, a poignant sense of comradeship, welled up within him.

He saw that the women had now stopped waving and were standing close together, a quarter of a mile away, staring at him. He noticed that one was holding a hand over her mouth and clutching the arm of her companion with the other. Von Werra was highly amused. Now that the party of prisoners had disappeared round the corner, the women were on a lonely stretch of road with a desperate escaped Nazi whom they had tried to betray! They were too scared to move.

Von Werra stood up cautiously and peered over the wall towards the bend in the road where he had staged his escape. Except for the two women, the road was clear in both directions. He jumped over the wall feeling so happy and excited that he quite forgave them their attempted betrayal, and as he dashed across the road he grinned and waved gaily to them. He squeezed through the thin hazel hedge on the other side of the road, and entered the wood.

The ground rose steeply, and for some distance there was thick undergrowth. As he picked his way through it as quickly and quietly as possible, he received the final signal from his comrades marching back to the camp.

It had been arranged that the prisoners would sing one of two marching songs. One song meant that the party had marched three hundred yards without the guards suspecting anything; the other that the escape had been discovered.

The song that von Werra heard told him that he had not been missed.

He began to move more rapidly, with less concern for stealth. Soon he was clear of the belt of undergrowth and entered the pine wood. The trees were tall and their thick trunks provided excellent cover. Round them grew bracken, turning yellow and withering. At first von Werra was glad of the extra concealment it gave, for in places it was breast high. But he soon began to curse it. The ground was so steep that he could not have run even if he had had a clear passage. As it was, he had to scramble through the bracken on all fours, his boots slipping on the stalks. In the silence of the wood, the rustling of the ferns as he groped his way through them sounded like the rattle of gravel tipped off a lorry.

At last he reached the top of the hill, the blood pounding in his temples, chest heaving, leg muscles a-quiver from the effort. He had climbed four hundred feet since leaving the road. He stood behind a tree and looked back. There was no sign or sound of movement in the wood. There was only the murmur in the treetops, the panting of his breath, the thumping of his heart. There was the scent of pines, the pungent smell of crushed bracken stalks and the

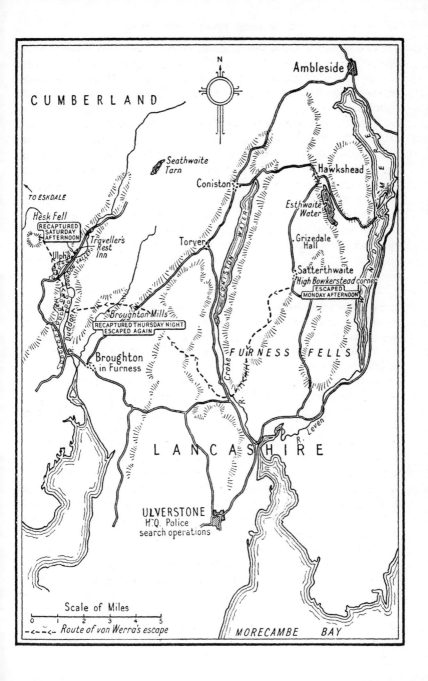

CUMBERLAND

Ambleside

N

Seathwaite
Tarn

Coniston

Hawkshead

TO ESKDALE

Hesk Fell

RECAPTURED
SATURDAY
AFTERNOON

Traveller's
Rest
Inn

Ulpha

Esthwaite
Water

Torver

Grizedale
Hall

Satterthwaite
High Bowkerstead corner

ESCAPED
MONDAY AFTERNOON

Broughton Mills

RECAPTURED THURSDAY NIGHT
ESCAPED AGAIN

FURNESS FELLS

Broughton
in Furness

LANCASHIRE

ULVERSTONE
H.Q. Police
search operations

Scale of Miles

0   1   2   3   4   5

-·<-·- Route of von Werra's escape

MORECAMBE   BAY

sweet dampness of the earth. And he was Franz von Werra and he was free.

Onwards he went, in a singing exhilaration. Down into a gully, where there was no bracken but a thick, springy carpet of pine needles, up the other side, down a deeper gully with a stream at the bottom of it, up again—and there was his first objective—the western edge of the wood.

He paused there and looked out. As far as the eye could see there was fold after fold of rough, stony moorland, with no sign of life except a couple of crows cawing testily over a gully, and the cry and wing-beat of a distant plover.

Onward !

To the south, along the edge of the wood. No need to consult map or compass yet. During the next hour he skirted woods that had delightful names—Cicely's Brow, Hob Gill, Low Fell, Higher Thorny Slack, Sale Moss, Green Hows, Ash Slack and Chamley Bank—but to him they were all *the* wood.

At last he reached his second objective, the tip of wood that stuck out like a thumb into the moors. He moved back into the wood a little way till he found a suitable thicket. He crawled into the middle of it and lay down to wait for nightfall. The time by his watch was twenty minutes to five and sunset was not until 6.23. He was breathing hard and his clothes stuck to his body, but he did not feel tired, only terribly thirsty. He recalled that two of his friends at the camp had sacrificed their lunch in order to give him a good start. He felt very happy.

An hour later it started to rain. For the next five nights and days it was seldom to cease.

Von Werra's comrades were in high spirits when they started back for the camp after the rest period at High Bowkerstead Corner. The guards were taken by surprise when, some distance from the corner, the prisoners burst spontaneously into full-voiced song, for singing on the walks was forbidden.

Then the trouble started. The mounted sergeant shouted, the officer shouted, cleared his throat, and shouted again. He waved his stick. The four leading guards showed signs of uneasiness.

The prisoners started to force the pace, those in front almost pushing the guards along. The repeated orders for the singing to be stopped were ignored. It was obvious that there would be no more such walks, at least for a very long time, and the prisoners were determined to make the most of it. All that mattered was that Oberleutnant von Werra had escaped.

The sergeant rode up and down the column trying to count the prisoners, but they adopted the tactics suggested by von Werra, moving from one rank to the next and back again, so that it was difficult to determine how many there were. After a word with the officer, the sergeant rode to the rear of the column and shouted orders to the four guards there, and then to the head of the column to the four guards in front. He continued a little way ahead, swung his horse round facing the party, drew his revolver and shouted.

"Halt!"

The guards in front turned, spread out a little so that they covered the sides of the column, and stood facing the prisoners with their rifles at the ready. The rearguard also spread out.

The prisoners shuffled to a stop and the singing gave way to sporadic shouting.

The party had reached a point just south of Satterthwaite, about two hundred yards from the telephone kiosk.

The officer went down the length of the column counting the prisoners. The count was twenty-three instead of twenty-four. To make sure, the officer and the sergeant counted again, moving from the rear to the head of the column. There could be no doubt about it : one prisoner was missing.

In the consternation, the telephone kiosk was overlooked, and the sergeant was sent back down the road towards High Bowkerstead. The prisoners' cheers as he galloped away were only partly ironic : they were pleased that the phone box had been forgotten, and thus a few more valuable minutes had been gained.

The officer gave the order to march.

Previously, it had been the prisoners who had tried to force the pace ; now the reverse happened—the guards stepped out and the prisoners hung back. As soon as the telephone box came into sight, the officer dashed ahead and put through an emergency call to the camp.

About ten minutes later, light trucks from Grizedale Hall began passing the party. Then a lorry halted a hundred yards in front of the column and soldiers with rifles jumped down and surrounded it.

The officer in charge gave the order :

"At the double!"

Whether they liked it or not, the prisoners ran the remaining distance back to the camp.

Meanwhile, a roll-call had been taken of the Germans at Grizedale Hall. Thus, the authorities were able to determine the names of the twenty-four who were out on the walk before they arrived back. A roll-call-cum-identification parade of the exercise party was made immediately it arrived at the camp. Within a few minutes it was established that the missing prisoner was Oberleutnant Franz von Werra. The police were then notified and given details of his appearance.

Hauptmann Pohle, who had been in charge of the exercise party on the German side, was hauled off to the Camp Commandant's office.

That night, the atmosphere in the camp was electric. There was a continuous coming and going of Army vehicles and a ringing of telephone bells. The singing of German songs, *Sieg heil!*-ing, the stamping of jackboots on the wooden floorboards, and the clapping of hands, went on far into the night.

Villagers still chuckle over the furore late that afternoon, though it is probable that they themselves were infected with it at the time. When the mounted sergeant reached High Bowkerstead Corner, he met the two women who had seen von Werra hiding behind the wall.

" Have you seen an escaped prisoner ? " he asked them.

" That's why we shouted and waved to you. He was crouching down behind the wall over there."

" Where did he go ? "

" Across the road and into the wood."

" Thanks ! " The sergeant spurred his horse, and plunged into the wood. They could hear him crashing about and cursing in the undergrowth.

Some time later he galloped back through the village. He was seen to have lost his cap and his face was covered with scratches and blood.

Lorries, staff cars, Bren gun carriers and motor-cyclists sped through Satterthwaite, first in one direction, then the other, with apparent confusion and purposelessness. Guards from the camp called on every householder and said that the prisoner who had escaped was a desperate and ruthless Nazi, who would stop at nothing to obtain food, clothing and money. They were asked to lock up such possessions, and women were advised to stay indoors until the man had been captured.

The escape occurred in Lancashire, but the police forces of neighbouring Westmorland, Cumberland and Yorkshire were also alerted. By five-thirty that afternoon the whole of the anti-escape machinery had been set in motion. Police, Special Constables or Home Guards began to replace the soldiers from the camp who had been sent out immediately to cover strategic points and encircle the area. These troops returned to the camp and were made available for direct search action. Between five and six o'clock troops were lined out on the road from High Bowkerstead Corner to the southern end of Bowkerstead Knott, ready to begin beating through the wood. They stood there in the rain waiting for the arrival of a party of police with three bloodhounds, who were being rushed by car from Headquarters in Preston. The beat could not begin till the hounds arrived for fear of spoiling the scent. The hounds were first taken to the camp and did not arrive at the wood until dusk. By then it had been raining heavily for some time, and the bloodhounds found no scent.

Von Werra disappeared completely for three days and nights. There was never a trace of him. As the days went by more and more police and troops were called in to take part in the search. Altogether several thousands were involved during the week beginning 7 October.

The B.B.C. reported the escape and gave details of von Werra's appearance in its late evening bulletins on Monday.

On Tuesday, 8 October, the national daily newspapers reported the escape. This was the first that Fleet Street had heard of von Werra. They seized on the detail that he was described as having no lobes to his ears, in spite of the fact that lobeless ears are quite common. He was dubbed " the lobeless Nazi pilot ". The description was to stick even when newspapers promoted him to " Baron ".

The police were worried and mystified by his disappearance. A great many wild rumours circulated in the district. It must be remembered that the general public thought Britain might be invaded any day. There was much talk about saboteurs and Fifth Columnists.

Ulverston Police Station was used as headquarters for search operations in Lancashire. Hundreds of telephone messages were received there from residents all over the Lake District and farther afield, reporting that they had seen suspicious-looking characters. Each one of these reports was investigated. Each one proved to have no connection with the escaped German.

Von Werra had vanished.

The camp authorities were able to state categorically that he carried no rucksack or bag with him, and this was confirmed by the evidence of the two women who had seen him dash across the road. Therefore, whatever food he had with him he carried in his pockets. It could not have been much. Enough to keep him going for two or three days, not more. He had to eat, somehow, somewhere. It was pouring with rain the whole time, and he had neither mackintosh nor overcoat. He would have to take shelter. But by nightfall on Thursday, the fourth day since his escape, there was still no trace of him. It was incredible, but he had simply disappeared.

The police could not understand how von Werra could have eluded them, in view of the scale and intensity of the hunt. They believed either that someone was harbouring him, or that he was injured as a result of a fall, or even dead.

That evening they issued a warning to local residents reminding them of the severe penalties for helping an escaped prisoner.

But von Werra was not being harboured, nor was he injured; and he was far from dead.

Even in the remotest and wildest parts of the Lake District, there are many small stone huts, known as " hoggarths ", used for storing sheep fodder. They are built in the same manner as fell walls —flat stones piled on top of one another without mortar binding— and usually they abut on to these walls.

Following von Werra's escape, police visited outlying farms and requested that all such buildings be padlocked and specially watched. At night, small patrols of Home Guards visited each " hoggarth " in turn, however high up on the fells, in their particular area. In view of the almost continuous rainfall since von Werra escaped, it was believed that sooner or later he was bound to try to shelter in one of these huts.

At about 11 p.m. on Thursday, 10 October, two Home Guards were patrolling fells in the Broughton Mills area, only four or five miles from the coast. Both were shepherds by calling. They were searching isolated huts on the moor between the Lickle and Kirby valleys. The older man carried a sporting gun, and the younger had a Colt in a holster at his waist. The latter also had a carbide bicycle lamp fitted with a hinged blackout hood. It was pitch dark and pouring with rain.

They came to a hut high on the fell overlooking the Lickle valley. The padlocked door had been forced open.

The light from the lamp fell on the white face and hands, and the glittering eyes, of a man standing a few inside. He was clutching a stick.

His clothes were dark with dampness and splashed with mud. His boots, the heels worn down and the toes turned up, looked like a tramp's throw-outs. He was freshly shaven and his face looked thin and drawn.

The Home Guard thumbed the safety catch of his revolver.

" Where's your identity card ? " he asked.

The man fumbled in his bulging pockets, but did not produce anything.

" I am sorry. I have forgotten it."

" That's what I thought. You are the escaped Nazi prisoner. You are coming with us."

One of the Englishmen tied a cord round the man's right wrist, and wound the other end several times round the palm of his own left hand. The other gripped the man's left arm firmly above the elbow.

They set off into the blackness down a steep and slippery hill, the younger Home Guard carrying the lamp in his right hand and gripping the cord with his left.

" Your name's Werra, isn't it ? " he asked.

" So ? I see you know all about me."

" Hundreds of people have been looking for you."

" I know. I've been watching them. What shall you do with me now ? "

" Hand you over. There's police and troops down there on the road."

" So ? I'm sorry then, gentlemen, but—I—must—leave you ! "

As he spoke, von Werra pulled his right hand, to which the cord was attached, behind his back, throwing the Home Guard who was holding it off his balance. Then, wrenching his right arm free, he struck out at him. The man went sprawling backwards. The lamp fell to the ground and went out. The prisoner jumped out of reach of the other Home Guard and at the same time snatched with all his might with his bound wrist. The cord came free. The man had probably opened his hand as he fell. The manœuvre was perfectly timed and was all over in an instant.

Into the darkness. Back up the hill to the left, where von Werra knew there was a wood. The older man with the useless sporting gun was panting a few feet behind him, but he soon fell back. He was not running for his freedom.

Von Werra got away. Half an hour later he was in hiding among some rocks high on the fell. It took him a long time to recover his breath. His head ached and now he really did feel exhausted. From his vantage point he could see the pinpoints of light from the hooded headlights of Army vehicles on the road in the valley below. Later, several flares were fired in the direction from which he had escaped. They were ineffective owing to the rain. For the moment he was safe, though he must descend and cross that road before daybreak. He sat huddled against a rock, getting what shelter he could. The rain streamed down his face and the back of his neck.

As he watched the flares he chewed an apple. Two nights previously he had found an orchard. Most of the fruit had been picked, but there were still dozens of windfalls on the ground. He had lived on apples since then, and still had some left in his pockets.

It was clear by now that the German was making for the West Coast, and that sooner or later he would endeavour to cross the River Duddon into Cumberland.

During the next two days the hunt was intensified and concentrated on the east side of the Duddon Valley, over the wild Dunnerdale Fells. By nightfall on Friday, the day after von Werra had got away from the Home Guards, the whole of the Lancashire side of the valley had been beaten without result.

It was believed that the prisoner must somehow have slipped through the net and crossed the River Duddon. While the east side of the valley is bare, there is a narrow belt of woodland all along the Cumberland side.

From daybreak on Saturday, 12 October, the sixth day of von Werra's freedom, police and troops began searching the woods, working south from Stonythwaite. Bloodhounds were used. The searchers reached the road running off west to Eskdale at about 2.30. No trace of the fugitive had been found, but this was not discouraging as it was believed he might be farther south. The prospects of rounding him up the next day, Sunday, seemed excellent.

During the night, the Eskdale road would be guarded in case he attempted to break back into the area already searched.

Superintendent W. S. Brown, in charge of a contingent of the Cumberland and Westmorland Constabulary, was waiting in a police car at the top of the hill above the Traveller's Rest Inn when the searchers reached that point at 2.30. After consulting with Lieutenant Blackburn, in charge of the party of about seventy troops from Ulverston, he agreed to call off the hunt for that day. At twenty minutes to three the searchers moved off down the hill from Hazel Farm to the Traveller's Rest for a much-needed " quick one " before closing time.

While they were drinking their pints, shouts were heard coming from the top of the hill. A man on Bleak Haw, 350 feet above the road, was making beckoning sweeps with his right arm and cupping his left hand to his mouth.

" *Tally-ho ! Tally-ho !* " he shouted, in the curiously high-pitched but far-carrying voice of the Cumberland shepherd.

The man was Mr. William Youdale, a sheep farmer, of Hazel Head Farm. He had been driving his sheep back to his farm when he saw a man come out of the bracken and gorse on The Pike, a sharp-pointed hill 1,200 feet high, overlooking the Duddon Valley, on the Cumberland side. The man walked along the side of a fell wall in full view of him and about half a mile away. With his dogs he quickly drove the sheep into the nearest " allotment "—a wall-enclosed field—and hurried to Bleak Haw to call back the searchers. He was able to keep the man under observation the whole time, and was glad to see him climb over a wall running round the base of Hesk Fell. The Fell extends a great distance, rises to 1,600 feet and is completely bare.

Nevertheless, by the time the search party got up the hill, the man had disappeared. Mr. Youdale was embarrassed.

" Two minutes ago he was walking round the side of the fell, yonder," he said, " about twenty-five yards inside the wall. He's simply vanished ! "

Superintendent Brown looked from the shepherd to the bare fell, and back again.

" What did he look like ? "

" He was about five foot six, had no hat or coat. He came out of cover on The Pike soon after you went down the hill."

" Well," said the superintendent, " if he was there two minutes ago, he can't have got far. Hiding behind the wall, no doubt."

The search party walked over a couple of fields to Hesk Fell. The man was not hiding behind the wall. There was no sign of him. There were no trees and no bracken where he could have hidden.

The soldiers and police, including the constable with the blood-hounds, spread out at the base of the fell. A whistle blew and they moved forward in line. There was a certain amount of ill-humour and chaffing, and sidelong glances at Mr. Youdale. A man could not disappear on an open fell with only close-cropped Cumberland turf for cover !

The line moved forward slowly. Mr. Youdale remained near the starting point with his dogs. He was joined by two other men, Mr. John Staples and Mr. C. V. Rawnsley.

The line moved farther and farther away, and the three men could no longer hear the searchers' voices. Mr. Youdale was very uncomfortable.

" He *must* be there somewhere ! " he said.

Then, as they watched the backs of the searchers, some of whom were now partly hidden in a fold in the fell, Mr. Staples noticed a slight movement among some tufts of coarser grass on a patch of damp ground only twenty yards from where they stood.

" Look ! " he exclaimed.

He ran to the spot. The damp patch looked firm, but he sank ankle deep in mud and water.

He almost trod on the man before he saw him.

" Here he is ! "

Oberleutnant Franz von Werra was lying on his back, his body and arms sunk in the mud, with only his white, freshly shaven face showing between two clumps of coarse grass.

A few minutes later he was handcuffed.

This time he did not get away.

Von Werra was immediately searched for arms. The only lethal weapon he carried was a bone-handled table knife, converted into a business-like dagger by filing and whetting, with which he had hoped to kill chicken, and, perhaps, a sheep for food.

His pockets also yielded a cocoa tin containing shaving gear, another tin containing the remainder of his " iron rations "—a bar and a half of chocolate ; his Iron Cross and insignia cut off his uniform, in order to prove his identity in case he got into serious difficulties while escaping ; several apples and about three shillings in cash. The home-made compass, the map, the list of prisoners and coded notes on military and intelligence matters were not found. He kept them in a separate tin, which he probably buried in the mud as soon as he was found.

Von Werra said little, and merely shrugged his shoulders when he was handcuffed to P—c. Patterson. He ignored the glances and comments of the troops and police surrounding him. He was not in the least disconcerted when the two leashed bloodhounds sniffed excitedly round his legs ; he looked down at them and made a soft clicking sound with his tongue. They raised their eyes and ears, whined, and tentatively wagged their tails. The constable in charge quickly pulled them away.

Von Werra's clothes and hair were covered with slimy mud. There were spots and streaks of it on his face.

Despite the circumstances and his appearance, despite his shortness compared with the constable to whom he was handcuffed, his bearing was not without dignity. When the party set off down the hill to the Traveller's Rest, he walked briskly, his head erect and his shoulders back. His jack-boots squelched at each step.

At the inn, Superintendent Brown arranged for the prisoner to be given a cup of tea. It was strong, hot and sweet. He had never tasted anything better. A soldier gave him a cigarette. As he sipped the tea and smoked, the reaction to his recapture, to the strain, exposure, hunger and physical exhaustion of the five days he had been on the run, slowly overcame him. It was all over. At last he could relax.

The tension lifted from his mind and body. He felt empty and light-headed. He became aware that his muscles ached, that his joints were stiff, even the knuckles of the hand holding the tea-cup. His very bones ached with fatigue. His eyelids smarted and were leaden, and there was a dull throbbing at the back of his head. If only he could sleep.

Somebody shook his shoulder.

" Time to go ! "

" Huh ? "

" Come on. Up you get ! "

He stood up with surprising alacrity, shaking the thoughts of sleep from his head, making a great effort not to betray his weakness.

On the way to Ulverston Police Station, Superintendent Brown asked him why he had escaped. He replied simply :

" It is the duty of a German officer to escape if he can."

At the police station, where the handcuffs were removed, von Werra was questioned by the police officer who had been in charge of search operations. He was very interested to know how many people von Werra had seen or spoken to while he had been at liberty. The German realised that he was trying to find out whether he had received any outside help and was able to reassure him on that point ; apart from the two members of the Home Guard who captured him temporarily, he had spoken to nobody.

The policeman showed him a pile of telephone messages from members of the public reporting they had seen the fugitive.

" You have given a lot of people a lot of trouble," he said.

He produced a large-scale map of the area and asked the prisoner if he could trace the route he had taken. Von Werra grasped the purpose of this : the policeman wanted to find out how and where he had broken through the cordon, so that the gap could be stopped in any future escape from Grizedale Hall. He studied the map closely, then said it was impossible for him to trace his route on the map : place-names meant nothing to him.

The policeman eyed him closely. He evidently did not believe von Werra, but did not press the point.

The interview was over. Von Werra's head was nodding, and soon his chin dropped on to his chest. He was allowed to sleep until the escort arrived to take him back to Grizedale Hall.

On his return to the camp, he was taken before the Commandant, who was correct without being friendly, business-like without being brusque. He sentenced von Werra to twenty-one days' close confinement for attempting to escape. He was asked if he had anything to say or any complaint to make about the guards or the other prisoners. As he had expected to get the maximum sentence of thirty days, he replied that he had none.

He was allowed to take a shower bath and was given a change of clothes. Partly dressed, he was taken to the Camp Medical Officer, who examined him thoroughly. He had lost weight, but the only thing he was suffering from was exhaustion. Apart from that, he was tougher and fitter than before he escaped. Not so much as by a sniff or a sneeze did he show that he had been soaked to the skin almost continuously for nearly a week.

He was taken to a cell in the basement of the building, given a meal and left alone. The bed was hard and narrow, but as he flopped out on it and covered himself with blankets it seemed to him the height of luxury.

He was awakened next morning when a German orderly, escorted by guards, brought in his breakfast. There was a plate of porridge, several hunks of bread with a little margarine and marmalade, and an enamel can of tea. The can had a dome-shaped, detachable lid, which served as a cup. When the orderly put the tray down on a little table, his back to the door and the guards, he tapped on the lid of the can and winked.

As soon as he was alone again, von Werra examined it. A groove ran round the inside of the lid, and a disc of cardboard, covered with margarine wrapping, had been fitted into it. Underneath was a wealth of treasure : notes written by his friends on small, rectangular sheets of tissue paper ; several cigarettes individually wrapped to ensure they would not be spoiled by the steam rising off the tea ; a little packet of non-safety matches ; a stub of pencil and sheets of paper for his replies.

Thanks to the tea-can lid, he was able to keep in touch with his friends throughout his dreary three weeks' sentence. Thus he learned that a group of prisoners, including Major Fanelsa, had been transferred to another prison camp.

Early on 3rd November 1940, two days before he was due to be released from the " cooler ", von Werra was handed a kit-bag and the few belongings he had left behind in the camp when he escaped, and told to be ready to leave immediately after breakfast. He was to be taken to another camp " farther south—somewhere in the Midlands ".

At about nine o'clock he was handcuffed to a Corporal and then, escorted by a Captain, led out into the courtyard where a weapons carrier was waiting to take them to the station. Somehow or other the other prisoners had got to hear that he was leaving and had gathered at the upper windows of the house. The instant he stepped out of the side door they started cheering and waving.

It was unexpected and confusing. There was a tightness in his throat as he passed through the pillared gateway of Grizedale Hall for the last time.

CHAPTER VIII

The Tunnel

AT FIRST von Werra had welcomed the news that he was to be sent to another camp. His three weeks' close confinement had in some ways been more of a strain than his interrogation at Cockfosters. Any change, he felt, was a change for the better.

The train journey gave him plenty of time to speculate on his new destination. It was long and tedious, owing to delays and diversions caused by bomb damage at several points along the line. He and his escort travelled in a reserved compartment with the blinds drawn. And the handcuffs, which had seemed a compliment at first, soon became irksome to the point of obsession. He had to fight down the urge, blind and panicky, to wrench himself free and move about.

In his autobiography von Werra claims that thanks to the sensation his escape in the Lake District had caused, and to the numerous photographs of him published in the British Press, people who saw him on stations and in trains during this trip recognised him at once, and gathered round marvelling, much to the embarrassment of his escort.

In fact, the national Press had published only brief paragraphs about his escape, and the War Office's laconic announcement of his recapture. No photographs of von Werra had so far been published in any British newspaper. Indeed, it was not until several weeks after his arrival at Swanwick Camp that he and other prisoners were photographed for War Office records.

What would the new camp be like? A *Straflager* probably—a punishment camp reserved for recalcitrant prisoners. Conditions would certainly be tougher, security measures more strict, than at Grizedale Hall. But he was determined to try to escape again. The exhilaration of his five days of freedom on the fells was not easily forgotten. Having got away once he was certain that he could escape again—even from a *Straflager*.

When von Werra and his escort reached Derby, after a six hour journey, there was an unexpected hitch. The Railway Transport Officer said that there were no more trains to their destination that night.

" Just my confounded luck ! " grumbled the Captain. " I've got to deliver this character to Swanwick P.O.W. Camp and return to Windermere by seven to-morrow morning. Can I ring the camp from here and ask for a car to pick him up ? "

Von Werra pricked up his ears. *Swanwick*. It was the first time he had heard his destination mentioned—though it meant nothing to him.

While the Captain was telephoning, he took stock of the dimly-lit office. Apart from closely-printed notices headed " Travel Warrants " and " Notice to Military Personnel On Leave ", the walls were decorated with graphic security posters, one depicting Hitler and Goering eavesdropping on the top of a bus. They bore such captions as : " Take Care—The Enemy May Overhear You ! "

The British had a nerve !

Then he saw a map—a large-scale railway map. In the middle of it he could make out the word DERBY.

When the Captain went off to find something to eat, leaving him in charge of the Corporal, von Werra's eyes examined the map more closely. Its surface reflected the light, and from where he was sitting he could not make out other place names. He asked the Corporal if he could move to the corner of the bench as he was tired and wished to lean against the wall. The Corporal obligingly shifted along. He too was tired, and was probably thinking of the meal the Captain was now enjoying.

From the corner von Werra could read the names of the larger towns. He must memorise them systematically. To the east of Derby were Stoke and Stafford, to the west Nottingham—all roughly on the same line of latitude. He repeated the names to himself, imagining how they would sound if he spoke them.

Now and again the R.T.O. glanced idly at the prisoner, who appeared to be dozing. It seemed that each time he glanced at the German he caught him in the act of shutting his eyes. Odd ! And if the man were dozing his chin should be on his chest, not stuck up in the air. Then, while he was explaining a route to an inquirer,

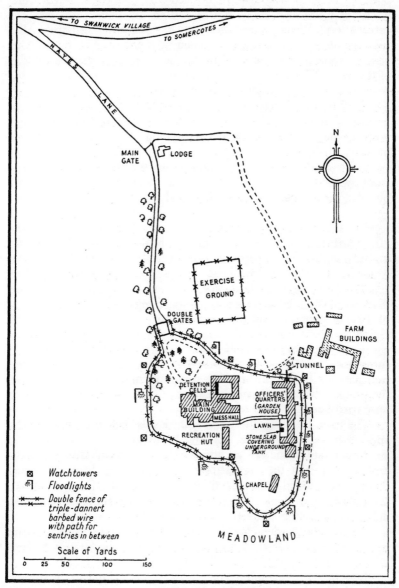

THE HAYES

pointing it out on the map, he noticed that von Werra's eyes were wide open and alert. The officer paused, then went on with his explanation. When he had finished, he glanced round the walls, rubbing his nose meditatively. Then he went over to one of the posters, took it down, moved back, and pinned it over the middle of the map. Whistling softly, and ignoring the prisoner completely, he went through the motions of dusting his hands.

The poster was headed : " Keep It Dark ! "

The Corporal shifted uneasily on the bench and wondered whether he should say or do something. Von Werra grinned broadly.

A few minutes later the Captain returned, followed by an officer from Swanwick Camp. Von Werra was formally handed over, and bundled into a truck in the station yard.

P.O.W. (Officers') Transit Camp No. 13 was a converted country house, called The Hayes, half a mile from the village of Swanwick, on the main road between Alfreton and Ripley. Originally a private residence, the property had been converted into a conference centre as long ago as 1911. In both world wars it was requisitioned by the War Office and used as a prisoner-of-war camp. Known to thousands of British people, it is thus also known to two generations of Germans.

While in peace-time the halls had often rung with the passionate summons to defend human liberties, they now rang with the frenzied *Sieg Heil !* and braggart songs of imprisoned Nazis. And the grounds where delegates had strolled on summer evenings, were now patrolled by armed sentries.

The main buildings are on varying levels, linked by brick paths and short flights of steps. On the lawns are several fine cedars. At the top end of the garden, about twenty-five yards from the main buildings, and at the highest point of the estate, there is a long, three-storey, wooden-frame building known as the Garden House. It contains 180 single bedrooms and is the main dormitory for delegates attending conferences at The Hayes.

Behind the Garden House, and only a yard or so from it, is the boundary fence. On the other side of the fence is the narrow lane which, from the lodge at the main entrance, runs round the boundary on three sides of the estate. The ground is still rising and the surface of the lane is roughly level with the window sills of the ground floor of the building. On the other side of the lane is a quickset hedge, and beyond it are open fields that slope down to the village of Riddings in the east, and south to the Pye Bridge and Ambergate Railway line.

During the war there was a triple-dannert barbed-wire fence on either side of the lane. Sentries patrolled the narrow pathway in between. The system of watch towers, set at intervals of fifty yards along the outside fence and equipped with searchlights and machine-guns, included one at either end of the Garden House. The fences were floodlit at night except during air raid alerts. When the lights were switched off the guard was reinforced.

The front door of the Garden House is half-way along its length. Immediately in front of one half of the building, on the right-hand side of the path leading up to it, there is a large rectangular lawn. From this quiet vantage point the gardens and most of the other buildings on the estate are in view.

Owing to the handcuffs, von Werra and the Corporal had to dismount together.

" This way, chum," the guard said to the Corporal. " Make for the blue light."

He was led into a porch lit by a low-powered electric bulb. When the outer door was closed the guard opened another leading into a brightly-lit hall. The officer was already there and handed the prisoner over to a sergeant, who wore a red cap. This cap caused von Werra a stab of dismay.

The presence of Redcaps at the camp, taken in conjunction with the uncompromising attitude of the officer who had fetched him from Derby, seemed to confirm von Werra's expectation of finding Swanwick to be a *Straflager*—a special camp for refractory prisoners.

The M.P. sergeant had cauliflower ears, a bulging neck and a vast, spreading monster of a nose, covered by a network of purple veins. He was known to the prisoners as *Feldwebel Saftnase* (Sergeant Fruity-Nose).

The sergeant unlocked the handcuffs and took him to the Camp Adjutant, a Captain with iron-grey hair, gold-rimmed spectacles and an icy, precise manner, which had won for him the nicknames *der Pädagog*, or *der Schulfuchs*—slightly contemptuous terms for " The Schoolmaster ". He spoke fluent, faultless German and prisoners felt he treated them as though they were new boys caught cribbing. He was invariably correct and often helpful, but he never unbent for one moment. Prisoners respected and feared him and did not bait him as they did some of the other officers. The Captain explained the rules of the camp to von Werra, and reminded him of certain articles of the Geneva Convention. He had von Werra's file open on the desk in front of him.

"You know better than most prisoners that it is impossible to escape from England. Why not accept the fact and employ your wits and energy more usefully?"

Von Werra was in no mood for argument and he did not think the Captain would be impressed anyway. So instead of pointing out that it was a prisoner's duty to try to escape, or wagering a magnum of champagne to a packet of cigarettes that he would escape, as he had done once before, he simply smiled and shrugged his shoulders. If the Captain thought he was a reformed character, so much the better.

A surprise awaited von Werra. After a shower, during which his clothes and kitbag were searched, a visit to the medical officer and a meal of bread and butter and cocoa, which he ate ravenously, the sergeant led him out of the main building and along a brickwork path flanked by barbed wire to another building.

"This here is the Garden House," the sergeant said. "I shall take you to see Mr. Fanelsa, who is camp leader. He will allocate you to your room."

So Major Fanelsa was now leader of Swanwick Camp! What was he doing in a *Straflager*?

They entered a hallway lit by the usual low-powered bulb. To left and right was a corridor running down the centre of the building from end to end. There were dozens of doors on either side of this corridor, and immediately ahead a stairway leading to the upper floors. Fire buckets, stirrup pumps, long-handled scoops for tackling incendiary bombs, and half-filled sandbags were lined up in front of a blocked doorway.

As soon as von Werra put his nose inside the building, his sense of smell sharpened by the damp night air, he felt a sudden, bitter-sweet pang of nostalgia: the place smelled of *Komiss*—of the German services; a mixture of odours: uniforms, leather, boot-polish and brilliantine.

The corridor was empty, but he could hear the sound of muffled German voices coming from the rooms, with occasional shouts, thumps and laughter. Somewhere on the upper floors a prisoner was expertly playing a mouth-organ; it sounded like the distant sobbing of a child.

The sergeant tapped on a door.

The booming voice of Major Fanelsa replied : " *Herein !* "

" Mr. Fanelsa, this here is Mr. Werra, who's just arrived. You'll see he gets fixed up all right ? "

" Yes, thank you, sergeant. Good night to you ! "

" Good night, gentlemen ! "

Von Werra clicked his heels and saluted Fanelsa.

" Heil Hitler ! Oberleutnant von Werra reporting after his release from close confinement and his transfer from Camp No. 1 to Camp No. 13."

The Major stood up and solemnly returned von Werra's salute. He did not appear to be particularly pleased to see the newcomer.

The interview that followed, was, from von Werra's point of view, most unsatisfactory. After a reference to his escape from Grizedale Hall, Fanelsa advised him bluntly to give up the idea of escaping for the time being. The Swanwick Camp Commandant was a reasonable man, and he, Fanelsa, had been able to win some privileges from him. He did not want to risk these good relations for the sake of any wild-cat escape plan. Of course, if von Werra hit on a really sound idea it would be different—but in view of the security precautions he didn't think that likely. Perhaps they could discuss the matter again in a month or two.

And with that Fanelsa showed von Werra to his room and bade him good night.

The corridor was dimly lit and von Werra was at first unable to find the switch of the room light. After fumbling in the semi-darkness he found it behind the door and turned it on. He was dismayed by what he saw.

A camp bed with two folded blankets. A locker in the corner by the window. A flimsy wooden chair, the cane seat of which had a large hole in it. And that was all. The room was smaller and contained less furniture than the cell in which he had passed his " solitary ". The stained match-boarding walls and the dark parquet floor, the bare light bulb and the dirty window gave the room a dreadfully shabby and uninviting appearance.

Loud, angry shouts from outside the building broke into his

melancholy contemplation of the room. He had forgotten to put up the blackout shutter. He found it in the corner of the room, beside the locker, and hastily fixed it in place.

The shouts had roused the occupants of nearby rooms. Doors in the corridor opened and sleepy or bad-tempered voices called out:

" What's going on? "

" Who's making all the row? "

" Switch off, man, or they'll shoot it out! "

Von Werra stepped out into the corridor and saw phantom figures converging on him, some in pyjamas, others in crumpled underwear. They peered forward to identify the culprit. One of them cried:

" Good lord!—Werra! "

All at once he found himself the centre of a laughing, gesticulating group. His arm was pumped, his back slapped by old comrades, and several men introduced themselves simultaneously. They clamoured for details of his arrival, his escape and recapture, and how he had been taken prisoner in the first place.

A tall, blond, broad-shouldered man had made his way to von Werra's side, and was now smiling at him and holding his elbow. The newcomer introduced himself as Leutnant Wagner, of the 54th Fighter *Geschwader*.

" Don't let them bully you," he said. " You get your head down to a good night's rest, and tell us all about your adventures in the morning. I just want to shake your hand—and wish you better luck next time! "

Von Werra immediately liked the look of this burly fighter type, and his eyes twinkled with pleasure when he heard Wagner's unmistakable Austrian accent. In the ensuing weeks they were to get to know one another well.

At 32, Wagner was the doyen of the fighter pilots at Swanwick. He was a reservist and had more flying and combat experience than many German pilots senior to him in rank, but his juniors by ten or twelve years. At that stage of the war it was hard for Austrians in the German Armed Forces to obtain promotion. Wagner was one of the most popular men at Swanwick Camp. He had plenty of Viennese charm, buoyant spirits, a sense of humour and the knack of getting on with everybody. He had an inexhaustible repertoire of Viennese dialect stories and comic songs and was a star turn at the nightly sing-songs. He was also an inspired inventor of nicknames, and was responsible for those given to the camp staff—the *Schulfuchs*, Lieutenant *Pivot*, Sergeant *Saftnase*, and others.

"Well, I don't know about you chaps," von Werra said at length, "but I'm going to bed."

Wagner was the last to leave. He looked back from the doorway and observed von Werra's expression with some amusement.

"Pretty bare, isn't it?" he said. "To-morrow you must look at some of the other chaps' rooms and get ideas for brightening it up and making it more comfortable. Some of them have worked wonders!" There was a note of raillery in his voice. Von Werra looked him in the eyes, weighing him up, then spoke with sudden passion.

"Damn the room! I don't want to brighten it up. I don't want to make it more comfortable. You don't suppose I'm going to stay in this hole one night more than I can possibly help, do you? I'm getting out, I tell you!"

Wagner shook his head in mock despair.

"Tut, tut, Werra," he said. "After all the sound advice the well-meaning *Schulfuchs* must have given you this evening . . . And perhaps the cautious Major Fanelsa as well?"

"Yes, what's he doing in a *Straflager*, anyway?"

"*Straflager*? Who said it was a *Straflager*?"

"Well, isn't it? I thought . . ."

"No more than any other British camp, as far as I know." After a pause Wagner added:

"I know how you feel. I'd like to get out myself. But you won't find it easy, you know."

"I'll find some way," von Werra replied categorically. "Have you any ideas?"

"H'm. Possibly. We'll talk about it to-morrow. You'd better get some sleep. I only came along to say hallo, and here I am gossiping like a Tyrolean post-mistress. See you to-morrow."

Von Werra was tired but it was long before he could get to sleep. The strange, new noises bothered him: the clock in the main building chiming the quarter hours, the periodic shouts of the sentries outside, the creaking of the wooden building, the hissing of the defective cistern in the lavatory a few doors away.

Within a few days of his arrival at Swanwick von Werra decided, after examining the various possibilities and discussing them with Wagner and a few other prisoners, that if he was to escape at all from Swanwick it would have to be through a tunnel excavated from a room in the north wing of the Garden House.

Unknown to Major Fanelsa, von Werra and Wagner then called a meeting of carefully selected prisoners, all of them Luftwaffe men, for the purpose of founding the *Swanwick Tiefbau A. G.* (Swanwick Construction Company). Major Heinz Cramer, one of the most experienced pilots in the camp, who had represented Germany in the 1936 Olympic Games, was elected chairman. Of the others, those who played the biggest part in the scheme were von Werra, Wagner, Manhard, Malischewski and Wilhelm. (Von Werra had been delighted to discover that this Leutnant Walter Manhard, pilot of a Me. 110, was the man who had scratched the defiant message on the window sill of Room 13 at London District P.O.W. Cage.)

It was proposed to begin the tunnel from an unused room near von Werra's in the north wing. It would lead under the two security fences and the lane in between them, and emerge in a small triangular patch of waste ground on which there were a few trees and bushes for cover. It would pass only a few feet from the base of the watch tower at the north-east corner of the Garden House, and the exit would be only about fifteen yards away from the tower.

There was one serious drawback to this exit: immediately after leaving by it, escapers would have to pass close to a farm-house and several outbuildings. But the risk of encountering people or dogs was one that would have to be taken.

Disposal of earth was a problem. There would be far too much from a tunnel 13 metres long to get rid of down the lavatories. Von Werra and his associates racked their brains to find a solution. Then one day Manhard, an ex-heavyweight boxer bursting with vitality and brute strength, who was always disconsolately looking for some outlet for his energy, spotted a large stone slab, sprinkled with bird-droppings and fragments of snail shells, on the edge of the rectangluar lawn in front of the Garden House. He decided to do a little weight lifting. He gripped the stone and tried to lift it bodily. It did not move. This only made him wild, and he tried again. The stone tilted sideways. What he saw underneath made his jaw drop. He let the slab down again gently and went rushing off into the house shouting excitedly for von Werra.

Underneath the stone was a circular hole two feet in diameter. About six feet down there was water. At first it was thought to be a well, but when it was examined with the aid of several flower canes " borrowed " from the out-of-bounds potting shed and fitted together like a fishing rod, it was found to be a huge underground tank used to store rainwater from the roof of the Garden House. It was big enough to take all the earth from a tunnel double the length of the one proposed.

Having solved the problem of disposal, von Werra and the board of the " Construction Company " worked out the plan in detail.

The tunnel was to be constructed as simply and quickly as possible. The roof and sides would be shored up only where necessary ; otherwise the tunnel was to be a " rabbit hole " just large enough for the man with the broadest shoulders (Manhard) to crawl through it.

The excavation was to be done by von Werra and Malischewski, working in turns. The earth would be carried away in fire buckets borrowed from the entrance hall. Manhard and Wagner would carry them from the room in the north wing along the corridor to the front door. There they would be taken over by two more men, Cramer and Wilhelm, who, when given a signal that the coast was clear, would carry them on to the lawn and empty them into the underground reservoir. Another prisoner would be standing by to lift the stone as the carriers approached.

British personnel were not normally in the Garden House except during the morning inspection and second roll-call between nine-thirty and ten-thirty, and during the evening inspection and final roll-call at 8 p.m. After the final roll-call the prisoners were locked in the building and guards patrolled outside.

There were roll-calls in the Mess Hall in the main building before breakfast at 8 a.m. and again before tea at five o'clock, but there was none at lunchtime. By missing the midday meal, therefore, von Werra and Malischewski could work on the tunnel from about ten-thirty until four-thirty. It was unlikely that they would be missed from lunch as there was usually only one British officer or sergeant in charge of the 150 officers in the mess hall.

A German look-out posted in the room above the entrance could keep the path flanked by barbed wire under observation. Look-outs would also be posted in the corner rooms on the first floor at either end of the building. Their duty would be to watch the guards in the nearby towers, which were level with the first-floor windows. This was especially important in the case of the tower at the northern end, as the tunnel would pass under the lane only a few feet from its base, and the diggers would have to be warned to stop work immediately the guards showed signs of having heard sounds they were unable to account for. Other men would be posted along the corridors, and at the foot and head of the stairs, to pass verbal signals.

Three warning signals were decided upon. In order not to arouse the suspicions of the guards, the names of actual prisoners were to be shouted. If one of the look-outs called " Oberleutnant Deike ! " it meant that the digger should stop work, but that there was no immediate danger. " Leutnant Manhard ! " meant " Danger approaching—close and camouflage entrance to tunnel—diversion crews move into positions and stand by ! " If the call was for " Leutnant Wagner ! " danger was imminent and the diversion crews would go into action. The principal diversion laid on was a free-for-all fight on the path leading to the Garden House.

The room in which the tunnel was to be started was kept locked. However, the British had provided " Vati " Schneider, who was in charge of the prisoners' shop, with a pass key as he used certain unoccupied rooms for stores. From this key Werra made a duplicate, using a nail file and a butcher's saw borrowed from the camp kitchen.

The tunnel was started on 17 November 1940. The " work-room " was tiny and contained only a single bed, a locker and a chair. There was a space of about a yard between the end of the bed and the outside wall. In this corner stood the locker and at the side of it a wooden blackout shutter for the window. The locker was moved out of the way and von Werra started work, using a crowbar and chisel fashioned by the German O.R. stokers. Malischewski kept watch at the window.

The floor was of oblong pinewood blocks laid herring-bone fashion. It took some time to remove the first block as great care had to be taken not to split it or mark its top side. After the first block was removed, von Werra was able to lever the others up easily with the flat end of the crowbar.

For the initial operations there was a third man in the room—a prisoner who was an amateur carpenter. The previous day he had obtained the blackout shutters from two empty rooms. He took them to pieces carefully and straightened and soaped the nails. Using the best battens from both shutters, he made a cover for the tunnel about 2 feet 6 inches square. As von Werra pulled up the pine blocks, the carpenter reassembled them on top of the lid in their original positions, nailing them firm from the underside, and cutting off the overlapping parts of the lid to correspond with the serrated edges made by the herring-bone pattern.

Below the parquet floor there was about six inches of breeze, sand and clinker. Below that was soil. There was no cement to break through. When the breeze was removed, a square frame made from an old fence post was fixed into position round the hole for the cover to rest on. The cover fitted over it perfectly.

By the time work ceased at the end of the first day the shaft had been sunk three feet. Fitted with a short handle, the scoops thoughtfully provided by the War Office for tackling incendiary bombs, had proved ideal tunnelling tools. The crowbar was then firmly wedged between the side of the hole and the underside of the cover, so that it did not sound quite so hollow when trodden on. The locker was moved back into its proper place—on top of the cover. The floor was cleaned and the room made normal. But it smelled dank owing to the soil that had been shifted. A prisoner coming in from outdoors said that even the corridor outside the room smelled like a freshly-ploughed field. Thereafter the window was opened a little way during working hours.

The next morning after breakfast von Werra was summoned by Major Fanelsa. He was furious. The first he had heard about the tunnel was when the " House Officer " had reported to him the night before.

Why had von Werra gone ahead without submitting his plans for approval ? He was undermining the Major's authority, acting in a manner prejudicial to good order and discipline, etc., etc. This was a prison camp for German officers, not an anarchists' club.

" Who's in this crack-brained undertaking besides you ? " Fanelsa asked.

Von Werra gave the names of the tunnel team, and of others who were helping indirectly. Fanelsa was horrified. He saw himself with a mutiny on his hands.

" Oh, yes," von Werra added innocently, " I forgot to mention that Major Cramer is on the tunnel team ! "

" Major Cramer ? You mean he's actually *working* on the tunnel ?"

" That's right, sir."

" Why on earth didn't he tell me about it ? "

" He said he wanted to, sir, but each time he's tried to find you, you've been tied up in conferences with British officers. He said he would report to you as soon as your official duties made it possible."

" I see. In what way is Major Cramer helping ? "

" He's carrying the buckets of earth, sir, and dumping them in the tank under the lawn ! "

Von Werra had no more trouble with Major Willibald Fanelsa for the time being.

As the days went by, the tunnel diggers ran into one difficulty after another. In order to minimise the risk of the guards in the nearby tower hearing sounds of the digging, von Werra had intended to sink the entrance shaft at least ten feet before beginning the tunnel proper. But when they got down about six feet, the earth became wet. When they opened up the next morning there was a foot of water in the bottom. There was nothing they could do but close down again and wait until the next morning to see if the water level rose still higher. But instead of rising it subsided a little.

" There's only one thing for it," said von Werra. " We shall have to start the tunnel just above water level. It's less than two metres down instead of three, but it can't be helped."

But Malischewski had had enough. He had become increasingly bad-tempered and nervous and when it was his turn to keep watch at the window, he was continually giving false alarms. He said the tunnel couldn't possibly be started at less than three metres—the guards were bound to hear the sounds of digging. He was relieved to have this excuse for dropping out of the scheme altogether.

Manhard took his place with the utmost gusto. He worked like one possessed and achieved prodigies of labour with which even von Werra could not compete. From the most disconsolate, he became the happiest man in the camp.

Meanwhile, some of the other members of the " Construction Company " had been working on the problem of lighting the tunnel. The wiring of a disused electric bell system was stripped from the top floor. From the odd pieces of wire obtained, two three-ply leads were plaited almost the estimated length of the tunnel. The wire was old and the insulation doubtful. To give extra protection, the two leads were lapped with strips of canvas cut from a kit bag. When the inspection light was finished it was quite a professional job. A hanging electric light socket was stolen from one of the empty rooms for the lamp, which was fitted with a handle, the bulb itself being protected by a jam jar. The other end of the lead was fitted into the ceiling light of the " workroom ", the bayonet-fitting adaptor being made from the brass base of a light bulb. In time, the insulation on the leads was affected by the dampness of the tunnel. This became a source of constant trouble and danger, and both Manhard and von Werra received nasty shocks from time to time.

When they had excavated the tunnel for a few yards, the diggers began to find large pieces of sandstone. Von Werra tackled the first one with the crowbar. The German look-out in the corner room by the north watch-tower immediately gave the preliminary warning signal, which was passed from one man to another along the corridor, down the stairs and back to the " workroom ", where Manhard transmitted it to von Werra by switching the light on and off in long dashes. Directly afterwards the second warning was given, and Manhard switched the light on and off rapidly. Von Werra was out of the tunnel, the lead disconnected from the ceiling light and dropped down the shaft, and the trap-door closed within a matter of seconds. Then they realised that their hurry was futile. If any of the British staff came into the room, having closed the tunnel entrance would make little difference. Von Werra was dressed only in filthy trunks with rags wrapped round his raw knees and elbows. He was grimed and perspiring from head to foot. Manhard was in a similar condition. Several fire buckets full of clay stood on the dirty floor. They could not talk their way out of such a situation.

After a few minutes there was a tap on the door, and somebody gave the agreed password. Manhard unlocked the door and the look-out man from the room upstairs came in.

" For God's sake don't make that noise again ! " he said. " The guards heard it and leaned right out of the tower listening. They were looking in the right direction, too! Whatever were you doing ? "

" There's a great lump of rock in the way," von Werra replied. " I was trying to lever it loose with a crowbar."

" It was like an earth tremor. You'll have to find some other way."

For safety's sake, they decided to close down for the rest of the day. When they had cleaned up, they consulted the other members of the " Company ". Thereafter, whenever the digging was hard, diversion crews went into action. A group of prisoners played *Skat*, a noisy German card game, in the corner room by the tower, with the window wide open, shouting and quarrelling at the top of their voices. At the same time and in the same room, Leutnant Bruns gave a recital on the very old and inefficient portable gramophone. He had only one record : " Hutch " singing " Begin the Beguine " on one side and " I paid for the lie that I told you " on the other. When Bruns got tired of winding up the gramophone and turning the record over, the prisoner with the harmonica played for a while. An alternative diversion was provided by practice sessions of a twenty-man choir under the direction of Leutnant Fritz Bein, a Stuka pilot with one leg encased in plaster.

As the tunnel grew in length, another problem became increasingly acute : ventilation. Many attempts were made to get a supply of fresh air to the tunnel face, but none was successful. Stirrup pumps were tried, but they were designed to pump water, not air, and proved useless.

Progress was now painfully slow. The length of time a digger could stay at the face grew steadily shorter. It was no longer possible for him to half fill a bucket and pull it back down the tunnel after him. The soil now had to be placed in a kit bag which was pulled out of the tunnel on a length of plaited string. Only a few pounds could be put into the sack at a time, otherwise the string broke.

The stage was reached when a digger could not stay at the tunnel face longer than a few minutes. He then crawled backwards down the tunnel and stood up in the shaft, sweating, gasping, retching. Going up the face and back was like completing the length of a swimming bath under water. After two or three trips the digger was in a state of collapse and had a blinding headache. It was as much as they could do to fill six fire buckets a day. And the tunnel was not half completed.

At the end of each day's work, Manhard and von Werra were dead-beat, haggard and thoroughly depressed. Prisoner-of-war rations were quite inadequate for the strenuous work they were doing, and they missed the calories of the lost midday meal. It seemed pointless to continue, for unless they could find some means of getting fresh air they could not hope to complete the tunnel.

But neither man put his fears and discouragement in words. Each morning they returned to work with stubborn hope.

Having been out-manœuvred and more or less forced into giving his blessing to the " Swanwick Construction Company ", Major Fanelsa kept a close watch on its activities and progress. Two or three times a week he managed to fit a hasty inspection of the tunnel into his day's full programme of pottering about asserting his importance as Camp Leader. On entering the " workroom " he removed his trenchcoat, which he folded carefully and laid on the bed with his cap on top. Underneath he wore only bathing drawers, which his batman washed after each inspection. Having crawled up to the tunnel face and back, the Major emerged grey, gasping but smirking maliciously.

" I say, Werra ! " he would exclaim. " You're not making much progress. Not slacking off, are you ? Must keep at it, you know. You ought to be there by now ! Well, I must dash off. Lots to do." And Fanelsa would hurry off to catch up with his schedule.

Then fate played the diggers a mean practical joke. Von Werra returned tremendously excited from a brief spell at the face. He told Manhard that the soil had suddenly become soft and easy to dig. Manhard hurriedly took his turn at the face. He came back a few minutes later, fighting for breath, with a twisted, savage grin on his face.

" This'll tickle the Major ! " he said. " This is where the *Swanwick Tiefbau A.G.* goes bust ! There's a sewer pipe bang across the tunnel bore—completely blocking it ! " Von Werra went back up to the face to look, and then came back and slumped down on the bed. Manhard stood beside the window keeping watch. They did not look at one another or speak. They were utterly dejected and ready to throw in their hand. In the silence the whole scheme hung in the balance.

" Well ? " said von Werra at last.

Manhard countered:

" Well ? "

" We obviously can't go under it, Walter. We should be below water level, and it's always wet under pipes, anyway. The pipe must run down the middle of the lane . . . where the sentries walk. The earth above the pipe will be loose : it's a filled-in trench. If we attempt to go over the top the roof may well collapse, especially if there's a thaw followed by rain. . . . A sentry might find himself swallowed up by a hole in the ground." Von Werra gave a wry grin. "Almost bound to arouse his suspicions!"

"Hell!" said Manhard. "Over the top and chance it! We'll have to shore it up very carefully, that's all."

Von Werra could have hugged him.

As it turned out, the sewage pipe proved to be the salvation of the tunnel, but not before total disaster had been narrowly averted.

With the utmost caution they excavated over the obstacle. They had to go back a few yards, sloping the roof of the tunnel upwards, using the earth to raise the level of the floor correspondingly, so that the top of the pipe would eventually be flush with the floor. It took them several days to complete this preliminary operation.

At last Manhard began to extend the roof over the pipe. Von Werra was at the bottom of the shaft, emptying soil from the kit bag into a bucket. Suddenly there was a rumble at the far end of the tunnel. He could no longer see the light where Manhard was working.

Von Werra went up the tunnel like a rabbit bolting from a ferret. Manhard was kicking madly, but stopped as soon as he felt his companion's hands. Von Werra inched forward over Manhard's legs and, as soon as he reached the fall, jabbed his fingers into the earth, pulling armfuls of it back towards him and to one side. After a few second Manhard began to kick again. Von Werra retreated, grabbed him by the ankles, digging his broken nails into the slimy, perspiring flesh to get a better grip, and heaved with a strength engendered by desperation. Manhard moved back a few inches, displacing more soil. A few more heaves and then von Werra could hear Manhard choking, fighting for breath. Another heave and another, and Manhard was free.

Von Werra collapsed on to his arms. He was finished. He seemed to be spinning giddily through black space. There was a singing and a banging in his ears. He hovered on the threshold of unconsciousness, then slowly returned. There was something different . . . a new quality in the blackness. He raised his head.

A breath of cold, dank air stole back along the fetid tunnel, stroking his clammy forehead like icy fingers.

He gulped fresh air.

He shook Manhard's leg.

" Air, Manhard! Air!"

Manhard lay still, gasping and spluttering. As he began to recover his senses, he panicked.

" Out!" he cried. "For God's sake, get out! We'll both be buried alive. Whole roof's fallen in over the pipe."

" Easy, Walter!" von Werra replied calmly. "Find the lamp. Let's have a look at the damage. The chief thing is, we've got air now!"

Manhard calmed down and began digging for the lamp, but could not find it. When von Werra thought he and his companion had regained sufficient confidence, they both left the tunnel and rested for a while. They were badly shaken and were tempted to close down for the day. But they went on looking by turns and eventually uncovered the lamp.

The damage proved to be less serious than they had feared. The fall had left a high dome above the sewer pipe. At the top, a few close loops of barbed wire were visible. Von Werra was mortified to discover that they were not under the middle of the lane as they had estimated, but directly below the first of the two security fences. On the other hand, if the fall had occurred under the lane the consequences might well have been fatal, if not for the tunnellers, then at least for the tunnel.

The British authorities had buried one concertina of barbed wire, filling in the trench loosely with clinker and rubble as well as earth. Air filtered through this trench into the tunnel. The coiled barbed wire acted as a reinforcement, preventing a total collapse above the sewer pipe.

The purpose of the buried wire was to stop prisoners burrowing under the fence at ground level. But by allowing air to filter through to the tunnel it had saved the " Swanwick Construction Company " from defeat.

CHAPTER IX

Von Werra Gets Out Again

AFTER THE earth from the fall had been cleared out of the tunnel, the dome was shored up by a framework of interlaced garden canes, behind which sheets of tin obtained by unrolling bully-beef and other cans, and even panes of glass, were inserted. It was rather a lash-up job, but it was secure enough.

Thanks to the air filtering through the roof over the dome, von Werra and Manhard were able to work undergound for long periods in comparative comfort.

From then on the tunnel advanced rapidly. Von Werra, and the other members of the team who were to escape through it, spent their evenings planning how they would get out of England once they had escaped from the camp.

They decided that the initial break-out would be made by the five prisoners who had worked on the tunnel scheme from start to finish. As soon as they got away the tunnel exit would be camouflaged in the hope that other prisoners would be able to leave by it later.

Of the team of five, only von Werra and Wagner had a fair knowledge of English. Cramer and Wilhelm understood it fairly well, but could put only the simplest sentences together. Leutnant Manhard, without peer as a tunnel digger, was no linguist and did not aspire to become one ; his knowledge of English was virtually nil.

As Wagner and Wilhelm had worked together disposing of the spoil from the tunnel, they decided to escape together. They would make their way to Liverpool in the hope of being able to stow away on a Swedish, Spanish or Finnish ship, or of getting across to Eire.

Cramer and Manhard were to keep together and travel by

buses and hitch-hiking to Glasgow, where they also hoped to be able to stow away on a neutral ship.

Von Werra was to make a solo bid to get back to Germany.

His experiences while on the run in the Lake District had convinced him that a German escaper in Britain stood very little chance unless he could somehow get out of the country before the search for him got under way. And the only means of getting out of the country quickly was by air. Von Werra therefore decided that after getting out of Swanwick camp he would make for the nearest R.A.F. aerodrome, wherever it might be, and try to get away in a stolen aircraft.

That was his basic plan. In order to put it into practice he had to devise some simple but completely convincing masquerade. It would have to be plausible enough to deceive not only laymen whose help he would have to enlist, but also R.A.F. officers—who might immediately detect any flaws in his story.

Von Werra knew he could not hope to pass himself off as an Englishman. Fortunately, however, there were now a great many Belgian, Czech, Dutch, French, Norwegian and Polish refugees serving in the R.A.F., speaking broken English and wearing uniforms with which the ordinary member of the British public was unfamiliar.

He decided he would pose as " Captain Albert William van Lott," a Dutchman, pilot of a Wellington of the " Mixed Special Bomber Squadron, Coastal Command," based at Aberdeen. He would not know until he got out of the camp where the nearest R.A.F station was, nor what kind of units were based there. However, he assumed that, being far inland, it was unlikely to be a Coastal Command base, and he chose to masquerade as a Coastal Command pilot for that very reason. Anyone he met at a Fighter, Bomber or Training Command station would not have an intimate knowledge of the workings of Coastal Command and would be less likely to trip him up. Moreover, the British public knew less about the activities of Coastal than of other Commands.

Von Werra got the idea for the name of the fictitious squadron from reading British newspapers. He had read an item about a Dutch pilot of a " mixed squadron " being decorated for gallantry. He was not sure, however, whether the " mixed " meant that the squadron was made up of British and Dutch crews, or that it carried out various kinds of missions. Its ambiguity was all to the good because it allowed him a certain latitude if he should be asked for explanations. He inserted the word " special ", making it " Mixed Special Bomber Squadron ", to give the designation additional vagueness. He selected Dyce, near Aberdeen, for its base, partly because it was a long way away, but mainly because a fellow-prisoner, who had been an observer in an anti-shipping unit of the Luftwaffe, had taken part in numerous attacks in the Aberdeen area from Norwegian bases, and was able to give him reliable information as to the location of airfields, factories, naval depots, etc.

So much for the background. As for the story itself, von Werra would say that he had been forced down somewhere north of Derby on the return flight from an attack on Esbjerg, on the west coast of Denmark, during which his Wellington had been hit by flak and seriously damaged. When he got in touch with the R.A.F. aerodrome from which he hoped to steal an aircraft, he would say that he had already reported the crash of the Wellington by telephone to Aberdeen, and had been instructed to make his way to the aerodrome, to which in due course a plane would be sent to pick him up.

That story should enable him to get on to the aerodrome. Once there, he would have to rely on luck and his wits.

As for his wardrobe for the masquerade, a certain Oberleutnant Podbielski had managed to retain his flying suit when he was captured, and he agreed to give it to von Werra. Another prisoner gave him a pair of fur-lined flying boots, and from another he got a pair of leather gloves. To complete his wardrobe, he bought a woollen tartan scarf from the camp shop.

The other escapers were to pose as civilians, and the " Forgery Department " were busy producing identity cards.

Von Werra thought he could dispense with identity papers ; if he were asked to produce them, he would point out that he had been on a raid and aircrew were not allowed to take papers into the air. However, he must be able to produce a service identity disc.

During the German offensive in France an R.A.F. Blenheim had been shot down near von Werra's airfield, and he had been detailed to bring in the survivors. He remembered that their identity discs were made of reddish-brown vulcanised fibre, and that they were stamped with the owner's name, number and letters denoting the religion to which he belonged. But he could not remember the size of the disc nor whether the owner's rank was also stamped on it. To get the details right von Werra and two members of the " Forgery Department " staged a little pantomime in the camp kitchens.

They approached the British Corporal in charge and asked him to settle a bet. Von Werra said he had once seen the identity discs of some captured British airmen, and was sure that in addition to name, rank and number, the owner's religion was given. His two friends ridiculed the idea that religion was among the particulars given. Who was right ?

" See for yourself," the Corporal replied with a grin. He pulled his own identity disc on a loop of string from his trouser pocket, and handed it to von Werra.

" What did I tell you ? " von Werra cried triumphantly. " You see—' C E '—' Church of England '. That'll cost you five cigarettes each ! "

" You were wrong about one thing, though," said the Corporal. " The rank is not given."

" Why, nor it is ! " said von Werra. " You'd better make it three cigarettes each."

While von Werra engaged the Corporal's attention with a rough description of German identity tags, the disc passed from hand to hand. Its weight and thickness were carefully noted, also the size, position and spacing of the stampings, and the number of digits in the regimental number.

As soon as they had left the kitchen, one of them took out his fountain pen and marked the faint circle in the palm of his hand, where he had pressed the disc hard against it.

The " Forgery Department " then set to work. First they tried with linoleum ; the upper surface was hard and shiny and ideal for the purpose, but the material was the wrong colour and it would not absorb their home-made dye. Moreover, it was too thick and the underside was rough and stringy. They tried with dyed cardboard, but was too light. Eventually they got over this difficulty by splitting a cardboard disc in half and inserting a small circle cut from a tooth paste tube. The three discs were then stuck together with glue made by melting little globules of resin scraped from knots in the woodwork of the Garden House.

It took a long time and much practice to imitate the stampings of a genuine disc. The letters and numbers were cut into the cardboard with the point of a nail file, which had been reduced and sharpened by much whetting on a lump of sandstone. At length a first-class imitation of a service identity disc was produced. It was left on a hot-water pipe for a couple of days to harden and give it the slight convexity that had been observed in the Corporal's disc.

The escapers were financed entirely by Oberleutnant Wilhelm. It was, of course, strictly forbidden for prisoners to have currency of any kind ; their pay took the form of book-keeping credits, the value of the items they bought in the camp canteen being debited to them. However, Wilhelm had a one-carat diamond solitaire ring, which he placed on the market. Being such a shady and dangerous deal for both parties, the highest bid he could get for it from selected camp guards was one pound. And even then he had the greatest difficulty in obtaining payment in small change instead of a note. The money was divided equally between the five escapers, thus each one would leave Swanwick Camp for Germany with four shillings in his pocket.

None of the prisoners was to carry any baggage except Manhard. He had acquired a fibre suitcase of which he was inordinately proud, and which he thought was just the thing for escaping. He had nothing to put in it except toilet articles and bars of chocolate. A non-smoker, he had always traded his monthly ration of cigarettes for chocolate, which he couldn't bear to leave behind. His " corner " in chocolate was one of the jokes of the camp, all the more so since he had never been known to eat any. When asked, chaffingly, what on earth he proposed to do with it, he would say darkly :

" Ah, that'll come in handy one of these days ! "

Meanwhile, the tunnel was nearing completion. One day von Werra noticed there were fine fibre roots in the soil he was digging out. The tunnel had reached beyond the two fences and the lane and was now under the hedge. He and Manhard therefore began to slope upwards for the exit.

Two days later a group of excited prisoners, including von Werra and Major Fanelsa, stormed to the window of a room on the top floor of the north wing. They were nearly twice as high as the watch tower and they could see the ground on the far side of the hedge, beyond the lane.

And there, waggling from side to side, about a yard from the hedge, was the flower cane Manhard was poking up through the surface from the end of the tunnel. It was a supreme moment for von Werra. He was proud, gratified and thrilled. New adventures were in the offing.

He turned to Major Fanelsa and said, not without a hint of malice :

" Well, Herr Major, is to-morrow the big night ? "

But the Major held himself aloof from the animation of the group. He frowned, and answered with a pompous, booming precision :

" I'm sorry, Werra, but as Leader of P.O.W. Camp No. 13 I cannot accept responsibility if you make the exit to the tunnel at that point. It's too great a risk. I require you to extend it at least another two metres."

There was dead silence.

Von Werra flushed with rage. The absurdity, the utter pointlessness of it ! And for such a childish reason !

" Oh, well," he muttered, " in that case we might as well keep going till we reach Calais. And then, I suppose, we shall be ordered to extend it to Wilhelmstrasse ! "

Some of the prisoners gasped, others tittered. Fanelsa asserted himself with relish, his Adam's apple bobbing up and down. He hinted at a post-war court-martial, ordered von Werra to find the other members of the tunnel team and to bring them to his office in five minutes, and strode out of the room.

Faced with the four other officers, including one of his own rank, Major Fanelsa was firm but a little less Prussian. He said that the tunnel scheme had turned the camp upside down. Every little *Gefreiter* was running round with a home-made duplicate key in his pocket, expecting to be allowed to escape.

" I am going to put a stop to this nonsense," he added. " I shall permit only you five, who have actually worked on the tunnel, to escape in the first instance. After that, if we succeed in camouflaging the exit after you've gone, we shall see."

As it had already been decided that only the five should break out for the time being, nobody offered any objections.

If Fanelsa wanted to take the credit for this decision—let him do so.

Von Werra and Manhard completed the extension of the tunnel in two days. To make quite sure there would be no further objections from Herr " Willibald ", they made it more than three metres longer.

The completed tunnel was ready for use on the night of 17 December —just a month after it was begun.

However, Major Fanelsa would not fix the date for the escape. A Medical Commission was due to visit Swanwick any day to examine seriously wounded prisoners with a view to their repatriation under the exchange scheme. It would create an unfavourable impression, he said, and perhaps prejudice the wounded men's chances of getting home, if the Commission arrived during the excitement of a recent break-out.

Three days later he changed his mind. Provided conditions were favourable at the time, the escape could be staged that night.

The five then decided the order of their going. Von Werra, wearing a beret made from a piece of blanket to keep his hair clean, and a pair of old pyjamas dyed with boot blacking to protect his flying suit, would crawl into the tunnel shortly after final roll-call and lock-up at eight o'clock. He would open the tunnel exit by breaking through the layer of frozen topsoil that had been left. As soon as the hole was large enough, a non-escaping prisoner in the tunnel behind him would crawl back and give the word to the other escapers, who would be similarly dressed. Major Cramer and Manhard would leave immediately after von Werra. There would then be an interval of half an hour, to allow the guards to forget any slight noises made by the first escapers, before Wagner and Wilhelm left.

The rendezvous for all five was a barn in a meadow beyond the farmhouse. As soon as the last man reached the barn and reported that all was well, the five would then go their separate ways. As the actual break-out would not be staged until 9 p.m., an hour after locking-up time, the rendezvous could not take place much before nine forty-five. The two pairs who were hoping to get away from the area quickly would have to hurry off to their respective bus stops. Von Werra had more time as his plan did not call for him to be on the nearest R.A.F. aerodrome until dawn.

Whatever Major Fanelsa's purpose may have been in delaying the escape until Friday night, when the time came the five men were glad they had waited. Conditions were ideal. The floodlighting over the fences was switched off between six and seven and shortly afterwards the air raid sirens sounded.

The sky was overcast, but the moon, almost in its last quarter and due to set shortly after midnight, tinged the clouds with a faint luminosity. There was a sharp frost and thin patches of fog.

There was also much German air activity. Liverpool, far away to the west, was more heavily attacked that night than at any previous time. Minor attacks of long duration developed on Derby, just a few miles to the south, and on Sheffield, not far to the north. It seemed to the escapers that the Luftwaffe had laid on these two attacks especially for their benefit. The night seemed full of the sound of aircraft, bombs and gunfire.

When the roll-call had been taken and the British officer and sergeant gone, and the prisoners had been locked in the Garden House for the night, the twenty-man choir under Leutnant Bein forgathered on the staircase between the ground and the first floor, and began their usual nightly concert. But to-night every available prisoner in the camp stood by to join in the singing at zero hour. Spirits were high, the atmosphere was supercharged, and von Werra's eyes sparkled.

That day he had suddenly remembered that the crew of the crashed Blenheim he had escorted in France wore their identity discs on a string round their necks. He did likewise. Later, this decision was to cause him chagrin and regret. Before he fastened the diagonal zip of his flying suit and put on the dyed pyjamas, he inserted that day's camp copy of *The Times*, which had been carefully kept clean for him. This, together with the packets of English cigarettes and bars of chocolate in his pockets, were all the props for his act.

At about eight-fifteen he shook hands with the friends he was leaving behind and crawled up the tunnel for the last time. It was harder work than he had expected to break through the frozen crust of earth. He puffed and perspired in the flying suit and fur-lined boots, for he was used to working naked. At last the hole was large enough and he gave the signal to the man waiting behind him.

Von Werra relaxed for a few minutes to recover his breath and composure. His head protruded a little way from the hole. He looked and listened. To the south, searchlights were ineffectively raking the cloud base. It was strangely quiet. No guns, no bombs, no aircraft and—horrible moment—*no singing*! What on earth had happened?

In the stillness close behind him somebody cleared his throat and spat. Von Werra's pulse raced.

Christ! He had completely forgotten the guards in the watch

tower. He turned his head, keeping his face under cover, and assured himself that he was screened from the watch tower by the hedge.

The guns opened fire again in Derby. Almost simultaneously the prisoners started singing. Von Werra grinned at the unexpected volume of sound. And he was hearing it from outside the wire! Then he realised they were singing that particular song for his benefit—*Muss i denn, muss i denn zum Städteli hinaus* . . . "I must away into the great wide world."

Von Werra listened for a moment longer. He could swear that he recognised the booming voice of Major Fanelsa. He emerged noiselessly from the tunnel and crawled towards some bushes. There he paused. On the next leg he would have to cross a path, skirt some farm buildings, cross another path, and enter the field in which was the barn fixed as the rendezvous.

He crept forward to the side of the path, out of cover. As he was rising off his knees he heard a gate slam behind the buildings. Then there was the sound of voices, male and female, and the ring of iron-shod boots on cobble stones. Von Werra fell flat.

The next moment the voices sounded much closer. Raising his head and peering between the fingers of his gloved hands, he saw several figures that had just turned the corner of a building and were now hesitantly coming towards him on the path. No doubt they had been attracted by the noise of the singing.

There were two men and two women. The women had coats slung over their shoulders.

There was a slight rustle behind him and the sound of quick breathing. Major Cramer. Then farther back, a squeak, unmistakably made by the handle of Manhard's accursed suitcase.

The figures on the path were not more than ten metres away.

The Illustrations

Franz von Werra

Von Werra's Me. 109 after he crash-landed—a photograph that contradicts his later statement that it was destroyed by fire

When they counted up the notches on the tail of von Werra's plane, members of the searchlight battery thought they had shot down a Luftwaffe ace

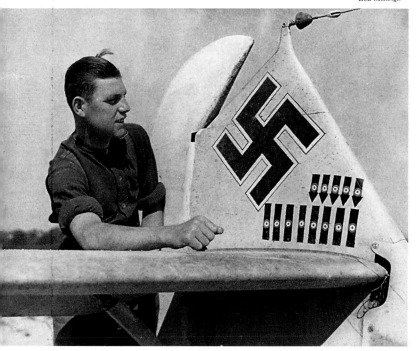

I am not at all happy to bee hier and I hop to see you again but not as prisonner of war but as a friend.

F. Ahlerra

German Luftwaffe

5 of September in the second year of war.

The small son of the station sergeant at Maidstone County Police Headquarters asked for von Werra's autograph

No. 8 Kensington Palace Gardens, the London District Prisoner-of-War Cage, to which von Werra was brought for interrogation

A lion cub mascot got von Werra on to the front covers of the German popular magazines

Pages from the German press with which von Werra was confronted by his British interrogator

Forestry Commission

Grizedale Hall (right; outbuildings centre), the prisoner-of-war camp in the Lake District to which von Werra was sent and from which he escaped twelve days later

LEFT: Major Willibald Fanelsa, senior German officer among the prisoners at Grizedale, and later at Swanwick. RIGHT: Hauptmann Helmut Pohle, member of the German equivalent of an Escape Committee at Grizedale

Mr. Sam Eaton, booking office clerk at Codnor Park Station at which
von Werra called after his second escape

The L.M.S. telegram blank on which Mr. Eaton asked the
" Dutch " pilot to write down his name and unit

The late Group Captain J. L. M. de C. Hughes-Chamberlain (right)
and Squadron Leader Boniface, respectively Station Commander and
Administrative Officer at Hucknall Aerodrome at the time of von
Werra's visit

DATE	NAME	NATIONALITY	ADDRESS	ORDER	TIMES OF ARRIVAL AND DEPARTURE
21.12.40	van Lott	Dutch	Aberdeen	Sec. ood (See Air)	09.⚹ 09.

Von Werra's entry in the Visitors' Book at the Rolls-Royce works on
Hucknall Aerodrome

An artist's impression published at the time in a German illustrated magazine of von Werra's leap from the window of the train

The point at which von Werra crossed the St. Lawrence. On the far bank, Prescott, Canada; in the foreground Ogdensburg, U.S.A.

Watertown Daily Times

Von Werra arrives in New York, his ears bandaged as a result of frostbite

Von Werra sends a picture postcard from the safety of the United States to the " Adjutant " at Hucknall (He has, however mistaken the date, which was the 21st)

Von Werra photographed in the grounds of the German Consulate in Mexico City, wearing the straw hat which formed part of his disguise for his escape from the U.S.A.

Von Werra was married on his return to Germany, to the girl he had first met when a crash, just prior to the outbreak of war, had made it unlikely that he would ever fly again

Von Werra, on the Russian Front, poses against the wreck of a Russian fighter—the last photograph of him to appear in the German press, in full colour

CHAPTER X

The C.I.D. Interviews
Captain van Lott

Von Werra lay and listened for the snuffle and padding of a dog, for the growl which would mean that the game was up.

There was no sound from Cramer and Manhard. They too must have spotted the figures and fallen flat.

It had taken four weeks to dig the tunnel; there were four people on the path, two men and two women: one week's heart-breaking toil thrown away on each! For they were bound to see him. They were less than ten metres away. Even now they must be looking in his direction, looking towards the prostrate figures of Manhard, Cramer and himself. Supposing the guards linked the voices on the path with the unprecedented row going on in the camp! Supposing, despite the air raid alert, they decided to switch on the watch tower's searchlights and investigate!

The moments went by. The people on the path had halted. Von Werra did not know that they had been warned not to approach too close to the barbed-wire fences after dark, or that the guards hearing female as well as male voices were completely reassured, realising that it must be the people from the farm.

The prisoners had finished their song. There was a pause, then tremendous, intermittent shouts. Leutnant Bein was reciting his P.O.W. *Abendspruch* (evening ode), and the others were shouting the responses.

As soon as the noise started, the people on the path turned round and retraced their steps. Then came the ring of studded boots on cobble stones, the slamming of a gate, more footsteps; a door was shut. Silence.

Behind, the slow regular steps of sentries patrolling the lane from watch tower to watch tower ; a desultory conversation between the two guards in the nearest tower.

As soon as the prisoners started singing again, von Werra darted silently across the path. A few minutes later he reached the barn. He leaned against the weather boarding. It was bitterly cold. Now that he was relaxed, his sweat-soaked vest felt as though it had been dipped in ice-water.

A shadow detached itself from the hedgerow and slid along the side of the barn. It was Major Cramer.

" Werra ? " he whispered.

" Werra it is, Herr Major ! "

" Where the devil did those people spring from ? I nearly blacked out. What fun, though ! I wouldn't have missed this party for a promotion ! "

" If they had had a dog . . . I was scared you wouldn't see them in time."

" I didn't see them at first. I heard some voices and then saw you hit the deck, so I did the same. Manhard must have taken the cue from me. Listen ! "

They could hear a faint, intermittent squeaking approaching them along the black shadows of the hedgerow.

They both chuckled.

" That damned suitcase ! " von Werra whispered. " He might have oiled the handle."

Manhard's masssive form disengaged itself from the inky shadows.

" Hallo, Walter," said von Werra. " Where d'you think you're off to ? "

" Berlin," Manhard replied loudly. " That is——"

" Sh, for God's sake ! You've a long way to go yet ! "

" It's getting late," said Cramer. " Manhard and I had better push off without waiting for the others, or we may not be able to get a bus."

" Right," von Werra agreed. " I'll help you get your pyjamas off and then, away you go ! "

They removed the old pyjamas and von Werra rolled them up and stuffed them under the hedge. He also threw away the others' home-made berets, but kept his own on for warmth.

Cramer and von Werra shook hands and wished one another

luck. Manhard picked up his suitcase. He stood rather awkwardly; he and von Werra had been through a lot together. The latter stretched out his hand.

"Well, so long, Walter!" he said. "Good luck—and don't forget: 'One for Nottingham!'" It was one of the few English phrases they had been able to make Manhard learn; it had been impressed upon him especially in case he became separated from Cramer on the bus they intended to catch.

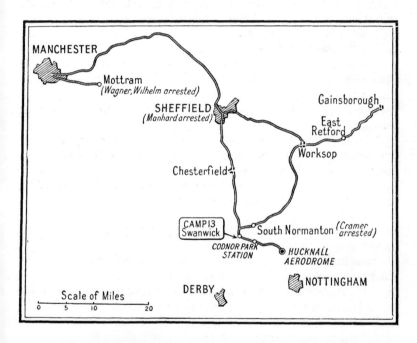

"So long, Sonny!" Manhard answered. "See you in Kranzler's Café on Kurfürstendamm! You'll be home first, so don't forget to ring up my girl-friend."

Cramer had already disappeared. Manhard hesitated, then made a gesture with the suitcase.

"She's crazy about chocolate," he said. "Tell her I'm on my way with a load." He was gone into the night.

So that was why he had hoarded his chocolate! Poor Walter, he had worked like a maniac on the tunnel, thinking all the time

of the chocolate he might be able to get home to his girl-friend!
With his inability to understand English, much less to speak it, his
chances were slight.

A few minutes later Wagner and Wilhelm, the last of the five
escapers, arrived at the barn and reported that all was well at the
camp. Then they went on their way and von Werra was on his
own. The camp was only two hundred yards away in the darkness
on the hill, but already it seemed curiously remote, part of another
existence, another world. He was no longer Oberleutnant Franz
von Werra of the Luftwaffe, prisoner-of-war of the British; he was
Captain Albert William van Lott, a Dutch pilot serving in the
Royal Air Force.

There was no hurry. With any luck, the escape would not be
discovered until roll-call at 8 a.m. the next morning—perhaps not
even then if the plans for covering the escapees' absence were
successful. He had at least ten hours' start on the camp authorities.
Perhaps by the time they found he was missing, he would be beyond
their reach.

It was better for him to keep off the roads until the sirens
sounded the "All Clear", otherwise he might be taken for a survivor
of a crashed German aircraft. Dorniers, Junkers and Heinkels were
still passing overhead from time to time.

He crouched down between the hedge and the barn, counting
the quarter hours by the chimes of the clock on the main building
of the camp. He was chilled to the marrow, but he did not mind.
He was free.

The moon went down and the night grew black. Activity in
the air diminished. Sometimes there was almost complete silence
from one chiming of the clock to the next. Released in these long
silences, his thoughts sped up and down the years, back and forth
across the frontiers, only to be recalled, in a spasm of blind panic,
by a sudden, sharp scuffle among the dead leaves under the hedge-
rows; but the hunter was not a guard with a gun, it was some
hungry small beast of the field.

Three o'clock struck and still the "All Clear" had not been
sounded. Von Werra dared not wait any longer. He emerged from
his hiding-place, cramped and shivering. He threw away his home-
made beret, combed his hair, tucked the copy of *The Times* under
his arm and set off across the fields.

He would have walked less jauntily had he known that police

were already scouring the district for four of the five escapees.

Major Cramer had already been captured.

After they left von Werra, Cramer and Manhard walked briskly to Somercotes, hoping to pick up a bus for Nottingham. They waited, but no bus came. They seemed to be attracting attention. Perhaps the last bus had left? Perhaps the place where they were waiting was not a bus stop—in the dim light it was hard to tell.

Men going home from the public houses shouted unintelligible phrases at them. Jovial greetings, information about the bus service, inquisitive questions—which? When they were accosted by an argumentative drunk, they decided it was time to make themselves scarce. They set off in the opposite direction—away from Nottingham. The reveller shouted after them, and they turned off on the first side road.

About midnight they passed through another village. There they found a bicycle, its masked lamp still alight, propped against a wall outside a shop. The shop was in darkness, there was nobody in sight.

Cramer grabbed the bicycle and they hurried away. The idea was undoubtedly good, but they chose the wrong bicycle.

It belonged to the village policeman. He had left it outside the shop while he made a routine check of the rear of the premises. Cramer and Manhard had gone only a few yards when he returned and saw that it was missing.

Shouting at the retreating figures, he gave chase.

" Run for it ! " Cramer said. " Good luck ! "

Manhard, still clutching his suitcase, raced off up the road, did a belly-roll over the first five-barred gate he came to, and ran off over the fields. He got away.

Cramer was a good all-round athlete. He leapt on the stolen bicycle as though he was starting a world record attempt. He pedalled furiously, but the three-speed gear did not engage. He remained stationary. His frantic pedalling achieved nothing but a loud grating sound.

" 'Ere ! " shouted the policeman.

Cramer saw that he had to act quickly. He sprinted down the road, pushing the bicycle beside him. He soon gained a substantial lead on the law and decided to have another try on the machine. He increased his speed and took a flying leap on to the saddle.

Carried along by the momentum of his run, he moved the gear handle to and fro, pedalling madly meanwhile. The gears refused to engage. The mechanism was, in fact, defective and only the owner knew how to coax it into action.

Cramer was now just short of the village hall. A dance had ended at midnight and the local lads were still standing in a group outside. The policeman shouted:

" Stoppim! Stoppim! Got my bike! "

One of the youngsters, quicker on the uptake then the rest, bowled the thief over as he went past.

Cramer was taken to the police station, where he did his utmost to save the situation for the other four escapers. First he said he was a Dutch refugee working in a munitions factory. That story lasted less than two minutes: his identity card was an obvious fake. He was searched. Under his civilian overcoat—a conversion job tailored in the camp—he wore his Luftwaffe uniform from which the insignia had been stripped. Some of it, including his Knight's Cross, was found in his pockets.

Cramer then admitted he was an escaped German prisoner, but gave the name of a prisoner who had not escaped, and to complicate matters still further, said he had broken out of Grizedale Hall, in the Lake District the previous day, and had made his way south by trains and hitch-hiking. He hoped this would satisfy the police for the time being and that, having got him safe in custody, they would not bother to check his story until daylight. But a call was made immediately through police channels to Grizedale Hall, and by 12.30 a.m. it had been established that no prisoner had escaped from that camp the previous day, and that the prisoner whose name Cramer had given had been transferred some time previously to Swanwick Camp.

The police then rang up Swanwick Camp and asked if any of their prisoners were missing. The camp authorities said they would investigate. Thus the alarm was given at Swanwick at about 12.45 a.m. The occupants of the Garden House were assembled under guard. Attempts to confuse the count were frustrated, and it was soon discovered that five prisoners were missing. However, their names were not determined until later, after an individual identity check of the Germans remaining in the camp.

About two o'clock the police were informed that five prisoners had escaped altogether, making four still at large. They did not receive the names, ranks and descriptions of the missing men until several hours afterwards.

Thus, the police began their quest for four escaped Germans an hour before von Werra set out on his quest for an aircraft in which to fly back to France.

The " All Clear " was sounded in the Nottingham-Derby area at 4.30 a.m. By that time von Werra had walked miles along country roads and through villages without encountering a soul.

Dawn was in three and a half hours' time. He had to be on the nearest R.A.F. aerodrome by then. And still he did not know where it was ; he might be walking away from it for all he knew. He was considering whether, as Captain van Lott, he should rouse the occupants of the next isolated house and demand help, when he came to a railway bridge. It occurred to him that signal-boxes and most stations were manned all night and that they had telephones. So he scrambled down on to the line. He thought he could hear the hissing of a stationary locomotive in the distance and he set off in that direction.

It was standing by itself in a siding. Somebody was scrambling about on the coal in the tender. The fire door was open and the cab was filled with flickering light.

" Hal-lo ! " von Werra shouted. There was no answer.

He climbed up to the cab. The driver was perched in the far corner, his head behind the canvas blackout curtain stretched between the cab roof and the tender.

" Hal-lo ! "

The driver's head appeared. When he saw the figure in the flying suit, with a newspaper tucked under his arm, his jaw dropped.

" What d'you think you're up to ? "

" I am Captain van Lott, formerly of the Royal Dutch Air Force, now serving with the R.A.F. I've just made a forced landing in a Wellington after being hit by flak in a raid over Denmark. I must get to the nearest R.A.F. aerodrome as quickly as possible. Can you help me, please ? "

The explanation sounded so incongruously matter-of-fact, that the driver laughed.

" But—but what can I do about it ? " he asked.

" Well, where's the nearest telephone ? "

" My mate's just going off duty. You'd better walk along the track with him to the station."

The engine driver's mate was a lad in his teens. He climbed down into the cab from the tender and looked at von Werra with surprise.

" An airman," the engine driver explained. " Been forced down, he says, and wants to use the telephone. Better take him along to Codnor Park, Harold. The signalman'll probably fix him up."

" Sure. I'm just going."

" Cheerio," said the engine driver to von Werra : " Harold'll put you right. Good luck ! "

" Cheerio ! " imitated von Werra. " Thanks."

" Better keep close behind me," Harold said, " or you'll trip up. Mind the wires ! Be all right once we get on the loop. It's not far."

" Good," said von Werra. " Where are you taking me ? "

" Codnor Park."

" Couldna Park—what's that ? "

" A little station."

" Is there a telephone ? "

" I 'spect so. The signalman'll know. You a pilot ? "

" Yes, of a Wellington."

" Over these points now and then we're on the loop. What happened ? "

" Hit by a shell over Denmark. I come back on one engine."

" And then you crashed ? "

" Yes, about two hours ago."

" You're not English, are you ? "

" No, Dutch Captain in the R.A.F."

" What about the others ? "

" None injured."

" Coo. You're lucky ! Me and my mate never heard anything."

They continued in silence on the sleepers between the rails. It was very cold. The sky had now cleared and the stars hung bright and low. There was just enough light for von Werra to discern the rime on the sleepers and the marks in it made by the lad's boots. The German had difficulty in adjusting his steps to the spacing of the sleepers. He stubbed his toes frequently on flints, and now and again one would strike the rails with an icy, metallic ring.

They reached Codnor Park L.M.S. Station about 5.30 a.m., where Harold handed him over to the signalman, Mr. R. W. Harris, of South Street, Riddings. But the signal box was not connected with the public telephone. Mr. Harris suggested he wait until the booking clerk came on duty ; there was a G.P.O. telephone in the booking office.

Mr. Sam Eaton, the booking clerk, arrived shortly before six, and the signalman handed von Werra over to him.

A dapper, mercurial little man with a ready smile and normally most obliging, Sam Eaton was not very pleased to have the stranger in trouble foisted on him. He had had an hour's walk along the tracks from his home at Langley Mill. It was a bitterly cold morning and the porter had not yet lit the fire in the office ; a train for Nottingham left at 6.22 and he knew he would be busy issuing tickets to munitions workers from about ten past six until the train left ; there was a considerable sum of money in the office, and on the wall of an inner room, visible through the open door, was a rack of Home Guard rifles.

" What's it all about ? " he asked. " What can I do for you ? "

Von Werra repeated his story. " I must get to the nearest R.A.F. aerodrome at once. It is most important. Will you please ring it up and say a car should be sent to fetch me ? "

" Whereabouts did you crash ? "

" Oh, I don't know exactly. Near the railway a long way down." "

" How far roughly ? "

" At least two miles."

" H'm. Which side of the line ? "

The booking clerk was manifestly sceptical.

" What's happened to the rest of the crew then ? " he asked.

" Oh, they are all right. None wounded. We were very lucky. We found a farmhouse, but there was no telephone. They stay there near the Wellington. Only I come to get transport for them and to report to my base at Aberdeen. It is most urgent. A plane from Aberdeen will fetch me from this nearest aerodrome. Please, you phone now ? "

While he was speaking, von Werra put the newspaper, title uppermost, on a small table, placing his gloves beside it. He partly unfastened his flying suit and pulled out an almost full packet of Player's cigarettes and a box of Swan matches.

" Cigarette ? "

"No, thank you. Not just now. I shall be very busy issuing tickets in a minute."

Von Werra lighted a cigarette and flicked the match into the fireplace.

The booking clerk seemed suddenly to make up his mind. He walked over to the telephone and picked up the receiver, resting his elbow on the desk and glancing back at the airman. Immensely relieved, von Werra smiled his thanks.

He glanced round the office. It smelled of sooty smoke and the foul paste used on the railways for sticking labels. He saw a long box in one corner, strolled over to it and sat down.

The telephone exchange took a long time to reply. The booking clerk impatiently pressed the hook. Passengers would start queuing for tickets any minute.

At last the operator answered.

"Put me through to the police, please!"

It was totally unexpected and von Werra showed his consternation.

"But why are you——" he began, but the clerk was already speaking and turned away from him.

"Is that Somercotes Police Station? This is Codnor Park L.M.S. Station. I thought I'd better let you know I've got a young fellow here who says he's a Dutch airman who's crashed in a Wellington down towards Langley Mill. He wants me to get in touch with the R.A.F. for him, but I thought I'd better let you know first . . . Captain van Lott. Van, like guard's van, L-O-double-T . . . No, he says he's serving in the R.A.F. . . . He says it was hit by anti-aircraft shells over Denmark . . . That's right, he was on his way back. No, he appears to be all right . . . They're not hurt, either. He says they're at a farmhouse . . . I wouldn't like to say, that's why I got through to you. At any rate he *says* he's Dutch . . . I don't know—I can't judge. He can make himself understood all right . . . Yes . . . Very good. It would probably be better if you did . . . Right . . . Right . . . Good-bye!"

The clerk replaced the receiver.

"I don't understand why you phoned the police," von Werra told him reproachfully. "I must arrive at an airfield as quickly as possible. It really is urgent. What can the police do? They will only waste time. I cannot tell to them more than I tell to you."

"Don't worry," said the clerk, "the sergeant said somebody would be along right away. Within ten minutes. They don't have far to come."

"They are coming here? What for?" von Werra was aghast.

"The sergeant said they wanted to see you. They are in a better position to help you than I am."

Passengers began to appear at the little window and ask for tickets. A porter came in through a side door from the platform. He rubbed his hands and called:

"'Morning, Sam. Cold 'un again, ain't it?"

He did not seem surprised to see the airman, but said, "'Morning!" and set about poking the ashes from the grate and laying the fire.

Von Werra had to make a quick decision. Get out while he still had the chance, or stay and try to bluff the policeman who was on his way to interview him? His instincts clamoured for him to go, to run for it, but reason told him that it would be fatal to do so. It would be obvious that he was an impostor, and the clerk or the porter would immediately ring up the police again. On the other hand, although he was obviously worried about something, the clerk seemed inclined to believe the forced-landing story. The police, von Werra thought, would know nothing about the break-out from Swanwick Camp; they would have no preconceived suspicions, and the constable who was on his way to the station would merely be making a routine check.

He stood up and paced the office. He happened to catch sight of his reflection in a little square mirror on the wall and was shocked to see how dishevelled he looked. He had washed his hair the previous afternoon and it was terribly untidy. There were smudges of dirt from the tunnel on his brow and face.

"May I have a wash?" he asked the clerk. "I got pretty dirty crawling out of the Wellington after we crashed."

Sam Eaton, fully occupied now issuing tickets, looked over his shoulder and indicated where the washroom was.

"You'll see soap and a towel there," he said.

When von Werra returned from the adjoining room a few minutes later, his face was clean and shiny, he had damped his hair and it was now flat and tidy. He returned to the box in the corner and sat down.

The rush for tickets began five minutes before train time, and the date-stamping machine by the little window thudded continually. Most of the latecomers were munitions girls, wearing brightly-coloured scarves tied turban fashion. The clerk seemed to know them all. Some were only half-awake, but others giggled when they saw the good-looking airman sitting in the booking office. Von Werra could not understand what they said, but he was quick on the uptake; he winked and smiled and said "Good morning!" cheerfully, making the most of this little opportunity of improving his standing with the booking clerk.

Passengers shuffled and stamped on the platform outside, their hands deep in their coat pockets. A bell clanged nearby. Levers slammed home in the signal box at the end of the platform; wires running along the platform by the rails vibrated and tapped together. The clerk was still issuing tickets when the train steamed in.

Doors banged shut. The guard's shrill whistle blew and the train moved out.

The porter came in again, shivering.

"Pretty nippy!" he said.

He had previously put a little soot-grimed kettle on the fire, which was now beginning to heat the office, and it was already singing pleasantly. He busied himself with teapot and enamel mugs, pushing von Werra's newspaper, gloves, cigarettes and matches to one corner of the little table.

Now that the rush for the first train was over, and the next was not until 7.5 the booking clerk was able to pay more attention to the "Dutchman".

Von Werra kept glancing at the clock on the wall. The ten minutes had already elapsed and at any moment a policeman would come through the door. Now that it was perhaps too late, the clerk seemed much more friendly: he had got over his initial fluster, he evidently felt happier after having informed the police and he seemed to think his visitor less dubious since he had spruced himself up. In fact, the "Dutchman" was obviously so worried and forlorn, that Sam Eaton was genuinely sorry for the delay and almost regretted that he had not telephoned the R.A.F. direct instead of the police.

Von Werra had been thinking hard about the line he should take with the policeman when he arrived. The clerk had unwittingly given him a valuable clue: his relief after he had passed the responsibility on to the police suggested that the policeman, in his turn, might be just as relieved to pass the responsibility on to the R.A.F. Von Werra decided that he would stand upon his dignity and insist that the nearest aerodrome be informed without further delay. The policeman himself must telephone to the R.A.F. from that office; he must be made to feel that he was helping the R.A.F. and rendering a personal service to a gallant Allied airman in trouble.

The kettle boiled and the porter made the tea.

"I expect you could do with a cup, Captain!" said the clerk.

"Yes, thanks very much. Just what I need!"

He moved over to the fire and sat down. He pulled a bar of Cadbury's chocolate out of his flying suit and offered it to his hosts, but they declined. He told them to help themselves to the cigarettes on the table. Then all three smoked, sipped their tea and chatted cosily round the fire.

"Ever bombed Berlin?"

"No. I'm Coastal Command."

"I see. Shipping, U-boats, and that?"

"Mostly. But last night we attacked the railway station at Esbjerg on the coast of Denmark."

"How did you get hit?"

"We were picked up by searchlights as we crossed the coast. I could not shake them off. I flew straight for the bombing run and just afterwards—*Ker-rump!*—the starboard wing was hit. We had an exciting five minutes."

"What happened? How did you manage to get back?"

"We were thrown all over the sky. The starboard motor died and . . ."

Von Werra continued in the most convincing manner.

He had concocted it all from pilots' stories of actual operations which he had read in British newspapers. He knew it all by heart. Inside out.

"You say you were bombing railway yards," the clerk said later. "You will be able to answer a question I've often wondered about: can you see railway signal lights from the air?"

"Only if you fly low along the lines."

"Ah!"

"Big night last night," said the porter. "They say Derby and Sheffield caught it pretty bad."

" Yes," replied the clerk, " but nothing like Coventry and London. We've been lucky so far, especially out here. How long do you think the war will last, Captain ? "

" Oh, two years at least."

" But we shall win in the end ? "

" Oh, yes," said von Werra. " We are sure to win ! "

The porter put his mug down and went out. The clerk moved to a desk and began to make up money for the bank. Von Werra glanced again at the clock. It was twenty-five to seven.

" When *is* that policeman coming ? " he asked. " All this waste of time . . ."

" Yes, they don't seem to be putting themselves out much."

" Perhaps he won't come. I could wait here all the morning for nothing."

" I'm very sorry, Captain. I don't understand it. The sergeant said ten minutes. . . ."

" I *must* get to the aerodrome. You don't know how urgent it is. Where is it, by the way ? "

" Hucknall."

" Ah, yes, of course, Hucknall ! There is a long range bomber squadron there, I think."

" Oh, is there ? I'd heard it was only a training school. They're buzzing about all day when it's fine."

" It's not far away then ? "

" About ten miles by road, though only about five as the crow flies."

" Look," said von Werra urgently, " I should not tell this to you, but I belong to a special bomber squadron. Last night we try out a new bombsight and other instruments for the first time. They are wonderful, marvellous ! Now you understand why I should get back to Aberdeen so quickly ? "

" Go on ! Really ? . . . I'm very sorry. If you'd said before . . ."

" But how could I ? I should tell it to no one. You must say nothing, or I shall be shot ! "

" Do you think . . . Should I ring up Hucknall now ? "

" Please do ! It will save time. Say they should send a car to fetch me at once. Perhaps the policeman will arrive before the car. If not, you can explain that I could no longer wait."

Sam Eaton lifted the receiver and asked for Hucknall R.A.F. aerodrome. He turned to the " Dutchman ".

" You'd better tell me the name of your unit, and so on."

" Wait ! I'll write it down."

The clerk handed him a thick black pencil and an L.M.S. telegram form.

Surprisingly, since he had not been able to give the number, the clerk was connected with Hucknall aerodrome straight away.

" Who shall I ask for ? " he whispered urgently.

Von Werra thought quickly.

" Ask for the Commanding Officer," he said.

" Hallo ? Is that the R.A.F ? . . . Can I speak to the Commanding Officer, please ? . . . What's that ? . . . You can't ? . . . It's a bit complicated, I'm afraid. This is the booking clerk at Codnor Park L.M.S. Station . . . Codnor Park . . . Not R.A.F.—L.M.S.—*railway* station. That's it . . . I've got a Dutch pilot here who crashed in a Wellington."

Meanwhile the " Dutchman " had written down his particulars on the telegram form, which he handed to the clerk.

It read (see reproduction facing page 96).

" Cptn van Lott
Coastl Command Staff
Mixt. special bomber sqūdr."

These " credentials " were, of course, full of glaring mistakes, which it is not hard to spot in retrospect. To start with, all Allied airmen serving in the R.A.F. were given R.A.F. ranks—and there is no such rank in the R.A.F. as " Captain " for which, in any case, the abbreviation is " Capt." Then to anyone who knew German, the stroke on the " u " in the equally wrongly abbreviated word *sqūdr*. would have been damning. Finally it was unlikely that even a Dutchman would write *Coastl* for Coastal and *Mixt* for Mixed, when spelling his own unit.

But one cannot blame Sam Eaton for not spotting these mistakes. To do so would be to overlook the impact of von Werra's personality. It was not the quality of his story in his pose as van Lott that mattered, but his ability to put it over.

Incidentally, this document was not produced at any of the five different official inquiries held after von Werra's escape. Few people knew of its existence. Mr. Eaton carried it about in his wallet as a souvenir for years, until the paper began to crack along the folds.

Then it was put away in a box where it remained until material for this book was being gathered.

Hucknall was being troublesome. First, the telephone operator said he could not disturb the Station Commander at that hour unless it was a matter of vital importance. What was the nature of the call? Sam Eaton explained Captain van Lott's plight in detail. The operator then said that since it was transport that was required, he would transfer the call to the M.T. Section.

Sam Eaton retold the story to the M.T. Section. The M.T. Section said they would need authorisation before sending out a vehicle to fetch Captain van Lott, so the call was transferred to the guard room.

Sam Eaton retold the story to the guard room. The guard commander said he would have to speak to the Duty Officer, and the call was transferred to him.

From von Werra's point of view, this little early-morning game of " passing the buck " was providential, for the clerk's confidence and the firmness of his delivery increased each time he related the story.

When Sam Eaton had first got through to Hucknall, his attitude had been : " Look, I'm simply going to tell you what this man van Lott says. He may be genuine, or he may not. You are the experts and it's up to you to find out and decide what shall be done, since the police don't seem to be bothering." But the delays and incredulity at the other end of the line reflected on his judgment. He became impatient and shifted into the position of himself *wanting* to make the story sound convincing. By the time he had gone over the story twice for the benefit of the Duty Officer, he was as word-perfect as the " Dutchman " himself. Finally, he handed the receiver to von Werra.

" He wants you to speak to him," he said. " Who is it ? " von Werra whispered. " The Commanding Officer ? "

" No, I don't think so. Some kind of officer—I didn't catch what he said."

Von Werra spoke into the phone :

" Captain van Lott. Who is that ? "

" This is the Duty Officer. I hear you've had a spot of bother."

" The which officer ? Perhaps I should speak with the Commanding Officer or the Adjutant, no ? "

" I'm speaking from the Adjutant's office."

" Ah ! Then you shall send a car for me ? "

Von Werra deduced quite wrongly that it was the Adjutant who was speaking.

" Well, what's it all in aid of ? What can we do for you here ? "

" A plane from Aberdeen will come for me there."

" I see. It's curious we've had no word of your crash. What happened exactly ? "

Von Werra told the story all over again in great detail, even mentioning the secret instruments with which the Wellington was equipped. Finally the Englishman said :

" Well, I suppose we shall have to do something about you. I'll send a vehicle to pick you up. Whereabouts is Codnor Park Station, for heaven's sake ? "

" No idea. I give you the clerk again. He will tell you. Thank you very much ! "

Sam Eaton gave necessary directions and then replaced the receiver. He turned to the " Dutchman " and smiled.

" Well, now I suppose you're happy ! " he said.

" Yes. Thank you for all your trouble."

The time was between a quarter and ten to seven. It was now a race between the R.A.F. and the policeman.

A few minutes later the telephone bell rang. The clerk answered it.

" Codnor Park L.M.S. Station . . . Yes, that's right . . . Yes, it's quite true . . . Just a minute, I'll put him on."

He handed the " Dutchman " the receiver.

" Who is that ? " said von Werra into the phone.

" You tell me who you are ! " a voice said at the other end.

" Captain van Lott. But——"

" What's your unit ? "

" Who are you ? "

" What's your unit ? "

" No. Tell me who you are."

" O.K. This is Hucknall again. I was just checking back. Can't be too careful these days ! Your transport's leaving now. Should be there in twenty minutes. 'Bye ! "

" It was the Adjutant again," von Werra told the clerk.

" I know. He told me not to say who it was. He's not taking any chances ! "

" No, he said he cannot be too careful these days ! "

They both laughed. The clerk thought the " Dutchman " looked extremely happy and boyish.

Just before seven, passengers for the 7.5 began to arrive. Soon there was a queue at the ticket window. The signal bell on the platform clanged.

At a minute past seven the office door opened and three men came in. The first wore a soft grey hat, a fawn raincoat, a check scarf and brown leather gloves. The second wore a heavy tweed coat and a cap of the same material. The third wore a peaked cap and a dark blue uniform coat; on one sleeve were three silver stripes.

The men nodded curtly to the booking clerk. He was too busy to do more than say over his shoulder :

" I'd given you up. I thought you weren't coming. I've already rung up Hucknall aerodrome now. A car's on its way to pick him up ! I'll be with you in a minute."

Von Werra stood up slowly and leaned against the wall by the fireplace. He felt sick. He could have wept with disappointment. Only another ten minutes . . . Worse, he had expected to have to deal with a village policeman, and here was the British " *Gestapo* ".

The three men advanced across the room and took up positions facing him round the little table in front of the fire. They eyed him in silence. Their looks were neither friendly nor hostile ; there was no flicker of suspicion, but a cold, casual, clinical interest. They might have been looking at a timetable.

They just stood there looking at him. Behind them, the queue in the waiting-room shuffled up to the little window, where the shirt-sleeved arms of the clerk were flying between ticket racks and stamping machine.

Then the man in the soft grey hat glanced down at the table. Fascinated, von Werra glanced down, too. *The Times*, gloves, an open packet of Player's, a box of Swan matches, the remains of a bar of Cadbury's chocolate, a blob of spilled milk, grains of spilled sugar—and the telegram form on which he had written his particulars.

The detective picked up the bit of paper and studied it. Suddenly he raised his head and rapped out :

" *Sprechen Sie Deutsch ?* "

Von Werra did not know that Major Cramer had been caught ;

nor that a widespread search for Manhard, Wagner, Wilhelm and himself had already begun; nor that the delay in the arrival of the police at Codnor Park Station was due to the fact that, *en route*, they had been investigating a report that one of the escapees had been seen elsewhere. Had he known, he would have thrown in his hand then and there.

As it was the odds against him seemed overwhelming. To him, plain-clothes police were the *Gestapo*. He knew about the methods of the German *Gestapo* by hearsay; he knew about the British *Gestapo*, " the most viciously cruel and sinister organisation in the world," through German propaganda.

The three policemen waited for his reply.

What should he say? His mind raced. The R.A.F. car was on its way. Hold on a little longer.

He answered in English:

" A little. Most Dutch people do. But not very well."

The detective who had put the question, gave a grunt. Instantly, the tension relaxed.

Perhaps the dramatic entrance, the subsequent stony looks and silence, the sudden question, had been carefully stage-managed? Three bluffers had met one and been out-bluffed? At any rate, " *Sprechen Sie Deutsch?* " was evidently the only German they knew between them.

The second plain-clothes man glanced over his colleague's shoulder at the slip of paper.

" Ah, so you're one of the Coastal Command boys, eh? "

And then von Werra *knew* that they had not come to Codnor Park to arrest him. They had come to check his story, to find out if he were genuine. Whether they arrested him, or whether they let him go in the R.A.F. car to Hucknall, depended on himself, on his ability to tell the tale convincingly. His spirits soared; he would steal that aircraft yet!

" Yes," he said, giving his most disarming smile. " Last night it was a wizard show, but we nearly bought it! "

The three policemen looked significantly from one to the other and grinned. The second detective, to show that he too was familiar with R.A.F. slang, said:

" Pancaked a Wimpey, didn't you? "

Von Werra, thinking perhaps this was a trick question, decided to play a straight bat to it. He knew what " to pancake " meant, but what the devil did the other word mean? What was a "wimpi"? Better be careful; leave it alone.

"We pancaked, yes," he said. "We were pretty lucky, though, to get back at all on one motor."

The 7.5 train pulled in. There was much scuffling of feet and slamming of doors. When the guard's whistle blew and the train started moving, the booking clerk shut the ticket window and joined the group round the fire.

"As you hadn't turned up at twenty to seven," he said, "I assumed you weren't coming. Captain van Lott explained why it was so urgent for him to report back to his base, so I got on to Hucknall aerodrome."

"Yes, I spoke to the Adjutant," von Werra broke in. "I explained the situation and he said he shall send a car at once. You see, it is most urgent."

"Spoke to him yourself, did you? Didn't he make any bones about sending you a car, especially this time of the day?"

"Please . . .? I don't quite . . ."

"He didn't mind, I mean."

"He was careful, of course. Later he telephoned back to make sure it was from here that I——"

"That's right," said the clerk, "he wanted to make sure it was all above board."

"Seemed quite satisfied, did he?"

"Yes, I think so."

"Why is it so urgent for you to get to Hucknall, may I ask?"

"I must get back to my base as soon as possible. A plane shall pick me up at Hucknall."

"Well, what about the rest of your crew? What's happening to them?"

"They are by a farmhouse. They are all right. I arrange with the Adjutant about them."

"Why didn't they come with you, then?"

"I did not think it would take such time and trouble to reach an aerodrome. I walk hours on the road, but nobody comes. Some crew must stay by the Wellington until the R.A.F. comes."

"You mean the crew had to guard it?"

"Yes, that's right. You see, we are of a special squadron. I can tell you: you are the police, and I mentioned it to this gentleman because you did not seem to come. Last night we attack Esbjerg in

Denmark to test a new bombsight and other instruments. I must report the results quickly."

" Go on ! " one of the detectives said with evident interest. Then he turned to the booking clerk and warned him :

" You're not supposed to know this, of course. You mustn't let it go any further."

" Of course not. But you see why I rang up Hucknall ! "

The police sergeant was not so easily impressed. He turned to his superior.

" What I don't understand, sir, is where the plane crashed and why we've had no report on it."

" Yes, what time did you land, and whereabouts exactly ? "

" Just before four o'clock. I don't know where exactly, but——"

" As far as I can make out from what he told me," the booking clerk interrupted, " it must have been in the fields on the west side of the line near Langley Mill. That was the one thing I couldn't understand. I live at Langley Mill and I didn't hear anything of the crash. I walked along the line to work, and I didn't see anything, either."

" It was very dark then," said von Werra. " You could not hear me coming in to land. I flew back from Denmark on one motor, and I have not crashed until all the fuel is finished and the other motor stops."

" As it was pitch dark, how could you see where you were landing ? " It was the sergeant who asked this. His stolidity was as dangerous as it was infuriating.

Von Werra shrugged his shoulders and answered rather shortly :

" As it was dark, so—I could not see. Have you not heard of airman's luck ? "

" As a matter of fact," said the clerk, " an aeroplane did make a forced landing in those fields some time ago."

With an abrupt return to his professional manner the leading detective snapped :

" Did you hear the ' All Clear ' ? "

" Yes."

" What time was that ? "

" About half-past four, I think."

" Was that before or after the crash ? "

Von Werra smiled fleetingly and answered without hesitation :

" About half an hour afterwards."

The detective grunted.

They asked him many more questions, but for the most part they seemed to be prompted by personal and private, rather than by professional, interest. The *Gestapo* seemed to have made up its mind that van Lott and his story were genuine.

Only the sergeant remained phlegmatic and troublesome. He even asked to see the " Dutchman's " identity papers.

The " Dutchman " was commendably patient.

" Do you not know," he asked, " that it is strictly forbidden for aircrew to take personal papers into the air ? With us, this rule is strictest. Perhaps you remember I said I am of a special squadron and that we last night test secret instruments ? "

After that, he was not asked to show his identity disc.

As often as he was deflected from it, he got back again to his story of the attack on Denmark, for he knew it inside out and could tell it glibly. His account of the amazing accuracy of the new bomb-sight went down particularly well. It is pleasant to feel one is being entrusted with the inside " gen ".

Making appropriate gestures with his hands, he described how the Wellington made its approach and bombing run, and how the " babies " went hurtling down.

" *Ker-rump* . . . *ker-rump !* " he said. " Bang on ! "

Whereupon the second detective slapped him on the back and said :

" Grand types, you Coastal Command chaps ! "

" Well, seeing that you are being taken care of by Hucknall," the senior detective said, " there's nothing we can do to help you. Anyway, jolly good luck to you ! "

The others expressed similar good wishes.

" Well, we'll have to be getting along. Some Germans broke out of a prison camp near here last night. We thought at first you might be one of them ! "

Von Werra joined in the laughter. At least, he opened his mouth as though he were laughing, but it was a moment before a strangled sound came out. Observing him just then, all Mr. Eaton's doubts about him returned.

The policemen filed out of the office.

" Good-bye, Captain. All the very best ! "

The moment after the door shut behind them was no mean one in Franz von Werra's life.

Five minutes later an aircraftman came in and saluted smartly. He wore a wide canvas belt bearing a pistol in a holster.

" Captain van Lott ? "

" Yes."

" Transport from Hucknall, sir ! "

Von Werra thanked Mr. Eaton for his help and hospitality and went out. He was still so dazed and cock-a-hoop that he forgot that in British vehicles the front passenger seat is on the left. He started to climb in on the steering-wheel side and then noticed that the driver was holding the opposite door open for him. He could have slid across to the passenger seat, but he could not forego the pleasure of being tucked into an R.A.F. vehicle by a respectful R.A.F. driver, so with complete unconcern he strolled round and got in on the left side, and the driver shut the door after him.

It was the crowning touch.

When it grew light that morning and he had a moment to spare, Mr. Eaton went on to the platform and looked south towards Langley Mill. The station is built on slightly higher ground, and except for the obstruction of occasional woods and thickets, dominates the fields on the west side of the line. He saw no sign of a crashed Wellington. However, he did see a number of uniformed police scouring the fields.

They saw no sign of it, either.

CHAPTER XI

The Duty Officer Turns on the Heat

CONTRARY TO von Werra's supposition, the vehicle was sent to pick him up, not because he had succeeded in convincing the R.A.F. that Captain van Lott was genuine, but because the Duty Officer strongly suspected that he was bogus.

After all the explaining the booking clerk had done on van Lott's behalf, the Duty Officer was surprised to find that the Dutchman was not only able to speak intelligible English over the telephone, but that he was glib and garrulous. He was especially struck by this because Hucknall was a Service Training School for Polish airmen, and he was accustomed to dealing with Poles who could usually make themselves understood in English when talking face to face, but were quite hopeless on the telephone.

Van Lott had talked far too much. The Duty Officer was himself a pilot and knew the district in which the Wellington was said to have crashed. It seemed incredible to him that a heavily-damaged bomber could crash-land anywhere there in the dark and none of the crew be injured. However, it was true that aircrew sometimes had the most amazing luck when they crashed.

When the Duty Officer stopped asking questions, van Lott gabbled on, going into all sorts of irrelevant details. The Englishman thought the caller was too anxious to prove that he was genuine; he seemed to be working overtime to keep him interested, to prevent him from ringing off.

Van Lott had said that the Wellington was equipped with new, secret instruments and that it was vital for him to report back to his base with details of their performance. That he should speak openly about such things on the telephone increased the Duty Officer's suspicions. On the other hand, the most extraordinary things happened in war-time flying. The man *might* be genuine, it *might* be vital for him to report back to his base as soon as possible. And then, he had given the impression that he had no interest whatsoever in aircraft at Hucknall, for he had said that one of his own squadron's planes would pick him up.

The Duty Officer did not know that five Luftwaffe pilots had escaped from Swanwick the previous night. He did not even know there was a prisoner-of-war camp fifteen miles away. At that time there was no machinery for warning aerodromes of the escape of enemy pilots. Such machinery was set up about a week later—as a result of von Werra's visit to Hucknall.

The Englishman decided that it would be much easier to check Captain van Lott's story on the spot. If he was an impostor, his dress, the papers he carried, and the way he told his story face to face, would give him away. A telephone call to his alleged base, put through in his presence, would settle the matter.

Having arrived at this decision, the Duty Officer summoned the Duty M.T. Driver. He explained that he suspected Captain van Lott was an impostor. He might be a saboteur, a spy or an escaped prisoner. But the driver was to treat him as he would any R.A.F. officer, and at all costs to avoid giving him the impression that he was under suspicion. He gave the driver his own .38 pistol and belt and told him to wear it. On no account was van Lott to leave the vehicle until they reached Headquarters, where he was to be brought straight to the Adjutant's office.

When the vehicle had left, the Duty Officer took certain precautions. Station Headquarters was a long, single-storied building. All the windows were barred. The Duty Officer locked the doors of all the rooms other than the Adjutant's office. Once van Lott, or whoever he was, entered the building, the only way he would be able to get out again was through the main door.

In all probability van Lott would be wearing a flying suit over his uniform. The Duty Officer wanted to see that uniform, or whatever it was the man was wearing. How could he induce him in as natural a way as possible to remove his flying suit? He built up the fire so that by the time that Captain van Lott arrived there would be a tremendous blaze. He placed one arm-chair in front of it and put the remainder out of the way. Van Lott would have to sit in front of the fire or else stand up.

He then sat down at the Adjutant's desk to wait.

At that time No. 16 Service Flying School was at Hucknall.

The Headquarters Staff was British but the Section Commanders, some instructors and all the trainees were Polish. The Poles, in fact, considered it their "own" airfield—their first in Britain. Others maintained that it was the Rolls Royce factory airfield—they owned some of the hangars there and from time to time strange prototypes flew about.

The Rolls Royce works were on the far side of the aerodrome. They had their own entrance and were fenced off from R.A.F. installations. The airfield was used by both service and Rolls Royce pilots, but otherwise the two establishments were entirely independent. The Rolls Royce side was strictly out of bounds to service personnel, officers and O.R.s alike, and both R.A.F. and private works police enforced this regulation. It was, in fact, a very hush-hush experimental station. Von Werra never realised that there were two separate establishments on the aerodrome, though this fact was to work in his favour.

It was still dark when von Werra left Codnor Park Station. It would be nearly daylight by the time he reached the aerodrome. He was exactly on schedule!

He was elated and excited, and had difficulty in stifling the urge to laugh gaily at everything.

The Duty Officer had said he was speaking from the Adjutant's office, and von Werra had assumed that he was the Adjutant. It would be useful to know his name, so he asked the driver. The driver explained that the Adjutant was on leave and that Squadron Leader Boniface was Acting Adjutant. Von Werra carefully memorised the name. Later, he heard the names of several other officers, but did not retain them. "Boniface" was the name he clung to. His confusion was understandable.

Von Werra asked the driver how he was fixed for Christmas leave, and commiserated with him when he replied that he had had to take his leave earlier.

"By the way," von Werra continued, "is Hucknall bombers or fighters?"

"Neither, sir. It's a Service Training School."

"For training pilots?"

"Yes, sir."

"Much flying done?"

"Quite a bit, sir."

" Saturdays and Sundays as well ? " (It was Saturday.)

" Yes, sir. There's flying every day the weather's suitable."

It was almost light. For some time they had followed twisting, narrow secondary roads. Now they emerged on to an asphalt highway. The grass verges and the hedges were white with frost. Above a hawthorn hedge, von Werra saw a high chain-link fence topped with barbed wire. Some distance inside the wire, their wing-tips and propeller blades showing above the top of the hedge, were groups of parked aircraft.

Von Werra caught his breath.

" Is this Hucknall ? " he asked.

" Yes, sir. The entrance is just down on the right."

Another minute to the crucial test. Would he get by the sentries at the gate ?

They overtook men in R.A.F. uniform walking briskly or cycling. Probably married men living out in the vicinity. It was a familiar and warming sight. Von Werra had seen it dozens of times before, but on previous occasions the men had been wearing Luftwaffe uniform.

The vehicle turned right and halted before a barrier at the entrance to the aerodrome. It was exactly, comically, like the barriers at a German level-crossing : a pole painted with wide black and white rings, reaching across the road. On the left was a low, brick-built guard house. An airman sitting at a window glanced out at the driver, who made a vague sign with one gauntlet-gloved hand.

Sitting squarely in his seat, apparently looking ahead through the windscreen, von Werra saw out of the corner of his eye a white-belted, white-gaitered sentry come out of the guard house and stride towards the barrier. The black and white pole rose smoothly. The car moved on.

Von Werra was on Hucknall aerodrome.

It had been incredibly easy ; there had been no check, no challenge ; the story he had ready to tell the sentry remained untold.

He did not realise that before leaving for Codnor Park the driver had called at the guard room, where the details of his journey had been entered in the traffic book ; that the return of the vehicle was a mere formality.

The next hour, von Werra realised, might bring him universal fame as the first German to get away from England in the war.

In an hour he could be nearing the coast of France. Success, lasting fame, universal admiration, liberty, everything he wanted were a hand's stretch away.

Alternatively, he would be dead or seriously wounded. How would the R.A.F. treat a " Hun ", a " Boche ", a " bloody Nazi gangster " caught trying to steal one of its aeroplanes ? Reverse the roles. How would the Luftwaffe treat an R.A.F. prisoner, a " murderer of innocent German children and civilians ", caught trying to get away in a Messerschmitt ?

The outcome depended on luck—about which he could do nothing—or on his wits.

First, to get rid of the driver.

" Take me to the control tower," von Werra ordered. " Then you can go. I shall see if there is any news of the aircraft which is fetching me."

" Sorry, sir," the driver replied. " My orders are to take you straight to Headquarters."

" But—but that is silly. Why ? I shall be only one minute at the control tower."

" Beg pardon, sir. I must obey orders."

The man had evidently been given special instructions. He was armed. Von Werra must regain his confidence.

" Of course," he said casually. " It does not matter. It would save time but I shall telephone from Headquarters."

They swung left on to the perimeter road, passing groups of parked aircraft.

Captain van Lott, the weary Coastal Command pilot, familiar with the appearance of a British airfield, stretched one arm negligently over the back of his seat. He seemed to be looking at the road ahead as though he couldn't care less about R.A.F. station, Hucknall.

Von Werra, the escaper with everything, including, perhaps, his life at stake, was all eyes and concentrated intelligence. Nothing escaped him.

A British airfield. Whitewashed stones at measured intervals at the roadsides. No scrap of litter on the grass, not a matchstick or a cigarette end on the smooth, cambered road. An asphalt path leading off to the left. A finger post on the corner. " M.T. Section

—something Workshops " in neat lettering. A similar notice underneath it. Some of the letters on the lower sign had accents. He noticed an inverted circumflex. *Polish !* Hell's teeth, an escaped German airman at the tender mercies of emigré Poles ! What had he let himself in for ?

" I see signs in Polish," von Werra remarked. " Are there many here ? "

" Hundreds of 'em, sir ! " the driver replied.

" Any of my countrymen—Dutch ? "

" No, sir. Only Poles."

" But Mr. Boniface is English, surely ? "

" Oh, yes, sir. All the officers at H.Q. are, sir."

Most of the aircraft at dispersal were twin-engined biplanes or monoplanes—trainers or obsolete bombers used for training purposes. Here and there, a single-engined trainer. They seemed to be unserviceable. Some were half dismantled, others partly covered with green canvas sheets, blotched with oil, stiff and glistening with frost. Most of them were anchored.

They were uninteresting, useless for his purpose. His spirits sank. Wasn't there a likely-looking aircraft anywhere ?

A segment of the sun showed orange-red above a dense cloud bank on the eastern horizon. Two hundred metres farther round the perimeter road was a group of camouflaged hangars. A gaggle of monoplanes stood on the tarmac in front of the farthest hangar. They were barely distinguishable against the mat green and black hangar doors. Their engine cowlings had not been removed. They were not sheeted. Squat, powerful-looking——

They were fighters !

Hurricanes !

Lined up ready for take-off. Perhaps reserved for airfield defence, kept in instant readiness.

One of them would get him home !

The vehicle drew up at H.Q. The driver ushered his passenger into the hallway. It smelled of floor polish, uniforms, stale tobacco smoke and stationery. The place seemed to be deserted. Von Werra saw that the first door in the left wing, facing the entrance, was marked " GENTLEMEN ". The driver wheeled right and knocked on the first door on the right-hand side of the corridor bearing the words " STATION ADJUTANT ".

" Come in ! "

The driver opened the door.

As soon as he heard sounds of the vehicle outside, followed by footsteps in the hall, the Duty Officer got up from the Adjutant's desk and began taking down the blackout shutters. He wanted to have something to occupy him when the Dutchman entered, so as to be able to observe him closely but covertly, and to put him at a tactical disadvantage. The R.A.F. officer did not glance back immediately the door opened and the two men entered. When he eventually did so he looked at the Dutchman, but addressed the driver.

" Switch the lights off, driver," he said.

The Dutchman, evidently with a greeting on the tip of his tongue, stood suspended, pointedly ignored, in the middle of the room. But the Duty Officer had taken a good look at him and was surprised, reassured and a little amused.

The man looked neither villainous nor Teutonic. He was so short that but for his kit and muscular build, the Duty Officer would have put him down as a jockey rather than a bomber pilot. He had curly hair, a frank, boyish face and a pleasant smile.

The Englishman was immediately struck by van Lott's flying suit. It was non-regulation and a type he had never seen before—pale grey-green with a long diagonal zip running left low to the right high. An inch of a brightly-coloured woollen tartan scarf showed above the collar of the suit. The Dutchman carried leather gloves in one hand. His fur-lined flying boots were also non-regulation. But their quality was most impressive.

Looking at and fumbling with the blackout shutters, the Duty Officer casually inquired :

" Van Lott ?—I won't keep you a moment. I expect you find it a bit fuggy in here. Take your flying suit off. Sit down, make yourself at home ! "

As the driver opened the door, the heat from the Adjutant's office had hit von Werra in the face. He sized up the situation with a glance : the roaring, glowing coal fire on the right and one arm-chair in front of it, all the others on the far side of the room. The room was as stifling as the stokehold of a ship.

" Mr. Boniface " was no fool !

The words of greeting queued up on von Werra's tongue. But the Duty Officer turned away from the window and spoke abruptly to the driver. Von Werra was momentarily disconcerted and the greeting he had ready remained unspoken. The Englishman looked him up and down. He wore pilot's wings, von Werra noticed. As he turned back to the window he glanced once more at the flying boots. Was there a flicker of a smile on his face, a barely perceptible relaxation of tension ? Had he recognised the boots as German, or had he been reassured by the Dutchman's appearance ?

Von Werra's glance swept round the room. Charts, maps, blackboards, silhouettes of German aircraft, a framed photograph of a group of airmen, a silver trophy on a wooden bracket, a calendar.

He had to do three things immediately : move as far away from the fire as possible, turn the situation to his own advantage and find out exactly what the Englishman's reactions were.

In reply to the invitation to remove the flying suit and make himself at home, von Werra said :

" It is not worth the trouble. My plane shall arrive any minute."

When the Duty Officer had finished stowing away the shutters he started to move back behind the desk. He dusted his hands. Von Werra seized the opportunity, strode across the room away from the fire. His right hand was outstretched and his smile was as friendly as he could possibly make it.

" I am so sorry to bother you," he said. " I wish not to make you trouble."

It was as though the Dutchman had waited politely until the Englishman had finished what he was doing before advancing naturally to shake his hand. It was now the turn of the Duty Officer to be disconcerted. He could not ignore the hand stretched out in a warm, friendly gesture. He shook it and smiled almost guiltily. In that unguarded moment he betrayed his real feelings to the alert von Werra.

" Mr. Boniface " was evidently extremely cautious rather than positively and specifically suspicious. He had harboured doubts but had been largely reassured and was feeling a little ashamed. On the one hand he was inclined to dismiss his doubts as idiotic and melodramatic, and was afraid they might make him look an ass ; on the other hand, he was not willing to take any chances.

Behind von Werra's back the driver standing in the doorway was making dumb signs to the Duty Officer. He was trying to ask whether he should hand back the pistol. He would also have liked to report that the Dutch officer had asked to be taken straight to the control tower, but he could not do it openly. Did the Duty Officer want him to stay in the room, in the building, or did he want him to take the vehicle back to the garage?

The Duty Officer understood the mime regarding the pistol, but it would have been pointed and embarrassing to have taken it back from the driver in front of Captain van Lott. He could not insult the man he had just shaken hands with.

He glanced at the driver and made a gesture of dismissal.

" I'll ring . . ." he said.

Von Werra took the initiative as soon as the driver left.

" You are most kind," he said, " but really I wish not to disturb you—I shall now go and wait by the control tower for my plane, yes ? "

" That's not necessary. Stay in here in the warm ! Control will ring me as soon as contact is made with your aircraft. Shall I have some breakfast sent over from the mess for you ? "

Von Werra glanced idly at his hands.

" No, thank you very much," he said. " But I would like to wash and so on in a minute—no hurry. I notice the lavatory as we come in. I have breakfast with the station man at Codnor Park. While we drink our tea the police arrive ! "

" You mean, the police came to Codnor Park station after all ? The booking clerk said they had not turned up ! "

" They come after you ring again. It was funny. There are two detectives in civilian clothes and one sergeant policeman. After they speak with me they are angry with the booking man because he waste their time. To me they apologise and wish to help and say good luck ! "

Von Werra was making the most of the fact that the police had interviewed him and had accepted his story.

The Dutchman remained standing by the desk—as far away from the fire as he could possibly get. He betrayed no signs of discomfort at the heat. He seemed to find it perfectly normal and gave the Duty Officer no opening to repeat the invitation to take off his flying suit.

Meanwhile the Duty Officer was being steadily grilled by his own coals. He pondered. If the C.I.D. had interviewed van Lott and were satisfied with his story, surely he must be bona fide! If they had been in any doubt about him they would never had let him come to Hucknall. The intervention of the C.I.D. put a rather different complexion on the matter. If the police more or less vouched for him . . .

But had they really interviewed van Lott, vetted him, seen his identity papers—or was the interview just one more episode in an entirely fictitious story?

Von Werra could almost read the Englishman's thoughts. He did not miss a flicker of his eyes, nor the shadow of a contraction of his brow. But at the same time he himself was thinking furiously about that row of Hurricanes out there on the tarmac. He must get out of the office. Other men would be coming on duty. Pilots would be taking off. Soon the place would be swarming with Poles. Time was running out.

He continued:

" The policemen would bring me here in their car but already the one you send is on the way." In a flash of inspiration he remembered an expression one of the policemen had used.

" They are grand types! " he added.

The Duty Officer smiled involuntarily.

" You certainly had the most amazing luck with that crash," he said. " The details sounded very confusing over the phone. I think you'd better tell me the whole story again from the beginning —you understand I have to make a report? I must also check with your station. Let's see, what's its name again? " He sat down at the desk to make notes.

" Dyce, Aberdeen. But is that really necessary? My plane must arrive any minute."

" Sorry. You know how it is—red tape, and all that."

The Duty Officer picked up the telephone.

" Anyway," he continued, " I may be able to find out what's happened to the aircraft they're sending. Hallo? Put through a call to the Adjutant at Dyce, Aberdeen, will you? Try to hurry it up." He replaced the receiver.

Von Werra shrugged his shoulders.

" Now," said the Duty Officer, " let me get the details of the crash right. First of all, what time did you take off? "

" Eighteen hundred hours. We set course———"

"—And what time did you crash ? "

" Soon before four o'clock."

" I see." That added up all right : the endurance of a Wellington was over ten hours.

" Tell me about the op. again. I believe you said you bombed the railway yards at Aalborg ? "

" No, I said Esbjerg. On the west coast."

" Ah, that's right, Esbjerg."

The Duty Officer looked his visitor in the eye.

" Aalborg or Esbjerg," he said, " this is the first I've heard of British raids on Denmark ! "

Von Werra returned the gaze, then smiled.

" We begin last night," he said. " We are a special squadron and make special attacks ! "

He hurried on to give details of the raid. The Duty Officer let him talk. Sometimes he thought the Dutchman was under a great strain. He smiled too often and his smiles dropped off too abruptly. His expression changed from a broad grin to dead straight, and vice versa, as though by the operation of a switch. But perhaps this was just weariness.

" I suppose you have your ' 1250 ' with you ? " (Form 1250 was the R.A.F. identity card.)

Von Werra looked puzzled.

" Twelve-fifty . . . ? "

" Yes. Mind if I see it ? "

Von Werra stuffed his gloves into a knee pocket and started to undo the zip of his flying suit.

" Ah, I've been admiring your handsome flying suit ! " the Duty Officer said. " New issue ? "

" No, it is my own. I wear it before the war when I fly for K.L.M. between Amsterdam and Batavia. I find it more comfortable than the R.A.F. one. You see, it is———"

The telephone bell rang.

The Duty Officer lifted the receiver.

" Hallo ? . . . Hallo ? . . . Hucknall here," he cried. " *Hallo ?* . . . Is that Dyce ? "

In his alarm von Werra backed away from the desk in the general direction of the door. He had taken only two or three steps when the Duty Officer, still speaking into the telephone, said in a flat, anti-climactic tone of voice :

" Oh, it's you . . . Right ho ! " and replaced the receiver.

It had only been Operations Room at Group Headquarters announcing air raid warning " white "—the " All clear," after another, short alert.

When the Duty Officer picked up the receiver, the wheel of fortune started turning. Von Werra moved in concert with it. When the Duty Officer replaced the receiver a few seconds later, the wheel of fortune stopped again, having completed one revolution. Von Werra had no clue as to who the caller was : all that mattered to him was that it had evidently not been Dyce on the line. Accordingly, he also reverted instantly to the *status quo*, and instead of carrying out the ruse he had thought of for getting out of the office, he feigned an absorbed interest in the photograph on the wall.

" You were about to show me your ' 1250 ', Captain," the Englishman said.

Von Werra gambled on his guess that a " 1250 " was some sort of identity document, rather than an identity disc. He turned his head away from the photograph and looked back over his shoulder, frowning. His expression and voice conveyed surprise and reproach.

" You know well such things cannot be taken over enemy land," he said. " And already I tell you I belong to a *special* squadron ! Of course, I have not my twelve-fifty with me. Why do you ask ? "

He turned his head back slowly, still frowning, to resume contemplation of the photograph.

There was a moment's pause before the Englishman replied.

" Yes, I know all about that," he said. " It's all very well . . . But surely you realise that you must identify yourself properly ? If that telephone operator would buck his ideas up and get through to Dyce . . . If you don't have your ' 1250 ', at least you'll have your identity disc. Supposing you show me that ? "

Von Werra turned towards the desk. He laughed tolerantly to show the Duty Officer that he bore him no malice for his insistence on formalities. He felt he could be magnanimous with complete confidence. Wasn't his home-made identity disc, a perfect replica of the genuine article—the ace of trumps—hanging on a string round his neck ?

" Of course," he said easily. " I show you my identity disc. You are very careful ! "

He opened the zip fastener of his flying suit a little farther and fumbled behind the tartan scarf, undoing first a button of his shirt and then a button of his woollen vest.

His fingers and thumb found the disc.

He touched it and gasped. Perspiration and the heat of his body had reduced the disc to clammy pulp. He dare not produce it.

The shock immobilised him. He was bent forward slightly, both hands at his neck, his elbows in the air. For the first time since his arrival at Hucknall, his wits were paralysed. He just did not know what to do next.

The Duty Officer had been looking on with mild but slightly embarrassed amusement.

" I'm sorry, Captain," he said. " Bit awkward, is it ? "

Von Werra looked up, grinned feebly, and resumed his fumbling.

The telephone bell rang. He was saved. The Duty Officer picked up the receiver.

" Right ! " he said to the operator. " About time ! Put me through . . . Hallo ? Dyce ? " He began shouting again. The line was apparently a bad one. He bent forward over the desk, screwing up his face, concentrating, placing one hand over his free ear.

But von Werra had no desire to hear the conversation.

When the Duty Officer glanced up, exasperated, he saw that his visitor had backed farther across the room and was now standing in front of the door, raising his eyebrows interrogatively, going through the motions of washing his hands and mouthing something in an exaggerated whisper.

" Eh ? " said the Englishman, momentarily uncovering his ears.

" Won't be long ! " said von Werra, and went out of the office, leaving the door open.

He stomped down the corridor to the door marked " GENTLE-MEN " which he opened and slammed—from the outside.

He tiptoed across the hall to the main door. As he opened it he could hear the Duty Officer shouting :

" . . . Captain van Lott . . . two words . . . Hallo? . . . a Dutchman . . ."

He could still hear shouts of " Hallo ? " as he passed outside the window of the Adjutant's office, crouching down below the sill.

CHAPTER XII

Flight Cancelled

VON WERRA had got away from the office and " Mr. Boniface ". But for how long? Time was now the supremely vital factor. Fractions of seconds mattered.

He sprinted back along the road he had travelled in the R.A.F. vehicle. There was not a soul in sight. When he reached the perimeter track he turned left, towards the group of camouflaged hangars and the gaggle of Hurricanes.

He slowed down to a walk near the first hangar, at the front of which construction work was being carried out. Builders looked down at him curiously from scaffolding. He dodged between a cement mixer and a heap of ballast, almost bumping into a labourer cutting open a cement bag.

He was out of sight of Headquarters. He did not start running again but walked briskly, purposefully. Past a wrecked aircraft and a row of twin-engined bombers. They were no good to him, but the sight of the staring roundels, the smell of aircraft dope and oil, the wide sweep of the airfield, made his nostrils twitch and his blood tingle. The orange red orb of the sun had risen above the rim of the airfield and frost sparkled on the grass.

The doors of the second hangar were wide open. It was full of aircraft in various stages of assembly.

Ahead was the group of Hurricanes. A mechanic wearing a black smock was dodging about near one of them. A trolley-acc. (accumulator trolley) was beside him. The Hurricane was about to be started up! There was only this mechanic in sight and von Werra needed someone to explain the controls of the British fighter to him.

The mechanic looked up wonderingly as the little man in the unusual flying suit approached.

" Good morning ! " said von Werra. " I am Captain van Lott,

a Dutch pilot. I have just been posted here. But Hurricanes I have not yet flown. Mr. Boniface, the Adjutant, send me down here so you should show me the controls and make a practice flight. Which one is ready for take-off? This one here?"

He looked the mechanic straight in the eyes and spoke with firmness and authority.

The mechanic looked puzzled. Then von Werra noticed that he was not in R.A.F. uniform, but wore civilian trousers and shirt and a striped tie.

"Haven't you come to the wrong place?" the man asked. "This is a private firm. We have nothing to do with the R.A.F. over there."

"I know. But Mister Boniface said it was to you I should come. I don't have much time . . ."

The mechanic pondered. Then the probable explanation dawned on him. The airman had said he was a "Captain", so he must be a ferry pilot from White Waltham, Headquarters of Air Transport Command. Apparently he had come to take delivery of a Hurricane. It was a common occurrence for civilian ferry pilots, known by the courtesy rank of Captain, many of them foreigners speaking hardly a word of English, to collect aircraft which had been sent to the Rolls-Royce works for modification. Moreover, when they had to fly a type of aircraft new to them they often asked for a practical demonstration of controls and peculiarities, in addition to the printed pilot's notes which were issued to them. Of course, von Werra knew none of this.

"Ah!" said the mechanic, "then you must be a ferry pilot?"

Von Werra did not know the meaning of the word "ferry" But he thought it best to agree.

"Yes, of course," he replied.

"That's different," the mechanic said. "You'll have to see the A.I.D.[1] blokes."

Aieyedeeblokes? Von Werra couldn't cope with it.

"Look," he said, "I have no time . . . You shall show me the controls now, yes?"

"I can't do anything until you've signed the Visitors' Book, and then you'll have to get your paper-work attended to. Hang on a minute, Captain, I'll go and fetch the manager."

The mechanic walked across the tarmac into the hangar. Von

[1] Aeronautical Inspection Directorate.

Werra stood leaning against the fuselage of the Hurricane. A brand-new beautiful Hurricane with not a scratch on it. A colossal beast, it seemed, twice as large as the Hurricanes he had encountered in air combat. He was tempted to climb into the cockpit and try to start the engine on his own. But it was no good. There were certain controls he must be sure about before he attempted to take off. If he got into the cockpit now it might wreck his chances altogether.

Familiar, nostalgic sounds issued from the hangar, as though from a cave : the beating of metal, the whirr of electric drills, somebody singing, somebody else whistling, the musical tinkle of a ring-spanner dropped on to concrete. At any minute " Mister Boniface " would know the truth. The alarm would be sounded and every man on the aerodrome mobilised to hunt for him.

The mechanic came out of the hangar with a man wearing a khaki smock. They approached the Hurricane in a leisurely fashion, talking and looking at one another from time to time, apparently discussing something quite unconnected with the Dutch Captain. Von Werra remained leaning negligently against the fuselage, one arm stretched out along it, one flying boot crossed in front of the other, his body half covering the roundel painted on the side.

The man in the khaki smock, presumably the manager, smiled pleasantly and said :

" Good morning, Captain ! " His manner was positive, as though his mind was already made up and he was dealing with an everyday occurrence.

" I hear you've come to collect a Hurricane," he continued. " If you'll come with me we'll get your paper-work fixed up."

" It shall take long ? I have little time," von Werra replied. " I just want to learn controls of the Hurricane."

" I'm afraid nothing can be done until you've signed the Visitors' Book. We'll soon fix you up, though."

Von Werra reluctantly followed the two men into the hangar. There was nothing else he could do. They walked with infuriating slowness. Fitters working on aircraft in the hangar stared down at him from staging, peered at him between undercarriages, craned their necks out of cockpits. He felt like a pickpocket at a police convention.

The mechanic remained in the works. Von Werra continued

behind the manager. They reached the rear wall of the hangar and passed though a door into an asphalt yard. On the other side of it was a gate and a glass-sided lodge. A man in a blue uniform was sitting inside the lodge. Evidently a works policeman. The manager entered and spoke to him.

Through the window von Werra saw a large, solemn, white-faced clock on a wall. A couple of minutes to nine. His mouth opened and his brown furrowed as he watched the thin, central second hand sweeping round the dial. Then he bit his lip and looked away.

What was " Mr. Boniface " doing between the time the second hand moved from 3 to 6 ? Perhaps that was the decisive quarter of a minute.

Though he looked away, the pointer continued to revolve in his mind's eye. He had to glance back. He expected to find the pointer at 8, but it was nearly at 10.

If only these idiots would hurry up !

The damned clock was making him lose his nerve. He fumbled for his cigarettes and matches with moist, quivering hands. Then he looked again at the pointer : 12. The two men came out of the lodge.

As they emerged von Werra put away his packet of Player's and the box of Swan matches, making sure that they saw them. Then he idly flicked away the match with which he had lighted a cigarette.

" 'Morning, sir ! " said the policeman brightly.

" 'Morning ! " von Werra replied in the same tone.

" If you'll just sign along the next line, sir . . ."

The entry had to be made across two pages, which were divided into columns. They were already half-filled with many different styles of handwriting. As he was afraid his German style might betray him, he decided to make his entry in printed characters. The first four columns were headed : Date, Name, Nationality, and Address respectively, and presented little difficulty. He wrote (see reproduction opposite page 97) :

21. 12. 40.   van Lott   Dutch   Aberdeen

His anxiety not to betray himself by his entry did not prevent him from once again making the telltale stroke over the " u " in " Dutch ".

The fifth column was head " Order ". He had no idea what he

should write under it, and the other entries in the column were indecipherable. He casually asked the policeman whether he wanted this item written out in full.

" No, it doesn't matter, sir. Just put ' See A.I.D.' "

Von Werra was none the wiser for his successful ruse. He asked the policeman to spell the words, but when he did so he was all the more confused. He had to write something. The manager was watching over his shoulder. The second hand was sweeping round the dial. Guards were probably searching every corner for him. Possibly Polish guards.

He made an entry of sorts, but the nearest he could get to " See A.I.D." was " Sicioed ". The proper entry was later filled in by the policeman.

The next column was headed " Time of Arrival ". The clock showed exactly nine o'clock, so von Werra wrote " 0900 " (hours). (It must have been the policeman who subsequently filled in the time of departure—perhaps just to keep his books straight.)

" That's it, sir. Now everything's in order ! " The policeman smiled happily and von Werra's spirits soared. If " Mr. Boniface " would only give him another five minutes ! He now felt so confident that when the manager asked him for his written orders covering the collection of the Hurricane, he replied firmly and without hesitation :

" My papers, parachute—all my kit—will come on a plane which shall land here soon—any minute. I will have instruction on controls to save time, yes ? "

" Right ho," said the manager. " We can do that all right now you've signed the book. Come with me, Captain."

Meanwhile, the mechanic in the black smock had come out into the yard and was hanging about expectantly. The manager went over to him and told him to take the Captain back to the Hurricane and explain its instruments and controls in detail.

The manager went off in a different direction with a smile and a cheery wave of the hand.

" He'll fix you up all right," he said as he left.

Von Werra followed the mechanic back across the yard. There was a large notice on the outer wall of the hangar : " No smoking beyond this door." Von Werra dropped his cigarette and trod on it.

Back through the hangar. Every second counted. Would he see a group of airmen looking for him when he emerged on to the tarmac? The mechanic did not dawdle, but von Werra felt an urge to push him along still faster. Instead, he had to keep pace non-chalantly.

Out through the open front. A glance right and left. No R.A.F. uniforms in sight!

And there was the beautiful, brand-new Hurricane, with a coating of rime on its wings and——

Hell's teeth!—the accumulator trolley was no longer beside it. Nowhere in sight. Some other mechanic must have taken it away while he was signing that blasted book. Oh, well, he would just have to hope that he could start the engine using the battery in the aircraft.

The mechanic climbed up on one side of the cockpit and slid back the perspex hood.

A couple of seconds later von Werra was sitting at the controls, the strange-feeling stick in his hands, aghast at the completely unfamiliar lay-out and instrument panel. Leaning over him into the cockpit, the mechanic carefully explained the controls and instruments.

Von Werra hung on to his every word. But there was much he was unable to follow, too many words he did not understand. He could not absorb and retain all that information in so short a time. He almost panicked. Never mind all those details—what were the essentials?

The compass. Heavens! What kind of compass was that? Nothing like a Messerschmitt's. How did you set the damned thing? (He had determined before escaping from Swanwick that 120 degrees was the most direct course to fly from the Midlands to the Continent.)

"Set the compass to 120 degrees, for instance," he told the mechanic. The mechanic obliged. Von Werra looked from the reset compass to the sun shining through the perspex. Rubbish. It didn't make sense. He could not make head or tail of the compass. To hell with it. Take off and keep the sun to port.

The stick. A monstrous contraption. As long as he didn't stand the aircraft on its nose when trying to take off . . .

The hydraulic brake system. Incomprehensible. He had never seen anything like it. Ah, never mind. Hope for the best. As long as he didn't stand the aircraft on its nose . . .

The starter. Most important. Try it. The mechanic had already pointed out the starter button and the injection pump. What had he said was the proper drill? Von Werra could not remember.

It was a cold morning. Would the aircraft battery be strong enough to turn the engine through the stiff oil? If so, then in a minute he would be on the edge of the field. He would have to taxi along the perimeter road until the engine warmed up. In five minutes he would be airborne, setting course by the sun. In half an hour or so he would be approaching the familiar French coastline. Then—throw the kite flat on the deck on the cliff tops—never mind about the undercart—before the flak started flying about. He would have made it!

He glared at the starter button. He willed the battery to be strong enough. God grant . . . It was almost a prayer.

Before the mechanic could anticipate his move, he jabbed the button.

Whirr—whirr. The propeller revolved twice then stuck. Not a cylinder fired.

"Don't do that!" the mechanic cried in alarm. "Can't start without the trolley-ac.!"

"Fetch it, then!" von Werra ordered.

He must have it. He must make the mechanic get it. He must *hurry* him to get it.

"It's not available just now. Somebody else is using it." Just who did this little man think he was?

Von Werra bit his lip. He could not possibly have more than a few minutes left. He must have the trolley-acc. He must have it. He must have it at once. But if he tried to boss and hurry the mechanic, it would probably have the opposite effect; he would sulk and deliberately take his time. Or not fetch it at all.

He turned on the von Werra smile.

"*Please* get it, yes? I really am in a hurry."

The mechanic looked hard at the smiling Dutchman, then grinned himself.

"All right," he said. "I'll see if I can find it."

The aircraft swayed slightly as he stepped down off the wing. He moved off in the direction of the hangar.

Von Werra glanced back up the perimeter of the airfield. Surely any second men would come running round by the scaffolding on the end hanger. He must not think about it, but use these last few minutes to concentrate on the controls and the instrument panel.

The air-speed indicator was graduated in miles per hour. He would have to convert that into kilometres. The altimeter showed height in feet. He would have to convert that into metres.

He heard a strange whining sound and looked out of the cockpit. The mechanic was coming across the tarmac standing on an electric truck, which was pulling the accumulator trolley.

Von Werra's heart thumped madly. His hands were clammy, his throat dry. Two more minutes! God grant nobody turned up.

The mechanic manipulated the truck with conscious expertness, swinging it round the starboard wing in a graceful sweep, halting it dead, with a clatter of couplings, so that the trolley-acc. was in exactly the right position. He jumped off the truck platform, went behind to the trolley-acc. and raised the armoured cable over his shoulder, preparatory to plugging in.

The aircraft swayed. For a second von Werra did not grasp the significance of the movement. He operated the injection pump a couple of times, hoping it would be enough. A voice above him on the port side said quietly:

" *Get out !* "

He jerked his head back. At eye level on the left-hand side of the cockpit, the sun was reflected on a highly-polished button of an Air Force officer's greatcoat. It gleamed too on the muzzle of an automatic pistol.

Von Werra's eye ran up the coat buttons, over a chin, a mouth twisted in a queer sort of grin and halted on a pair of cold, blue eyes.

It was " Mr. Boniface."

Von Werra got out.

The mechanic, busy on the other side of the Hurricane, had no idea what was going on. After a few seconds he called out. The engine did not turn over, so he called out again. Still nothing happened. He dodged under the wing, looked into the cockpit. It was empty. He heard footsteps and looked behind him. He saw the little Ferry Pool pilot walking away with an Air Force officer.

The mechanic was furious.

" Hey, Captain ! " he called out. " Aren't you going to use the trolley-acc. after all that fuss and bother ? "

The Captain was too disgusted to reply, or even to look back.

The Duty Officer remained silent. Von Werra's disgust and bitter disappointment changed to uneasiness. What was going to happen to him?

"I have never flown a Hurricane," he said. "Only bombers. But always I want to. I just got the man to show me the controls..."

The Duty Officer said nothing. It was unnerving.

"Do you sometimes fly Hurricanes?" von Werra asked brightly.

At last the Englishman spoke, not in reply to the question, but to make it clear that the bell had rung for the end of playtime.

"I spoke to Dyce," he said flatly.

In the course of the long walk back to the R.A.F. side of the field, the two men were joined by aircraftmen who had been out looking for the Dutchman. In the end quite a group collected round them. Von Werra noted with growing alarm that most of the men had a flash with the word "Poland" on their shoulders. Finally a sergeant came up and asked the officer if he could fall the men out.

"For God's sake, no! Post them all round Headquarters until this bird has been dealt with!"

Dealt with? What did that imply?

"See," said von Werra, "I had better tell you. I am not Dutch, but an escaped Luftwaffe officer. I am sorry if I get you into trouble, but I——"

"Save it!" the Duty Officer broke in. "It's useless to talk to me. Keep your explanations for somebody else."

"But I wish to surrender to you and prove who I am."

The Duty Officer lost his temper.

"Cut it out, I tell you!" he shouted. "Prove you're not a saboteur to somebody else. I've had enough!"

They approached Station Headquarters.

Von Werra was very frightened.

The line to Dyce had been very bad and the Duty Officer had been able to make himself understood, and to understand the man at the other end, only a few words at a time, by constant shouting and repetition. Several times communication was cut altogether.

After van Lott left the room the Duty Officer was torn with anxiety as to his whereabouts, but pinned down by his call to Dyce —the one certain way of discovering the truth about van Lott.

It was probably the most frustrating five minutes of his life. At the end of it he knew that van Lott was bogus.

As he now expected, he found the lavatory door was unbolted. The place was empty.

A Hun or a saboteur—he could not be anything else—was at large on Hucknall aerodrome. And he was responsible.

The Duty Officer took the swiftest and sanest action possible. He rang up the guard room and M.T. section in turn and ordered every available man out on the airfield to look for a short, bareheaded man wearing flying boots and a pale grey-green flying suit with a diagonal zip. The man was to be arrested and taken, by force if necessary, to Headquarters. He also warned R.A.F. workshops and hangars on the other side of the field. There was no internal line to the Rolls-Royce works, or he would have warned them too. He then rang through to the mess to get hold of another officer who would look after Headquarters while he himself went in search of the Hun.

All this took time. In the meantime he had got his pistol back from the driver and had buckled it on.

The Duty Officer made for the Rolls-Royce works by the shortest route, which involved passing through a guarded wicket gate in the dividing fence. He reasoned that a Hun, whether an escaping airman or a saboteur, would not be interested in the R.A.F.'s slow trainers, but would make for the Hurricanes and the secret experimental station.

By the most extraordinary luck, von Werra had penetrated into the Rolls-Royce works by way of the perimeter track, without being observed by the works police, perhaps as a result of the confusion caused by the construction work going on at the boundary.

The Duty Officer got involved in an argument with the policeman on the gate, who did not want to let him pass, and who insisted that nobody answering van Lott's description had previously passed that way.

Much against his will, the policeman eventually allowed the officer to enter the premises. A minute or so later, the Duty Officer saw the mechanic manœuvring the truck with the trolley-acc. And then he saw the back of van Lott's head in the cockpit of the Hurricane.

The door and windows of the Adjutant's office were open to clear the room of the "Duty Watch fug". The real Squadron Leader Boniface was standing with his back to the window, flipping through a file. Another officer was seated at the desk. They heard footsteps in the corridor, but paid no attention. Somebody came a few paces into the room and halted. Both officers glanced up.

A little man in a curious flying suit stood there. His face was white and drawn. Behind him stood the Duty Officer with a drawn pistol. Then something even more extraordinary happened. The little man clicked the heels of his flying boots together, bowed stiffly from the waist and announced in a loud but rather shaky voice :

" I surrender. I am Oberleutnant Franz von Werra, fighter pilot of the Luftwaffe. Last night I escape from Swanwick camp. I claim the protection of the Geneva Convention."

Squadron Leader Boniface looked at the phenomenon and screwed up his face as though he were facing strong sunlight.

" I say, easy on, old boy," said the officer at the desk. " Steady the Buffs, and all that. Have a cigarette, for God's sake ! "

It was their introduction to what was to become known as " the Hucknall Incident ".

" Perhaps von Werra's worst moment," Squadron Leader Boniface recalled later, " was when the Station Commander (the late Group Captain Hughes-Chamberlain) appeared for a moment in the doorway of his office, which adjoined that of the Adjutant. There were about five of us in the room then. We stood up and said, ' Good morning, sir,' and so did von Werra. An uneasy silence followed. I think von Werra wondered just what was going to happen next. He was obviously under a great strain. But the Station Commander merely said, ' So that's the Jerry ! ' and then turned his back on him.

" I had some breakfast brought over for him from the mess —eggs and bacon, toast, marmalade and coffee. He ate it while awaiting the police escort which had been telephoned for. Breakfast seemed to convince him that nothing dreadful was going to happen to him, and he became cheerful and talkative.

" He had a most engaging personality. It was impossible not to admire his enterprise and audacity. I suppose the situation in which he found himself had something to do with it, but he struck me as being totally unlike the conventional idea of a bigoted, fanatical Nazi. But then, I saw him only after he had surrendered.

" Two policemen arrived while von Werra was eating his

breakfast. They waited until he had finished and then took him off.

" He deserved to have got away in the aircraft. However, thank heavens he didn't."

Von Werra was driven to Police Headquarters, Nottingham, where he was kept in a cell for twenty-four hours until a military escort arrived from Swanwick camp to collect him. He was searched when he reached Police Headquarters and according to the inventory of his possessions preserved in police records, the search yielded two boxes of matches, one pencil, one packet of chewing gum, a pair of spectacles and 2/3d. in cash.

The escape of the five prisoners from Swanwick camp and von Werra's subsequent exploit at Hucknall aerodrome resulted in the calling of no fewer than five separate inquiries : by the War Office at Swanwick ; the R.A.F. at Hucknall; the police ; the Rolls-Royce Company, and the L.M.S. Railway.

Of course, everybody was wise after the event. It was then perfectly clear to all concerned what should have been done and what should not have been done.

It is inevitable that the reader following the course of events on Hucknall aerodrome on the morning of 21 December should see the gaping holes in van Lott's story and its utter implausibility.

But the fact remains that von Werra *did* succeed in inducing the R.A.F. to send out transport and bring him on to an aerodrome where he all but took off in a Hurricane. For such a unique feat of audacity and enterprise he deserves great credit. So far as is known, no British escaper in Germany ever succeeded, or for that matter, tried, to induce the Luftwaffe to convey him on to a German airfield.

Security at R.A.F. stations was tightened up as a result of von Werra's visit to Hucknall, but that did not prevent two other escaped Luftwaffe pilots from actually taking off from an R.A.F. aerodrome in a stolen plane a year later. However that is another story.

A statement has been obtained from Mr. R. Dorey, then Manager of the Rolls-Royce Flight Establishment at Hucknall, speaking in a private capacity. It sums up rather well the feelings of all the British concerned in the Hucknall Incident.

" I actually saw and spoke to von Werra myself. What with his delightful personality and the twinkle in his eye, it was not difficult to realise afterwards how he had carried through his escapade. Furthermore, a lot of us, sporty types, were rather sorry he did not make it ! "

Mr. Dorey reveals a fact of which von Werra was, and always remained, completely ignorant. The aircraft in which he received his instruction was one of the first Hurricane Mark II's to be produced. Only one or two had been delivered to the R.A.F. and they had never been used operationally.

If von Werra had got back to France with one he would have made the Luftwaffe a present of the latest, top secret British fighter before it had ever been encountered in combat.

Von Werra earned fame for the purely imaginary feat of skittling nine Hurricanes out of the sky over one British airfield. But he acquired real merit by his unsuccessful attempt to get a single Hurricane into the air at another.

CHAPTER XIII

Mr. Spittle and Mr. Winks

ON HIS way back to Swanwick, von Werra learned that his four fellow escapers had all been captured within less than twenty-four hours. He saw them again, briefly, the following morning, when the Camp Commandant sentenced them to fourteen days solitary confinement for attempting to escape.

It was a light enough sentence—they had expected twenty-eight. They put this down to the fact that the Commandant was a sportsman and that Christmas was in two days' time. Both these explanations may have had something to do with it ; another possible one was that the Commandant already knew that in two weeks' time he would be rid of the lot.

Von Werra's " cell " was a small, pleasantly furnished room in the main building, much more comfortable than his room in the Garden House had been. The others had rooms on either side. There were two guards armed with pistols in the corridor. By speaking through the hole in the wall, through which the heating pipes passed, von Werra was able in the days that followed to piece together what had happened to his companions.

It will be recalled that Manhard had accompanied Cramer as far as South Normanton, and that he had made off across the fields when the policeman gave chase.

Manhard kept walking. His objective was Sheffield, which he knew was to the north. Setting course by the pole star, he walked throughout the night along lanes and by-roads.

The next morning, a single decker bus was on the route from Gainsborough to Sheffield. The driver was Mr. Harry Winks, the conductor Mr. Colin Spittle. At East Retford they, in common with all other road users, were warned by the police to be on the look-out for four German prisoners who had escaped from a prison camp the previous night. As the bus started after stopping at Gateford Toll Bar, near Worksop, a figure, appearing from nowhere, leapt on to the platform. It was a broad-shouldered, dark-haired young man wearing an ill-fitting sports jacket and old flannel trousers. He carried a suitcase.

" What the . . .? " exclaimed the conductor. " Where did you spring from ? We're full up."

The young man grinned sheepishly, but said nothing. There was no room in the gangway and he had to stand on the platform beside the conductor. He put his case down and started fumbling in his pockets.

" Fares, please."

" For Sheffield," said the newcomer, still fumbling.

" Single or return ? "

" Sheffield," he said, finally producing a florin. That was insufficient for a return ticket, so Mr. Spittle clipped a one-and-fourpenny single and handed it and eightpence to the passenger. Then a curious thing happened.

The young man made a slight, stiff forward movement from the waist, and clicked his heels as he said : " Thank you."

At Handsworth, about four miles from Sheffield, the conductor walked round and spoke to the driver.

" Harry," he said, " stop the bus if you see a policeman. I've got one of those escaped Jerries on board ! "

" Go on ! Where did we pick him up ? "

" Gateford Toll Bar."

Two miles farther on, at the junction of Staniforth and Atter-cliffe Roads, the driver spotted a police sergeant and a constable, and called them over to the bus. When the conductor saw this, he alighted, sliding the door of the bus shut behind him. He walked round to the cab.

" What's this about an escaped German prisoner ? " the sergeant asked him.

" We were told by the Retford police that four Jerry prisoners had escaped. I think I've got one of them on board."

" What makes you think so ? "

" He clicked his heels and sort of bowed when I gave him his ticket and change."

" Not much to go on, is it ? Are you sure ? "

" It's a German mannerism. I'm certain he's one of the four escaped prisoners."

" It's nothing to go by, lad. What do you want me to do ? "

" Well, you could ask to see his identity card."

" H'm."

" I know it's not much to go on. But if you don't ask him for it, I will. I'm a Special Constable and carry a warrant. But I'd rather you do it as you're in uniform."

" All right, get him off ; I'll ask him."

The suspect was by now standing in the gangway at the front of the bus. The conductor tapped on the window to attract his attention, but as he took no notice, the conductor pointed to him and the passenger standing next to him tapped his shoulder. He took his case from the rack and worked his way to the back of the bus, where the sergeant, the constable and the conductor waited for him on the pavement. He seemed quite unperturbed.

" Where are you going to, son ? " asked the sergeant.

" Sheffield."

" Then where are you going ? "

" Sheffield."

" May I see your identity card ? "

The young man looked blank.

" Haven't you got it with you ? "

He started to move away.

" I go," he said.

The conductor grabbed his arm.

" Oh, no, you don't," he said. " You're going along with these policemen. You're one of the Germans who escaped from near Derby last night, aren't you ? "

The young man shrugged his shoulders and was silent.

The sergeant took him to the nearest police call-box and summoned a patrol car. On the way to Attercliffe police station it was established despite the language difficulty, that the suspect was, in fact, an escaped German prisoner, and that his name was Leutnant Walter Manhard.

At the police station his case was found to contain fifty-six quarter and half-pound bars of chocolate.

Wilhelm and Wagner had hoped to reach Liverpool, where they thought they might be able to stow away on a ship bound for

Sweden or one of the Baltic countries. Alternatively, they thought they might be able to get across to Eire. Wagner spoke quite good English, having lived in Canada and the United States.

They managed to get on a north-bound bus soon after their escape, and the same night they reached Sheffield via Chesterfield.

It was nearly midnight when they arrived and there were no more buses. They set out on foot to the west. It was an eerie experience trying to find their way out of a bombed city in the blackout. They seemed to see policemen in every shadow, but although they encountered several patrolling constables, they were never challenged.

They kept walking. Between five and six o'clock they noticed that workers were beginning to collect at bus stops. They joined a queue and finally got on to a bus filled with working men in caps and scarves. The bus was dimly lit and was filled with high-pitched, gabbling voices, speaking a language that seemed to bear no resemblance to English. Wilhelm found the ride something of an ordeal.

The bus reached the outskirts of Manchester, which had also been bombed during the night. Roads were blocked and there were many detours.

Wagner says that the next couple of hours were a nightmare. After leaving the bus, they had to pick their way through bombed streets where rescue squads were still at work under arc lights. They would walk down a long street only to find near the end of it that it had been roped off, and there was a dimly-lit sign " DANGER —UNEXPLODED BOMB ". And then they had to walk all the way back.

It grew light as they were making their way westwards across the city. The streets were now full of people, grim, silent, strained, with hate in their eyes. The fugitives dared not stop, nor ask directions. They kept on the move, seldom speaking to one another.

Eventually they came to a main road leading to the south-west. They could not get out of the city fast enough. As they had little money, and did not want to spend it all on fares, when they reached the suburbs Wagner started trying to thumb a lift. The driver of an open lorry stopped and invited them to get into the cab with him. Wagner dared not risk it in view of Wilhelm's inability to speak English. He asked the driver if they could get up in the back and lie down as they were very tired. He also made the mistake of saying that they were soldiers on their way home to Liverpool for a short Christmas leave.

The lorry driver's suspicions were aroused. His feelings had been hurt because the cosy hospitality of his cab had been spurned ; no man, however tired he might be, would prefer the jolting, bouncing back of an empty lorry on a bitterly cold morning to a ride " up front " ; the two men were shabbily dressed in civilian clothes, though they claimed to be in the army ; Wagner did not sound a bit like a Liverpudlian Tommy. However, the driver shrugged his shoulders, and the two fugitives climbed into the back of the lorry.

Some miles farther on two genuine soldiers in uniform hailed the driver. They got into the cab. Apparently the driver told them about the queer birds in the back and after a while the lorry stopped again. The two soldiers got out and asked to see Wagner's and Wilhelm's identity cards. Both escapers were blue with cold. They were at a disadvantage which even Wagner's Austrian charm was unable to overcome. The soldiers handed them over to the police at Mottram, in Cheshire.

Christmas Eve. It was snowing. The sentry in the courtyard outside wore a Balaclava hood and khaki gloves. The five prisoners in the punishment cells asked to be allowed to spend the evening together in one cell. This was refused. Each was served the same special dinner as was served to the rest of the prisoners ; as a further concession they were allowed to have their bottle of " Christmas " wine sent in from the camp. When they had finished their meal, they sang traditional carols. The guards suffered in silence.

Then on the last morning of their sentence the Adjutant visited each of them in turn and said :

" To-morrow you will leave with the rest of the prisoners for Canada."

CHAPTER XIV

Prisoners in Transit

IN THE early years of the war the usual cause of "trouble" at prisoner-of-war camps in Britain was the announcement of an impending transfer of captives to Canada. There were several minor riots and many unpremeditated escapes and disappearances when prisoners were told they were about to be shipped across the Atlantic.

There were several reasons for this. The prisoners boggled at the idea of being sent so far away from home. It made many of them take their captivity seriously for the first time. The majority thought wishfully that if they remained in Britain they would soon be liberated by invading German armies ; they could not conceive of a long internment here. But if they were sent to Canada, thousands of miles from the theatre of war, there was no hope of their being liberated, and they might be interned indefinitely ; for even if Britain was overrun, the chances were that the Empire would continue the fight.

And if it was almost impossible to escape across the English Channel from Britain, what chance would there be of escaping across the Atlantic from Canada !

The basis of the Germans' complaint was that transfer to Canada contravened the Geneva Convention in as much as they would be unnecessarily exposed to danger while crossing the Atlantic. Victims of their own propaganda, they were inclined to magnify the risk of being sunk to a virtual certainty. However, this argument was unlikely to carry much weight with a country whose very existence was being threatened by unrestricted U-boat warfare. In any case, the Geneva Convention also required prisoners to be interned in areas sufficiently removed from the fighting zone to be out of danger; owing to bombing and the promise of invasion, the whole of Britain was a fighting zone.

Of course, the more responsible prisoners did not protest against transfer because they felt they had serious cause for complaint, but according to the old-established P.O.W. principle that no opportunity should be lost of making the enemy's life a misery. Having exploited this chance of making a nuisance of themselves, for what it was worth, these prisoners looked forward to the change of scene with stoicism if not eagerness.

And von Werra?

As soon as the Camp Adjutant left his cell after telling him that he and the rest of the fit prisoners were to leave for Canada the next day, von Werra called through the wall to Wagner, the " expert " on Canada:

" You know Canada. Where are they likely to send us? "

" It's a big country. Anywhere."

" What are the chances of escaping into the United States— *a neutral country*? "

" You've got something, Werra. I should think the chances are pretty good."

" You must tell me everything you know about Canadian geography and customs. We'll keep together on the crossing! The other chaps will be on to you, too, but I claim priority. Agreed? "

Wagner laughed.

" Right-ho! " he said. " But don't get any false ideas. My knowledge is limited. Even if it's possible to escape, it won't be easy. Think of the vast distances."

Von Werra's head was once more back in the clouds.

" Never mind how difficult it is," he said. " I'll find something, don't you worry. I'm sure about it. Wagner, I've got a feeling. It's more than a feeling—in Canada I shall be lucky! "

It was prophetic.

In the afternoon the Adjutant visited the " cooler " again and gave each prisoner a printed Red Cross postcard bearing the message: " I am well. I am being transferred from England to Canada."

Prisoners were not permitted to write anything on the cards

other than their names and numbers and the address of their next of kin. Nevertheless, being P.O.W.s, they dispensed with permission and utilised every scrap of space to write a bonus letter home.

In the evening they were escorted from their cells to the mess hall, where piles of kit were ranged on long tables. There was a small mountain of civilian overcoats, thick and well-made, most of them still bearing the manufacturers' sewn-on tickets. There was nothing *ersatz* about the materials used—only thick, heavy tweeds. The prisoners held up one coat after another, each more beautiful than the last.

The only trouble was, they were all the same size—" youth's, large ". Von Werra was one of the few in the camp they fitted. He chose a smart, beltless model in navy blue. They fitted big fellows like Wagner, Wilhelm and Manhard as snugly as strait-jackets. During the next couple of weeks the sound of seams splitting developed into a standing joke, and a burst button spinning across the floor was the signal for ironic cheers.

The prisoners were also offered kitbags, gloves, woollen cardigans and underwear and other items. Naturally, the British Government did not supply the goods free of charge, but as few men had enough pocket-money left to cover their essential requirements for the trip, credit had to be given. As a result, all the prisoners bought everything they could lay their hands on and far more than they required.

If they were going to be torpedoed, their debts did not matter, anyway; on the other hand, they might as well make their demise as costly as possible to the British Government.

Even von Werra, who thought it was bad psychology to waste time making one's quarters more pleasant to live in, and was against the collection of impedimenta of any kind, on this occasion indulged in an orgy of spending. His purchases, he computed, would mortgage his pocket money for the next three years.

By the time the tables were cleared, and the camp was swarming with prisoners wearing undersized overcoats and carrying cardboard boxes, untidy bundles of clothing, or bulging kitbags slung over one shoulder, it looked almost as though The Hayes Conference Centre had come into its own again with a Rag-and-Bone Men's Convention.

After the distribution of kit, von Werra and his fellow escapers were allowed to return with the rest to the Garden House. That evening there was a special issue of cigarettes and chocolates for consumption on the Atlantic crossing. Then " *Vati* " Schneider, the " Canteen General " Put up a notice : " Closing Down Sale— All Stocks Must Be Cleared ". There was a rush to buy everything from surplus chewing gum and chocolate to pipe cleaners and darning wool. The shelves were cleared in a few minutes. Manhard's broad shoulders took him quickly to the front of the crush round the counter, where he quickly laid in a stock of chocolate for his next attempt to escape. He was to become one of the most persistent and daring escapers in Canada, making at least half a dozen attempts and sometimes getting far into the United States before being recaptured by the F.B.I. and handed back to the Canadian authorities. He finally escaped successfully from an Ontario camp in August 1944 ; but that is another story.[1]

An end-of-term atmosphere prevailed in the Garden House that night. Prisoners dashed excitedly hither and thither, laughing, shouting, bartering, packing and questioning. The U-boat men, a minority who had hitherto been kept in their place by the airmen, were now the centre of attraction. What were the safest places on a ship ? How many survivors could a U-boat take on board ? How long would it take to cross the Atlantic in convoy ? How long did it take for a large ship to sink ? etc., etc.

But if the dominant feeling was of excitement, there were undertones of anxiety and sadness. Far into the night, after the excitement had died down, groups of men sat smoking and yarning about their homes, which they were soon to leave so many thousand more miles behind them.

The prisoners were assembled early the next morning. Each man was required to sign a chit for the goods he had purchased the previous day. The British soldiers dropped their reserve and hostility. They were surrounded by prisoners and replied patiently, to the best of their ability, to their questions. Sergeant *Saftnase*,

---

[1]To-day Manhard is still listed as " Wanted " by the Royal Canadian Mounted Police and the F.B.I. in case he remained on the North American continent as an illegal immigrant, as did some 200 other German and Italian escapers. In 1953, when he was the only wartime escaper in Canada still not accounted for, the R.C.M.P. assumed that he had either got back to Germany, was living illegally in the United States, or was dead. According to his fellow-prisoners, none of these assumptions is correct ; they say that Manhard has made an entirely new life for himself elsewhere.

carrying a board with papers clipped to it and a stub of pencil behind his cauliflower ear, dashed hither and thither, flustered but good tempered.

The last roll-call. One hundred and fifteen officers, plus eight more seriously wounded who were remaining behind for repatriation. Major Fanelsa was ready with a few suitable words which he boomed with feeling.

" In this hour," he said, " our transfer to Canada begins. Whatever fate may hold in store for us, whether we remain together or are separated, the spirit of this camp will live on, and we shall continue to exhibit the soldierly qualities which have made such a deep impression on the English people. In this hour, we think of our Fatherland and of our beloved Führer."

" *SIEG HEIL ! SIEG HEIL ! SIEG HEIL !* "

As the last shout died away and the prisoners' arms dropped from the Nazi salute, Captain Allen, the Camp Adjutant, said in a matter-of-fact voice :

" Collect your sandwiches on the way out."

In the drive stood a line of double-decker buses. A new guard company of young soldiers—the guards at the camp had mostly been veterans of the First World War—had been brought in and now formed a lane from the door to the buses. They were smart and aloof and not to be drawn into conversation.

At Butterley railway station the prisoners were transferred to a train waiting in a siding. During the long train journey which now began, they passed the time between the game of Find the Bomb Damage, the U-boat men hooting derisively at the sight of small craters in open fields, and guessing their port of embarkation.

Liverpool ?—Wiped out long ago.

Bristol ?—That was *kaputt*, too.

London ?—There had been no docks left in London since last September.

Southampton ?—One of the first places to be destroyed.

It was generally agreed that the only ports still usable were on the west coast of Scotland.

The following morning the train reached Clydeside. A ship at anchor. Then another. Then nothing but ships, of many types and sizes. Some jet black, some grey, some still in their peacetime paint.

The Luftwaffe officers hooted derisively.

" What *is* this ? Hey, where are those U-boat line-shooters ? What's the explanation of this, Kapitänleutnant ? Why haven't these been sunk ? "

" Must be one of the convoys the Luftwaffe said it could deal with ! "

Uproar. A fierce argument, superficially good-humoured, but with undercurrents of real animosity and bitterness on both sides. A German counterpart of the Brylcreem Boys versus Bloody Matelots argument.

The train pulled into Greenock station. The dispute was instantly forgotten. On a neighbouring platform stood two long lines of German prisoners—N.C.O.s and men from camps for O.R.s.

The officers detrained and began shouting across to the men. One bomber pilot recognised his rear-gunner, another his wireless operator, a third his observer. U-boat officers saw members of their crews. There was much yelling and hallo-ing, and inquiries after Hunz and Kunz and Hans and Heinz. The only way the guards could put a stop to it was by marching the O.R.s off the station.

Then the men from Swanwick, who had been at the head of the train, noticed that prisoners from Grizedale Hall were getting out of the rear carriages, which had been picked up somewhere on the way. As though there was not a second to lose, there was a wild scuffle and scramble to greet old friends and comrades ; then much laughter, hand-shaking and back slapping, as they waited on the platform in the icy, stinging wind.

A large passenger ship was moored alongside the quay, the *Duchess of York*, of the Canadian Pacific Line. Some of the O.R. prisoners were already on board, others were lined up under guard near one of the several gangways, waiting for their turn to embark.

The officers went aboard two at a time. A British officer and a sergeant stood at the bottom of the gangway, ticking the prisoners' names off the roll as they embarked.

As each man, already struggling with a kitbag or a cardboard carton containing his belongings, moved along the deck, various things were thrust upon him : a ticket showing his deck and cabin, two buttered rolls, a can of corned beef and finally, boiling hot cocoa in a beaker without a handle.

Von Werra and Manhard scarcely had time to find their cabin when there were shouts all over the ship. English voices calling :

" Werra ! Werra ! "

Now what ? Had he been included in the contingent by mistake ? Was he going to be taken off the ship ?

He went out on deck.

A guard officer and two soldiers hurried towards him.

" Are you Werra ? "

" Yes. What have I done wrong now ? "

The officer seemed relieved.

" Nothing, yet. Where's your cabin ? "

" In there—35."

" I'm sorry. You'll have to come with me. There's a special cabin for you where you must remain under guard until the ship sails."

" That is unfair. I did my time in the ' cooler ' with the others."

" Sorry. Special orders. Leave your kit here, if you like. You may come back as soon as we sail. Until then, these two guards will not let you out of their sight."

When he knew that he was not going to be left behind, von Werra went away docilely with the escort. To tell the truth, he was rather flattered.

CHAPTER XV

Third Time Lucky

AFTER A false start, designed, the prisoners decided, to deceive German spies in Scotland and through them the German Navy, the *Duchess of York* finally sailed from Greenock on the evening of 10 January 1941.

In addition to the German prisoners (250 officers and 800 O.R.s) there were over a thousand R.A.F. recruits on board, on their way to take part in the Empire Air Training Scheme. The prisoners were heavily guarded and barbed wire screens and gates separated future R.A.F. pilots from the ex-aircrew of the Luftwaffe. When the Germans had first seen the R.A.F. men coming on board they decided that the British must have notified the German Navy, through the International Red Cross, that the *Duchess of York* would be filled to capacity with prisoners. This would guarantee the ship immunity from U-boat attacks. Some Germans went so far as to say that the whole purpose of sending prisoners to Canada was to enable R.A.F. trainees to cross safely.

The next morning there was no land in sight. The prisoners saw that they were in a convoy of about fifteen large ships, escorted by the battleship *Ramillies*, a London class cruiser, a small cruiser and about ten destroyers.

The prisoners were assembled on deck early for life-jacket drill. On the first morning the drill lasted two hours. It was repeated every morning throughout the crossing, but with practice the time was reduced to half an hour. On the deck of one of the other ships in the convoy they could see hundreds of troops doing physical training. The rail of another was lined with hospital nurses, their blue capes billowing in the wind. Now and again a destroyer would sweep ahead across the course of the *Duchess of York*, signal lights winking, its quarterdeck stacked with depth charges. Both cruisers carried a fighter on a catapult launching ramp.

On the second morning an air raid alarm was sounded. The prisoners took up their positions on deck, the *Duchess of York's* anti-aircraft guns were manned. One by one, barrage balloons rose up off the ships. But it was only a test alarm. U-boat and Luftwaffe prisoners alike were tremendously impressed by the convoy, by British seamanship and the display of defensive power. The stock of the U-boat prisoners reached rock-bottom. They herded together disconsolately in their groups and had little to say for themselves.

After the first few days von Werra began thinking seriously about his next escape attempt. He spent a lot of time getting information about Canada and the United States from Wagner, and with his help drew a rough map showing the boundary and the principle towns near either side. He found a bathroom with a sea-water cock. Preparing for the possibility of being able to drop out of a porthole and swim ashore when they reached Canada, he and Manhard tried to harden themslves by increasingly prolonged immersion in the ice-cold water.

He also volunteered to take the place of one of the German rankers assigned to kitchen duty and spent a whole morning peeling potatoes and chatting with the ship's cooks. In this way he learned that the *Duchess of York* would dock at Halifax, Nova Scotia, as it was impossible to get up to Quebec on the St. Lawrence at that time of year, owing to the ice, and that the prisoners would go from Halifax by train, possibly to camps in the far west. The ship was due at Halifax on 21 January.

Von Werra soon ingratiated himself with the cooks and began wandering out of the kitchen, gradually increasing the length of his periods of absence, and penetrating farther into forbidden parts of the ship. He got as far as the engine room. There were no guards and he was never challenged.

These clandestine excursions gave von Werra an idea. Would it be possible for the German prisoners to seize control of the ship and sail it into a German-held French Atlantic port?

That evening he discussed the matter with several U-boat commanders, and with the peacetime captain of the German liner *Europa*.

A plot was hatched. It was taken for granted that at some stage of the voyage the *Duchess of York* would separate from the convoy, which was no doubt bound for North Africa. The decks of some of the merchant vessels were covered with army vehicles ; neither these, nor the nurses, nor the troops seen doing physical training were likely to be bound for Canada. The question was, would the *Duchess of York* be on her own after separating from the convoy ? There could be no question of attempting to seize control of the ship unless it was unescorted.

The next day half a dozen picked prisoners disguised as members of the crew made a series of individual sorties into various parts of the ship, getting past the sentries without once being challenged. Their unexpected success gave a tremendous fillip to the scheme. Between them they had located or reconnoitred the wireless cabin, armoury, bridge, engine room and other strategic points of the ship.

A plan of action was worked out. Assault parties would be formed, each one being assigned a single objective. First, the wireless cabin was to be stormed, suddenly and silently, and the operators overpowered. Next, the armoury would be captured and weapons distributed to the other assault parties, who would go into action simultaneously. The remainder of the prisoners would then deal with the guards and R.A.F. personnel. If the operation succeeded, all the U-boats in the Atlantic were to be called up immediately to escort the ship into port.

Von Werra and the other conspirators went to bed in a fever of excitement.

At dawn next morning one of them looked into von Werra's cabin and beckoned him to go outside.

" We've left the convoy ! " he whispered.

Von Werra dashed out.

Not a ship or a smudge of smoke to starboard.

They ran across the ship to the rails on the other side. Not a ship or a smudge of smoke to port.

They ran aft to look behind.

And there, wallowing a few hundred metres dead astern, was the faithful *Ramillies*.

The R.A.F., it appeared, was in the market for German or Swiss wrist watches. Von Werra had a wrist watch, but it was too useful a piece of escaper's equipment for him to want to sell it. On the other hand, he was extremely anxious to get hold of some cash. He remembered that his old friend, Oberleutnant Karl Westerhoff, had just the sort of watch that was in demand—one with several hands and dials, and special buttons round the case to operate them. He persuaded Westerhoff to let him sell it for him on a commission basis.

After two day's bargaining he accepted a bid from an R.A.F. sergeant, who gave him one pound and two ten shilling notes. Von Werra kept one ten shilling note for his commission.

As it turned out, the sale of the watch benefited nobody but the man who bought it. In Canada it could have been sold at a much higher price in negotiable dollars; sterling was a useless and dangerous currency for an escaped prisoner to have in the Dominion.

In the second week of the voyage, escape preparations reached fever pitch. The schemes were so numerous and absurd that Major Fanelsa ordered all officers planning to escape in Canada to report to him in the stateroom used as prisoners' mess and common room.

Seventy-three of the 250 officers reported. Each man was required to outline his escape plan. It was evident that the majority of the men had no real aptitude for escaping, and that their plans were born of frustration and boredom and the desire to be in fashion. Plans that seemed brilliant and foolproof when conceived on one's bunk before going to sleep, became utterly absurd and impracticable when put into words publicly. Most of the plans were greeted with roars of laughter, and the meeting was the great success of the crossing.

As a result of the meeting, Wagner was asked to give a series of lectures on Canada to would-be escapers. Although a large proportion of this " class ", comprising several dozen men with more serious intentions, did manage to escape for short periods in the course of the next three years, Wagner himself did not try for eighteen months, despite his knowledge of certain parts of the country ; he was too busy helping others. It is ironic that when he did escape he was given credit by the authorities for succeeding where von Werra had failed. He was said to have taken off in a stolen aircraft. In fact, he got away by train—but not far enough.

Land in sight !

The last few days of the crossing had been tempestuous and most of the Luftwaffe prisoners were seasick. The smirking U-boat men had their little revenge for the airmen's earlier sarcasm.

But now, approaching harbour, the sea was calm and the sun shone in a clear blue sky. The cold was of an intensity von Werra had never experienced before. Coming out of the heated cabin on to the deck, the thin, clear air stabbed into the lungs like ice. Everything was a-glitter: the sea, a string of red buoys across the harbour mouth, the snow on land, the windows of tall buildings, icicles on the superstructure of the ship.

The U-boat men said that the string of buoys supported an anti-submarine net. After a while, two tugs with the word " Halifax " in white letters on their sterns, pulled open the boom. First *Ramillies*, and then the *Duchess of York*, sailed through the gap into the western passage of Halifax harbour. There were curiously exciting smells of fish, oil, tar and fresh-sawn timber.

After a couple of hours' wait the prisoners began to leave the ship. British guards with lists clipped to a board ticked each man's name and P.O.W. number as he stepped on the gangway. Canadian guards did the same as he stepped on to land. The prisoners were a motley, dishevelled, seedy-looking crew. With their cardboard cartons or kitbags of belongings, their undersize civilian coats, some with white padding protruding from burst shoulder seams, their rather hang-dog air, they bore no resemblance to the swaggering, goose-stepping Nazis of the propaganda pictures. The bystanders felt thay had been cheated.

Newsreel camera operators went into action and Press photographers dashed hither and thither, taking close-ups and angle shots. The prisoners passed between a double cordon of soldiers keeping back the sightseers, into a long, low customs building. There was some half-hearted booing and shouting in a mixture of French and English, but the prisoners were such a sorry-looking lot that they were hardly worth bothering about.

In the customs house the prisoners were " frisked " for weapons, and the contents of their kitbags or cartons were tipped on to the floor and examined. But their clothes were not searched and the inspection lasted only a few minutes.[1]

[1]Owing to the epidemic of escape activity that broke out among this contingent of prisoners after its arrival in the Dominion, the Director of Internment Operations in Canada ordered that in future all prisoners were to be thoroughly searched as soon

The prisoners were shepherded out of the other end of the building. From there they proceeded, officers to the left, men to the right, between long double rows of armed soldiers to two trains, each of fourteen coaches standing one behind the other in a siding.

In the coach in which von Werra was to travel there were thirty-five officer prisoners and twelve guards. A third of the coach was taken up by the guards, the remaining two thirds being allocated to the prisoners. There were far more seats than prisoners and they were able to spread themselves in comfort. There was a central gangway with comfortable seats arranged in pairs, back to back, on either side.

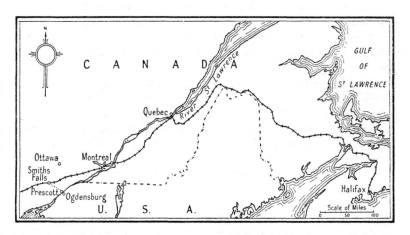

The guards were members of the Veterans' Guard of Canada. Three were on duty at a time. They stood in the gangway, one at either end of the section occupied by the prisoners, the third in the middle. They were armed with pistols.

The coaches were heated and had double windows for insulation against the cold. One army blanket was loaned to each prisoner.

Von Werra sat by a window and Manhard beside him. Facing them were Wagner, by the window, and Wilhelm next to the aisle.

The train left Halifax at about 7.30 p.m. It was snowing heavily.

---

as they came ashore. Among the clothes of the next contingent to arrive were discovered one prismatic and many home-made compasses, maps, sail-cord, cash in several different currencies, a variety of small tools including hacksaw blades, identity papers stolen from a seaman and a considerable part of the ship's cutlery.

The outer windows were almost completely covered with ferns of frost on the inside. There was a thick layer of ice on the bottom of the frame between the inner and outer windows. The prisoners could see the blazing lights of Halifax through the small areas of glass that were frost-free : floodlit shops and departmental stores, the uncurtained windows of office blocks, street lamps, winking neon signs, a myriad glistening snowflakes slanting across the dazzling headlamps of automobiles. The war, Europe, home were far, far away.

Soon after the train started a Canadian officer entered the coach and gave the following orders, which Wagner interpreted :

Prisoners would not be permitted to move from that coach to the next.

Prisoners could move about within the coach, but in each bay of four seats not more than one man was to stand up at one time.

Anybody wishing to go to the toilet was to hold up his hand. Prisoners would be escorted to the toilet one at a time in turn.

Windows were not to be opened or tampered with. The guards knew what to do if they saw anyone violating this order.

At night, after the seats and the luggage racks above them had been converted into bunks, there was to be no further movement of prisoners about the coach.

The officer announced that meals would be served to prisoners where they sat.

The coach became unbearably hot. Von Werra sat in his shirt sleeves next to the ice-covered window and perspired like a stoker. It took the prisoners some time to find an equable setting of the heat regulators. The guards seemed as indifferent to the intense dry heat inside the coach as they were to the intense dry cold outside it.

Several hours later German orderlies came in and erected in the bays the long, collapsible tables that were stored under the windows. One of them handed out thick slices of new white bread liberally spread—*with butter !* Other orderlies carried in large containers of food. Grinning broadly and winking, they whipped off the covers. There were exclamations all over the coach. Potatoes fried crisp and brown in bacon fat, baked beans with tomato sauce, thick slices of fried " sow-belly " ! Afterwards there was canned fruit. And coffee. Not acorn *ersatz* with saccharine. Not concentrated coffee and chicory diluted from a bottle, as in British camps. But real coffee, made from coffee beans, black, piping hot, sweetened with sugar to taste.

After the meal the prisoners were in a benign and expansive mood. So this was Canada ? Most of the men eyed their guards with a new tolerance, a musing interest.

Von Werra was tickled to see that one good meal had been enough to undermine the determination of half a dozen escapers, men with no experience who had talked about escape *ad nauseam* during the crossing.

Good-natured extroverts that they were, the guards responded at once to the more friendly atmosphere and were drawn into the conversation of various groups through prisoners with a knowledge of English. It soon became known that the German officers were being taken to a new camp in the bush on the north shore of Lake Superior, Ontario.

This piece of information was vital to von Werra. It meant that the train would in all probability pass through Montreal and Ottawa, and according to Wagner, the best place to escape from the train would be between those two cities, for the Canadian-U.S.A. border, the River St. Lawrence, was within a day's hitch-hiking distance.

There were other places along the route where the U.S. border would be closer. For instance, in north-west New Brunswick, at an early stage of the journey, the railway ran near to the border of the State of Maine. But for several reasons von Werra regarded this an unpromising place. All the other would-be escapers seemed to know about it, and any who had serious intentions would almost certainly try there. No doubt the train guards, and the Border Patrols of both countries, would be particularly alert while the train ran near the New Brunswick-Maine border.[1] Even if an escaper succeeded in crossing into Maine, the country was wild and snow-bound, and the chances were he would get lost in the vast forests and perish from a combination of exposure and starvation.

Von Werra decided that it would be best to try to escape as late as possible in the journey. This would give a chance for the excitement of any other escape attempt to die down. Above all,

[1]Eight prisoners escaped from the train at various stages of the journey. All but one were quickly recaptured ; all suffered frostbite and one broke a leg. Guards caught others in the act of leaving the train. Several O.R.s spent days cutting a hole in the floor of their compartment with a hacksaw blade stolen from the ship, only to find an accumulator box underneath which completely blocked the exit.

he did not want to get off the train in the backwoods. The point where he escaped must be reasonably close to the U.S. border, within reach of main roads, and not too far from human habitation. The obvious choice was somewhere between Montreal and Ottawa.

There was no chance of getting out of the lavatory window. The door was wedged wide open and a guard stood near the doorway all the time the prisoner was inside. It would have to be the coach window. But with a guard standing only a few yards away, this looked impossible.

The attempt would have to made while the train was in motion. As soon as it stopped, at signals or in stations, the three guards on duty in the coach were immediately on the alert, and other guards kept both sides of the train under observation. The other prisoners would have to stage a diversion at the critical time for the benefit of the three guards on duty; a quarrel farther along the coach might be the thing.

Owing to the height of the window above the floor, and the narrowness of the aperture, he could not jump out feet first, but would have to dive out, head first. But to do so while the train was travelling at speed would be suicidal. He would have to choose a moment when the train was travelling slowly, preferably just after it started following a halt. He would need the cover of darkness; the best time would be shortly before dawn.

But how was he to get the windows opened unnoticed? He observed that when the train halted for any length of time, the heat inside the coach partly melted the frost on the inner panes and the ice on the frame between them. After a long stop it should be possible to open the inner window fairly easily. If he opened it just a little way—less than a centimetre would do—the heat from the carriage would melt some of the ice on the frame between the two windows, and make it possible to open the outer window.

After the next long halt this plan was put into effect. Wagner stood up and kept an eye on the guards while von Werra, hidden by the backs of the seats, knelt down in front of the window and raised it a quarter of an inch. He wedged it with paper in case the vibration of the train closed it again.

Thereafter, whenever a guard happened to pass by the bay in which they were sitting, von Werra or Wagner would lay his arm negligently along the window sill, thus concealing the opening.

During the next long halt they had the satisfaction of seeing water from the melting ice trickle from the gap.

The volume of ice between the windows was greatly reduced in the next twenty-four hours. The process of freeing the frame would probably be accelerated if the coach temperature was raised to maximum. Von Werra therefore arranged with other prisoners to open all heat regulators to " Full " as soon as the train left Montreal.

There were several other difficulties to overcome : how to keep watch on three guards at once and to open the window when their attention was distracted ; how to conceal the open window ; how to shut both windows afterwards, for it would make all the difference if his disappearance were not discovered for some time ; he must be wearing his overcoat when he dived out, but how, having been sitting in his shirt-sleeves, could he put it on without arousing the guards' curiosity ?

An escaper must have luck, and luck solved most of these problems for von Werra.

The train reached Montreal late the following night. There was a long halt during which the heat was cut off while the locomotive was changed. The temperature in the coach dropped rapidly, and thus it was quite natural for the regulators to be fully opened when the heating was reconnected.

At the evening meal that night they had tomato soup, goulash, and a whole case of dessert apples. The prisoners were starved of fresh fruit, and they ate the lot.

This surfeit of apples following the unaccustomedly rich and plentiful food of the past twenty-four hours proved too much for their systems. In von Werra's coach from midnight onwards there was a long queue for the toilet, and some of the traffic had to be diverted to the guards' toilet at the other end of the coach. The three guards on duty were highly amused. Their attention was diverted, and at times there was only one guard left in the coach.

In spite of the stifling heat in the coach, one or two of the prisoners, white-faced and shivering from sickness, wrapped their coats or blankets about them, and sat hugging their stomachs. Von Werra was able to put on his overcoat without arousing the slightest suspicion. Afterwards he sat with his head in his hands. The guards were not expecting any of the prisoners to escape in their present condition.

But the train would not slow down. It went on and on exasperatingly at high speed. It was hours before the brakes were applied with a gradually increased pressure that indicated a coming halt at a station.

Through his fingers von Werra glanced at his three companions. All were wide awake and looking at him questioningly. Manhard and Wilhelm sat facing one another in the seats beside the gangway, each watching a guard. Their thumbs protruded from the blankets above their knees. Von Werra watched those thumbs. One thumb was horizontal, the other vertical.

Now both were sticking up. Von Werra stood up, opened out his blanket and shook it. Wagner knelt down behind it in front of the window. A second later he was back in his seat. Von Werra finished folding his blanket and sat down again.

The inner window was wide open. No word had been spoken.

The train stopped at a station. The remaining ice on the window frame and the frost on the glass were now fully exposed to the heat of the carriage. The guards stretched their limbs on the platform. The frost quickly melted on von Werra's outer window; through it he could see their silhouettes, massive against the station lights. If he could see them, they could see him. All the other windows were pearl-grey and opaque from frost. His was black and must be as noticeable as a gap in a row of teeth !

Would the guards spot it ? The minutes dragged interminably. The halt was much too long.

A bell clanged, the engine whistle sounded. The guards climbed aboard, banging the snow off their boots on the steps. Two of them got in the prisoners' end of the coach and had to walk back down the gangway to their seats. They would have to pass the defrosted window. Von Werra held his breath, keeping his head in his hands, peering between his fingers. The train was already moving. The first guard passed by looking straight ahead. The second approached more slowly. He was feeling his way. His spectacles were misted and he was squinting over the rims. He passed by.

Von Werra glanced at his friends. They were ready.

There were several prisoners now with raised hands, for during the halt there had been no visits to the toilet. A guard escorted the first man out. Two guards were left.

The train clanked and lurched over points outside the station. It was gathering speed rapidly. Manhard's thumb was up.

Wagner, holding two corners of his blanket in his lap, looked at von Werra in anxious inquiry. Von Werra nodded. Wagner stood up, and opened out the blanket. Wilhelm slid along into Wagner's corner seat.

Masked by the blanket, von Werra stood up, caught hold of the outer window, and jerked upwards. It did not move. Another fierce jerk and then a steady, sustained lift. The window opened smoothly.

A rush of cold air pressed the blanket against Wagner's body. He continued to shake the corners up and down, looking up the coach towards the two guards.

Von Werra felt the icy blast on his face, heard the unexpectedly loud and hollow beat of the wheels over the rail joints. Snowdrifts flashed by at a terrifying speed. The train was still accelerating.

It was sheer madness. Suicide. He couldn't possible do it.

The next moment Wilhelm saw von Werra's jack-boots disappear through the middle of the open window. For a split second, which he will never forget, he saw von Werra's body, rigid, arms straight out above his head, suspended almost horizontally a foot or so outside the coach.

It dropped back and was gone. There was nothing but the icy draught and the whine and the beat of the wheels on the rails.

Wilhelm shut the outer and inner windows and slid back along the seat. Wagner folded the blanket deliberately, slowly, and sat down.

No word was spoken.

All three were aghast, incredulous.

A few brief seconds ago von Werra had been sitting there with his head in his hands. Now he was gone.

The three of them watched ferns of frost sprout rapidly over the window. Inside a minute the glass was completely covered. It was as though the window had never been opened.

They never saw von Werra again. They had not even had time to wish him luck.

At daybreak, Major Cramer, who was officer-in-charge of the prisoners in that coach, walked down the gangway to see how the men who had been ill during the night were getting on. When he reached the bay occupied by Wagner, Manhard and Wilhelm, he paused. All three were lying on their bunks. Von Werra's was empty. He raised his eyebrows interrogatively. Wagner nodded his head slowly.

Cramer passed on, smiling.

It was not until late the following afternoon that von Werra's absence was discovered. The train was then several hundred miles from the point where he had dived out of the window.

CHAPTER XVI

Patrolman Delduchetto Arrests
a Tramp

VON WERRA landed on piled snow at the side of the track. The force of the impact drove all the breath from his body. He lay for a minute, feeling sick from the shock. He had ricked his neck in the fall, and he ached all over.

He stood up dizzily and looked around him. The cold struck him like a blow—he had jumped from stifling heat into thirty degrees of frost. The perspiration congealed on his skin.

There was snow everywhere, the smell of pine trees. In the distance, a red pin-point of light. The train's rear lamp. Then it was gone.

He felt a sudden surge of exhilaration.

His temples throbbed, his neck ached, he was stiff, chilled to the marrow, and his nose stung like hell. But he was free.

He became aware of the silence—the silence of snow. It was as though his ears were plugged with cotton wool.

The sky was clear and the stars hung low and large. The snow reflected their diamond light.

Heavens, it was cold!

What a fool he had been not to think of getting a cap. He would have to do something or his ears would drop off with frostbite. He pulled from his pocket the tartan scarf he had bought at Swanwick, and wrapped it over his head.

Having taken a bearing on the pole star, he crossed the railway track and set out southwards across a stretch of open country. The going was difficult. Each step he took he sank up to his calves in snow. The harsh, rasping sound of his boots in the snow seemed to fill the universe.

He began to imagine noises, and when he glanced back quickly over his shoulder, it was not only to check his bearing by the pole star.

After about an hour he saw the serrated outline of a pine forest, black against the pale horizon. There was no road or track along the edge of it. There was nothing for it but to find his way through.

The forest was full of noises—creakings, scufflings, whisperings, sighings, rustlings—breaking the awesome silence.

Sometimes he was in the open, knee-deep in snow, sometimes groping, stumbling in the blackness under the trees. After a while he came to a broad avenue. It was a hundred yards wide— probably a fire break. The snow in the middle had been flattened by a tractor. It was like walking on a road. Ahead of him the tree tops formed an elongated V against the stars. Behind him the sky was paling. Dawn was near.

He hurried. The hard track was a godsend, but he was afraid that as soon as it became daylight he might encounter lumberjacks, or perhaps the man with the tractor. How could he explain his presence in the middle of a Canadian forest in such clothes at that time of day? He must get on to a highway. The sun rose. The tips of the trees on his right were edged with gold and silver. The pines cast gigantic shadows. He hastened onwards, sometimes running. He was reluctant to leave the hard track.

He must have walked several miles, but still the end of the avenue was not in sight. Suddenly he heard the sound of an engine. It sounded like a car, and it seemed to come from the trees on his right. He listened intently. The noise grew louder, and after a few moments a car flashed across the avenue half a mile away ahead of him, snow chains rattling.

A road! In a few minutes he had reached it.

For an hour he followed it without seeing any more vehicles. Then it joined a wider road. There was a signpost.

According to the announcement put out by the Canadian authorities, von Werra escaped from the train near Smiths Falls, Ontario, about forty miles south-west of Ottawa. If that is so, he had only about thirty miles to cover to reach the St. Lawrence which at that point forms the border between Canada and the United States.

When eventually he reached New York and was besieged by reporters, sensing the sort of story they were after, he gave it to them. He said he had leapt off the train 100 miles north of Ottawa ; this gave him far more elbow room for an extravagant account, in the true von Werra manner, of his achievement and of the daring and aplomb with which he had brought it off. No one enjoyed more than von Werra telling a good story for the entertainment of his audience, and if their legs were pulled in the process, so much the better !

His story having been accepted by the American Press (which after all would have no means of knowing the real route taken by the prisoners' train and presumably did not bother to discover for themselves that no east-west rail track passes within a hundred miles of " a hundred miles north of Ottawa ") there seemed to von Werra no reason to vary his account when he came to write it in book form for the German people. Indeed he improved on it.

First of all a truck had come along and he had thumbed a lift in the manner Wagner had taught him. He had a story ready for the driver. He was a Dutch seaman. He had been twice dive-bombed crossing the Atlantic and had seen too many ships sunk by U-boats. He had had enough. He had relatives in Ottawa who would help him get a land job.

After some miles the lorry driver set von Werra down where he was due to turn off the main highway. " Plenty of stuff heading for Ottawa on this route," had been the driver's parting remark. " You'll soon hitch a ride, bud."

Sure enough, after a quarter of a mile, von Werra had heard a rattle of snow-chains coming behind him. He removed his hand from his pocket ready to carry out the Wagner drill again. When he looked back his heart missed a beat. He quickly put his hand back into his pocket and turned his back on the approaching vehicle.

It was a big saloon car. On its bumper there was a large red shield bearing the word " POLICE ".

Von Werra pretended to ignore the car as it drew level, but the driver braked and pulled in beside him.

So his third attempt had not been lucky after all. Had he been a fool to walk along the main highway instead of keeping to the forest where he would have been safe ?

The policeman was beckoning him to get in. He had no option. Inside he noticed the radio receiver. That explained it. Police cars were probably out scouring every highway looking for a short, fair man wearing a blue overcoat and no hat.

But from the policeman's opening remarks it appeared that he was more concerned with von Werra's half complete hitch-hiking gesture. What Wagner had been unable to tell him was that since the beginning of the war begging a lift had been made illegal in Canada. " You changed your mind just in time," the policeman had said. " If you'd hailed me, I'd have run you in. As it is I'll run you in to Ottawa." For von Werra had told him about his " relatives " in Ottawa.

Whether any policeman ever did help von Werra on his way we are unlikely to know. If the policeman did not exist, at least he could not come forward to contradict von Werra's story ! If, as von Werra said, the policeman dropped him off outside police headquarters, it was certainly not in Ottawa where he also placed some other daring adventures. He had gone into one of the big banks and asked to change English currency into Canadian dollars ; he had not revealed that all he had to exchange was a ten shilling note. When the clerk behind the grille had demanded to see his papers, von Werra had once more escaped from a desperate situation. He had another story for American newspaper men, that he had narrowly escaped arrest by police guarding the Parliament Building while he was sightseeing in the capital ; but this one he must have forgotten by the time he came to dictate the notes for his book.

If, as the Canadian authorities stated, and as his companion, Wagner, confirms, von Werra left the train near Smiths Falls, he certainly never went near Ottawa, which lay in the opposite direction —i.e. northward—to that in which he wanted to go.

What his object can have been in making up such a tale, is left to the imagination of the reader who has already had experience of von Werra's gift for extemporising.

One incident must have had some truth in it, for von Werra describes a ruse by which he acquired a road map from a garage, and an " Imperial " road map of Ontario State was among the items later found in his possession.

The indisputable fact remains that in due course, from whichever direction and by whatever means, von Werra did arrive at Johns-town on the north bank of the St. Lawrence and saw the twinkling lights of the United States beckoning him from the other shore.

He had no idea how he was going to cross the river. According to his map, there were international bridges at Cornwall, forty-five miles downstream, and at Thousand Islands, forty miles upstream. Between the two bridges there were ferries at Morrisburg, Prescott and Brockville. Prescott was the nearest, only a few miles away, and he decided to investigate that first. But would the ferry be working at that time of year? It seemed unlikely in view of the ice he had seen on the river from the train, farther downstream between Quebec and Montreal.

He walked south and came to what appeared in the gathering dusk to be a wide, flat, snow-covered valley. It was a few seconds before he realised that this was the River St. Lawrence. It was frozen over. He was tremendously excited. All he had to do was to wait until it was quite dark and walk across to the United States.

It was far better than a ferry or toll bridge where he would have had to run the gauntlet of customs, passport officials and police of two countries.

But the size of the river was terrifying. How wide was it? Five hundred metres? A thousand? The dusk and the snow made it impossible to judge. But it was a long, long way to the winking lights of the American city on the other side, which he reckoned from his map to be Ogdensburg.

He set out along the bank, wading knee-deep through the snow. He was dead tired and ravenously hungry. He had eaten nothing for nearly twenty-four hours. It had been cold enough all day, but with the approach of night the temperature dropped rapidly. There was a bitter wind at his back. It pierced his clothing like a knife. The cold and fatigue had made him drowsy. He fretted with impatience.

He had travelled so far; now there was only three-quarters of a mile at most between him and final freedom.

He struggled for about two miles along the bank. It was desolate and silent. There was only the hum of the wind round his ears, the occasional flurries of powder blown along the surface of the snow.

He waited until long after dark. A haze of light hung over Ogdensburg. Some distance to the east of it there were three isolated points of light forming a triangle. Perhaps they were street lamps. He made them his objective.

At seven o'clock he left the comparative shelter of the bank and set off across the open ice of the river.

The snow had been blown into deep drifts near the bank. He floundered, fought his way forward foot by foot. Fifty yards out the going became comparatively easy, but the wind swept over the ice straight up the course of the river. It seemed to be laden with splinters of glass. Ice formed on his eye-brows, on the scarf over his head and on the upper part of his coat. Snow from the drifts he had struggled through turned into ice as he walked ; the flaps of his coat were like boards.

The glittering stars and the lights of Ogdensburg merged and traced scintillating lines across the snow. The merging of land and sky gave him the illusion that he was about to look over the edge of the world. The illusion vanished as the lights of the city ahead became more distinct.

Now and again he heard the sound of the ice cracking—a sharp snap followed by a rapidly receding rumble. He knew that cracking ice was not dangerous so long as it was freezing. But when he reached what he thought was about half-way, the sounds of cracking became very loud and menacing. Sometimes they were close and he could feel the slight sudden shock wave. An odd sensation.

He tripped over something and went sprawling. The ice was no longer smooth under its thin covering of snow, but jagged and rough as a road surface broken up by a pneumatic drill. He was so numb from cold that it was a minute or so before he felt the full hurt of his tumble.

He was winded and shaken. He lay for a moment, almost overcome by the urge to sleep, his senses pulling one way, his will the other. There came to his mind the memory of a summer evening on a lake near Berlin : green reeds rustling, sun-spangled water, white sails billowing, ripples lapping against glistening, varnished woodwork. Lapping . . . lapping . . .

The wind dropped momentarily and he clearly heard the sound of a car horn. He got up, aching all over, slipping and stumbling on slabs of ice larger than paving stones.

He was only a quarter of a mile from the American shore. Cars rolled along the waterfront, headlights blazing.

He hurried forward eagerly, then paused. Ten, fifteen yards ahead the snow seemed to stop. Beyond was blackness. The shore already ? But why was there no snow ?

Then he saw the lights reflected on the blackness : water ! He could not grasp it. How could there be water when the whole river was frozen over? He frantically hacked with the heel of his boot at a slab of ice. A corner broke off and he tossed it forward into the blackness. It fell with a hollow splash, like a pebble into a well.

There was an ice-free channel between him and the American shore.

To swim in that temperature meant certain death. He had to go back.

Von Werra returned to the Canadian bank and walked along it towards Prescott. He came to a collection of chalets—a deserted summer holiday camp. He floundered about in the deep snow on the foreshore and eventually found what he was looking for—a long, cigar-shaped mound of snow. He scraped away the side with his boot and came upon something hard. It was an upturned rowing boat.

He went back to the chalets and found a wooden fence. After much kicking and wrenching he managed to free two palings. They were too wide and too thick and ice made them heavier still, but they would have to do. He used one of them as a shovel to dig away the snow from the boat.

It was a large, cumbersome affair, and was frozen to the ground. He had to lever it free, a little at a time, with one board, using the other as a wedge. When he had freed it he still had to turn it the right way up. It took all his strength and the aid of the two boards but finally he righted it.

There were no oars or rowlocks. The boat was a six-seater. How ever was he going to row it—even assuming he could manage to drag it as far as the water?

He groped around, looking for another boat. He found nothing, so returned to the six-seater.

He had got to do it !

In a sudden, desperate rage, he threw himself at the stern of the boat and pushed wildly. It scarcely moved.

He felt a snowflake on his cheek. He looked up at the sky. The stars were obscured. He looked across the river. The lights of Ogdensburg were barely discernible through a curtain of flurrying snow.

It would be fatal to give way to rage and panic. He must conserve his strength, use his wits to spare his muscles, and make every scrap of effort count.

If he tried to *drag* the boat, he would waste a lot of effort, for he would tend to pull the bow down into the snow. He must *push* it. When he got out beyond the drifts, where the snow was only ankle deep on the ice, he could tie his scarf to the mooring ring in the bow and pull the boat behind him.

He tossed the boards into the boat and began pushing it towards the river. He advanced a foot to eighteen inches at a time. At first he thought he would never reach the river. But gradually he stopped thinking. He became an automaton, oblivious to everything except the rhythm of his movements, the rasping of his breath and the taste of his saliva. Fatigue, hunger, thirst and cold were forgotten.

At last he reached the open ice. He crouched down on the lee of the boat out of the wind and the driving snow, resting. When he got up again and tried to push, the keel was frozen to the ice. He had to wrench with all his might to free it. It was wasted effort—he must not rest any more until he reached the pack-ice.

He tried to tie his scarf to the mooring ring, but his fingers were without feeling and for the life of him he could not tie a knot. He would have to continue pushing.

Half-way across.

Sometimes for minutes at a time the lights of Ogdensburg were completely obscured by snow. Von Werra kept pushing. He dared not stop. Now and again he slipped and fell on to his knees. But he got up and went on.

He was brought to a halt by the pack-ice near the water's edge. How could he get the boat over the ice and into the river?

He pulled the boat back a few feet, then pushed it up on to the pack-ice using the two boards as runners under the keel. Again, using the boards alternately as runners, he managed to push the boat forward, a length at a time.

At last he reached the open river. He tipped the boat three-parts of the way into the water, jumped in and pushed off against the ice with one of the boards. The whole boat slid into the water, rocked violently and in the struggle to regain his balance the board slipped out of his numbed hand.

He sat down and picked up the remaining board, trying to use it as a paddle. But it was too long, too heavy and too clumsy. He could neither feel it nor grip it. It slid out of his hands into the water.

Rudderless, oarless, the boat floated away into the darkness, rocking and turning lazily round and round in the 10 miles an hour current. Now and again small icefloes thudded against the sides.

An escaper must have luck. Farther downstream the ice-free channel followed the contour of a toe of land jutting out in the river. The boat, steadied now and facing upstream, gradually slid across the channel and eventually bumped and scraped along the jagged ice bordering one side of the headland.

Von Werra was no stranger to excitement. But even he found the thrill of that trip on the St. Lawrence a little too hectic and sustained. Time seemed to stop. He had the impression that the boat was spinning round and round in the darkness, and hurtling down to the sea.

When it bumped and grated against the margin of ice by the headland, he needed no time to make up his mind. The boat grated : he leapt. He managed to fall on the ice. The boat recoiled, then slowly returned. The last he heard of it, it was bumping and scraping slowly downstream.

He got to his feet, staggered across the ice and scrambled up the bank. He was very anxious. It seemed to him that he had been in the boat for hours, and that he had drifted miles. And he knew from the map that farther downstream the U.S.A. border was some way south of the St. Lawrence—that *both* banks were in Canada.

He saw a huge building some distance away on his left. The windows were ablaze with light. Then he had a shock. He noticed that every window was barred. Had he landed in the grounds of a penitentiary ?

He moved away to the right as quickly as he could. He was reassured when he saw a car pass by ahead of him. There must be a road. Then he saw two cars parked farther down on the right. He got on to the road and walked towards them. The leading car was unoccupied. The bonnet of the other was raised and a man was tinkering with the engine. A young lady in a snow-sprinkled fur coat stood by him and there was another girl sitting in the car.

On the licence plate of the rear car were the words : " New York ". It was the same with the other car.

He dared not believe it. He had seen cars in Canada with New York licence plates.

The man went to the car ahead, presumably to get some tools. He looked hard at von Werra but did not speak.

Von Werra moved across the front of the car. The headlamps shone on his overcoat, which was stiff with ice. His legs cast long shadows on the snow. The woman stared at him and then glanced in the direction of the river from which he had come. She laughed and asked lightly :

" What's the matter with you ? "

" Excuse me. Is this America ? "

" Are you sick, or something ? "

" No, truly. What is that house over there ? What place is this ? "

The woman was struck by his accent and by the tiredness of his voice. She replied straightforwardly :

" That is New York State Hospital. I am a nurse there. You are in Ogdensburg."

" *Ogdensburg ?* But——" Von Werra could not believe it.

Instead of having drifted miles downstream, he had travelled barely half a mile.

But what did it matter ? He was in America.

He smiled wearily.

" I am an officer of the German Air Force," he said. " I escape across the river from Canada. I am "—he corrected himself, " I *was* a prisoner-of-war."

The nurse gave him a cigarette. He had difficulty in holding it in his frostbitten fingers. The nurse explained that she had been setting out "uptown" when her car had stalled. She had telephoned a garage and the proprietor himself, Mr. Al Crites, had driven out to see what was wrong. There were, she said, many Canadians in Ogdensburg, including frontier officials.

It was not until some time later that von Werra realised that the nurse had been trying to tell him that Al Crites was a Canadian.

Crites gave von Werra a lift into the city. The German insisted on getting out at the traffic lights on the corner of Ford and Patterson Streets. Although he did not then know that Crites was a Canadian, he wanted to make sure that he surrendered to an American policeman.

A few minutes later Patrolman James Delduchetto, of the Ogdensburg City Police, having been tipped off by Crites, arrested

Oberleutenant Franz von Werra as a tramp, loitering in the precincts of the Presbyterian Church.

"Come on, you!" said Patrolman Delduchetto. "Head-quarters!"

"Excuse me. You are American, or Canadian?"

The policeman tapped the badge on his cap. It bore an eagle and the letters "U.S.A."

Von Werra smiled.

"Okay!" he said. "Sure!"

At police headquarters, von Werra was charged with vagrancy. But with the aid of his uniform jacket, complete with Iron Cross, and various censored letters addressed to him in British internment camps, he was able to convince the police he was an escaped German prisoner-of-war. The vagrancy charge was dropped, and he was turned over to Immigration Inspector David K. J. Benjamin.

An Immigration Board held a preliminary inquiry at Ferry House the same night, and von Werra was arraigned on a charge of illegal entry into the United States. The hearing was adjourned to the next day to enable him to get in touch with the German Consul in New York, and to obtain legal representation. Later, he was handed back to the police for safe keeping.

Since diving out of the train early that morning he had passed an eventful and utterly exhausting day. Physically, he was dead beat. Somehow he managed to keep going on nervous energy. His eyes pricked for want of sleep and he was in a waking dream.

Things had moved fast after his arrest. When he arrived back at Police Headquarters, photographers and reporters milled round him. He was given food and drink and then he told his story.

And now the other side of von Werra's character took over. He committed one indiscretion after another. He boasted, bragged, exaggerated outrageously and spoke of the British war effort with contempt. If this performance had been limited to the night of his arrival, it would be easy to overlook it, but it was continued throughout the next day, after food and a night's sleep, when some of the famous feature writers arrived from New York to interview him.

The following morning, Saturday 25 January, the story of his escape, and many pictures of him, were front page news throughout

America. The local paper, the *Ogdensburg Journal*, devoted several pages of news and pictures to his " saga ".

Following are a few extracts :

. . . Von Werra boasted of German supremacy in the present war and said his " big ambition " was to " get back to my squadron in time to take part in the all-out invasion of England." Asked by Police Chief Herbert S. Myers to " put it in writing ", von Werra wrote out the date " May 12 1941 " and said : " Remember what I am telling you, on May 12—that will be the big day and I will be back flying over England with my squadron."

. . . He boasted that he would get away from the States as easily as he had gotten away from the English in England on two occasions and from the Canadians . . .

. . . Von Werra was idolised as a hero and trailed by crowds of sympathetic admirers after he was apprehended by local police . . .

. . . At his mass press conference he spun stories that would have amazed Horatio Alger, Joseph Conrad or the author of the Arabian Nights.

On 27 January the London *Times* published an account from its New York correspondent, under an appropriate heading :

BARON MÜNCHAUSEN ESCAPES

GERMAN AIRMAN TELLS THE TALE

. . . He said that he shot down three British aeroplanes that day, but had come into collision with another German aeroplane when coming out of a dive. He said he had flown over England so many times that he was unable to count the flights. He had escaped this time, he said, so as to take part in a " knock-out blow " against England in March. The Germans had been experimenting with the transport of troops in gliders towed by bombers, each glider carrying 45 to 50 men. He asserted that United States help was " too late " to " save " England, and predicted a British capitulation in September. Praising British morale, he declared that German bombers had done " terrific " damage to London.

CHAPTER XVII

A Borderline Case

VON WERRA was the third German prisoner-of-war to escape from Canada into the United States.

The first was a U-boat rating who dropped at night through a port-hole of a prison ship sailing up the St. Lawrence in the summer of 1940. He swam ashore to Quebec province and later crossed into Maine, U.S.A., on foot. There he surrendered to an American border patrol and was held in Bangor, Maine, city goal for several weeks until immigration authorities decided what to do with him. He was then released under a bond paid by the German Consul in Boston and handed over to him for safe keeping. A few weeks later the man skipped his bond and returned to Germany via Japan and Russia.

This escape from a prison ship was in some ways more spectacular and daring than von Werra's escape in a rowing boat. Moreover, it was the first incident of its kind. But whereas von Werra's story was treated sensationally and splashed across the front pages of American newspapers, the escape of the U-boat rating was reported only briefly and then not until he was released from gaol. His later disappearance from the States was never mentioned in the Press.

The explanation for the disparity of Press interest in the two escapes is simple : the U-boat man did not have von Werra's brash, colourful personality, he was not a baron, and far from having a flair for personal publicity, he said little to reporters and referred all their questions to a Consular official who acted as his spokesman.

The second prisoner who escaped from Canada was a merchant seaman named Emmanuel Fischer. His ship was seized in a British port the day war broke out. The crew was interned in Scotland and later transferred to Canada. Fischer escaped from a prison camp in Ontario, in August 1940, and crossed the border into the United States at International Falls, Minnesota. The Americans kept him in gaol for three months and then handed him back to Canada where he was reinterned.

It was primarily von Werra's personality which saved him from a similar fate. He told reporters the sort of things they wanted to hear from an escaped German baron. He caught the imagination of the American people. Nation-wide publicity was given to his case by Press, newsreels and radio with the result that it became an international issue.

America was then in a state of " armed neutrality " and the sympathies of its people were divided. A large section of the public, made up mainly, of course, of Americans of German or Italian origin, was anti-British. The Bund and other German-American societies, and on a higher level, the America First Committee, exercised a powerful influence on American public opinion. Nazi sympathisers in America flooded prison camps in Canada with gift parcels. Postal regulations required senders to show their addresses on the parcels. German prisoners made secret lists of these addresses: they proved useful to men who escaped across the border.

Von Werra got in touch by telephone from Ogdensburg with the German Consul in New York. The Consul instructed an Ogdensburg lawyer, Mr. James Davies, to take up the case immediately. Davies was present at the resumed hearing by an Immigration Board at Ogdensburg the day after von Werra's arrival. Von Werra waived examination on a charge of " entering the United States without reporting to an immigration officer " and elected to appear before a Federal Grand Jury at Albany, N.Y., several days later. He was released from custody under a bond of $5,000 paid by the German Consul in New York.

The Consul was anxious to get the fugitive away from Ogdensburg and the Canadian border as quickly as possible. One of the reasons for haste soon became manifest: a few hours after von Werra left Ogdensburg the Canadian authorities made the first move to secure his return. The Ontario Provincial Police delivered a summons to the Ogdensburg police to be served on von Werra, charging him with plunder and theft of a rowing boat valued at $35.

If the summons had been served on him in Ogdensburg, he

would not have been permitted to leave until the matter had been settled. The charge was a criminal one and could not be settled simply by payment of the $35. The case could not be tried by a U.S. court, and the charge might well have led to von Werra's extradition to Canada. The Canadians later applied for an extradition order on the basis of the theft charge, but by that time von Werra was in hiding in New York, and his case had been lifted from the $35 local level into the arena of international politics.

The German diplomatic representatives in America must have been horror-stricken by the indiscretions committed by von Werra in his rapturous interviews with newspapermen in Ogdensburg. It was not only what he said—his wild boasts, his insouciant revelation of war secrets—but the way that he said it : the day after his escape newspapers described him as " garrulous ", " cocky ", " boastful ", and so on.

These were hardly the kind of epithet German diplomatists liked to see applied to a dashing young hero of Hitler's Third Reich. It is clear from contemporary newspaper reports that he did not have things all his own way at his mass Press conferences at Ogdensburg. Hard-boiled, dead-pan New York newspapermen " jollied him along " and provoked him into making ever wilder boasts and statements. It is unlikely that he ever realised to what extent they were " taking the Mickey " out of him. At Ogdensburg the Press had free access to him ; he could say what he liked, how he liked ; there was no cautious Consular official at his elbow to advise and restrain him. No doubt this was another reason why the German Consul in New York was so anxious to get him away from Ogdensburg.

From the time he arrived in New York, von Werra was kept out of the way of newspapermen and forbidden to speak to them. He stayed at the Westchester home of Bernhard Lippert, one of the German Vice-Consuls. Whenever he went out he was accompanied by Consular officials or lawyers, and later by a professional body-guard. " Werra is a soldier," they said, " and as such he cannot talk to the Press." On some occasions his movements were invested with all the thrills of a film chase. To shake off reporters and camera-men he and his escort would dodge into a building by one entrance and leave by another ; cars would be waiting with doors open and engine running. One reporter stated that his taxi, doing fifty miles an hour, had been unable to keep contact.

He spoke to reporters only once more—at La Guardia airfield, on his return from one of the frequent and mysterious trips he made by air to Washington. Then he was reported next day as being "cheerful but reticent." Asked what he thought of the U.S.A., he replied: "It's very nice here." He posed politely for photographers, but declared that newspapers in America were "a funny business". He referred reporters to the German Consulate for further information about himself, and answered most questions with: "No comment. I am a soldier."

This was a very different von Werra from the one who had been so voluble at Ogdensburg. But although he spoke no more to the American Press, the American Press spoke a great deal about him. At first its tone was not unfriendly, and tribute was paid to his courage and resourcefulness. But if the papers gratefully published his tales of derring-do, most of them commented caustically on his extravagances.

His reception was in the nature of a *succès de scandale* and one newspaper openly referred to his success as "tainted".

There was much speculation about what would happen to von Werra, and it was reported that officials in Washington were looking up precedents in international law. On 25 January the American Department of Justice stated that "Baron von Werra . . . will probably be deported to Germany. War conditions, however, make it virtually impossible to execute deportation orders, and von Werra may be released under bond until his transportation to Germany can be arranged. International law prohibits the United States from returning prisoners to the country from which they have escaped. A deportee may be sent to a country other than his native land, provided he asks to be sent there and the country is willing to accept him."

Fortunately for von Werra, in the search for precedents nobody seems to have discovered the one of the previous year, when, as has been told, Emmanuel Fischer was handed back to the Dominion after spending three months in an American gaol!

In the end the Department of Justice in Washington cancelled von Werra's appearance before a Federal Grand Jury. According to the London *Times* (6/2/41), the reason for this was that the only charge that could be made against him was that of illegal entry into America, which was a misdemeanour, not indictable offence. At the most he could have received a year's imprisonment followed by deportation to Germany at the earliest opportunity.

In lieu of the grand jury proceedings, the Department of Justice imposed a further bail of $5,000 in addition to the $5,000 already paid. When this had been paid by the German Consul, von Werra was formally handed over to him to keep in " protective custody " pending a final decision on his case by the Attorney-General.

A few weeks later von Werra was again summoned to Ellis Island and questioned for several hours. At this hearing the amount of his bond was doubled, and once again it was the German Consul who paid the money. He had now paid a total of $15,000 for von Werra's provisional liberty.

It was in New York that von Werra first learned that Hitler had awarded him the Knight's Cross of the Iron Cross in recognition of an exploit " unique in the annals of fighter aviation in this war " —the attack he claimed to have made on a British airfield. Thus, the prophecy of the R.A.F. Interrogation Officer had in part come true, but the party to celebrate the award was held in New York— not in a British prisoner-of-war camp. Three of the German-American guests who attended that party were, in 1943, to be tried as Nazi agents.

In Germany, the publicity given to von Werra's escape quickly elevated him to a national figure. Reports running to thousands of words, together with pictures, appeared in the daily Press, while two-page features, accompanied by maps, photographs and drawings illuminated the magazines.

The Propaganda Ministry not unnaturally suppressed many of von Werra's boasts and indiscretions, and did not scruple to alter details to suit its own purpose. German readers, for instance, would not have heard of Hucknall, so it was stated that von Werra almost got away from the better-known Croydon aerodrome. The epithets " cocky ", " boastful ", etc., applied to von Werra by the American press, were omitted in German versions of the story. Von Werra was presented as an eager, earnest hero of the National-Socialist Reich, who did and dared all for the Führer and the Fatherland.

A great fuss was of course made over the warrant issued by the Canadian police charging von Werra with the theft of a rowing boat. " Canada Weeps for $35 " and " Canada Covers Itself with

Ridicule " were typical headings to Nazi newspaper reports dealing with this aspect of the story.

However, it is clear that the Germans in Washington were very worried about the possible consequences of the Canadian warrant. On 29 January the German Embassy issued a special statement about it to the Press. The simple truth about the warrant was confused at great length, and the statement concluded : " In view of the great importance Canada appears to attach to the boat, Franz von Werra will gladly place at the disposal of the American authorities the sum of $35, which in the Canadian view represents a reasonable hire charge for a short period, so that the warrant against him may be withdrawn."

Nobody, of course, least of all the Canadians, really blamed von Werra, or any other prisoner-of-war, for stealing a boat to make good an escape. What the Germans could not see was that if it was legitimate for von Werra to use the boat as a means of escape, it was equally legitimate for the Canadians to use it as a means of getting him back !

Behind the scenes in Washington a great tussle was going on for possession of von Werra's " body ", with the Germans pulling one way, the Canadians and the British the other, and the Americans acting as referee. Von Werra's escape was a serious threat to British security. The British were not only concerned at the possible return to Germany and to operations of an experienced pilot ; they were concerned at the possible return of one who had been sub-jected to their interrogation methods, and who had been sufficiently astute to hold out against them. They therefore used every possible means to prevent his getting back.

They were not to know that the harm had already been done. As soon as von Werra reached New York the German Military Attaché instructed him to write a preliminary report on his ex-periences as a prisoner-of-war, with special reference to procedure at British Air Interrogation Centres. This report was immediately communicated in code to Luftwaffe Headquarters in Berlin. The Intelligence and Operations Branches were so impressed by it that extracts and instructions aimed at tightening up aircrew security, were teletyped to all operational units of the Luftwaffe. The effect of this measure was soon felt by British Air Intelligence. German aircrew captured after von Werra's report and the issue of new instructions based on it, were extremely security-minded. They knew what to expect from guards and interrogators.

A booklet entitled *How to behave if taken prisoner*, based on von Werra's observations and experiences was made available to all flying personnel a little later. It advised German airmen that if they had the ill luck to fall into British hands " complete and persistent silence is the only defence against enemy interrogators."

They were warned not to try to lie to or mislead enemy interrogators. " They are up to every kind of trick and know their job inside out. If you try to beat them at their own game, *you* will be the loser." They were warned that one simple remark, apparently quite harmless, might enable the enemy to unravel something that was puzzling him. Particularly they were warned against letting themselves be provoked into argument or indeed into conversation on any subject. Franz von Werra had forgotten none of the lessons he had learned at Cockfosters.

While a decision on his case was pending, von Werra made frequent air trips from New York to Washington, ostensibly to confer with the German Ambassador and legal experts, but really to write reports and answers in response to questions from Berlin.

The F.B.I. kept a close watch on these comings and goings, and on the people he met. This was borne out at later trials of various German spies in America, when times and places of their meetings with von Werra were specified. In 1945, the F.B.I. revealed that for many months before America entered the war, people arriving at and leaving the German Embassy in Washington were secretly photographed from windows of houses across the street and from innocent-looking vans parked nearby.

Naturally, one of the first things von Werra had done on his arrival in New York was to cable news of his escape to his foster-mother, and to the girl to whom he had become engaged at the outbreak of war. He also cabled the German state publishing house, the *Deutscher Verlag*, offering them the rights of a book dealing with his experiences as an escaper. The offer was accepted by cable the same day.

In the course of his unexpected holiday he wrote many " wish-you-were-here " picture postcards to old friends and comrades. He did not forget more recent acquaintances—the various Army and R.A.F. officers he had met in England. One such postcard is reproduced opposite page 161. It was addressed to "Mr. Boniface" who happily preserved it as a war souvenir.

The weeks passed. At first von Werra had a wonderful time in New York, visiting theatres and night clubs and attending social functions, though always in the company of Consular officials. "Escaped Hun Baron Women's Pet in U.S." was the heading to a news item in the London *Daily Mirror* (21/3/41). He was described as "leading a life of luxury in New York as the darling of dozens of doting German-American women." Every morning "masses of expensive flowers" arrived for him and notes from women who wanted him to be their guest at dinners and parties.

"At night," the report continued, "the baron eats and drinks at his admirers' expense, repaying them with fantastic stories of his 'bravery' . . ." describing dramatically how he shot down fourteen British planes and how he hoped to return to Europe to shoot down many more. When he dined out with his bodyguard, it was said, "you can't see the baron for skirts."

Behind the scenes, the tussle for his "body" was intensified. During March there were indications that public and official American opinion was hardening against von Werra. He went out less often and his professional bodyguard was reinforced. The Germans did not rule out the possibility of an attempt to kidnap him.

On 22 March two more German prisoners crossed the St. Lawrence at a point where it was completely frozen, with a posse of Canadian police on their heels. The Canadians could not shoot for fear of hitting an American border patrol which was coming out to meet the escapers. The Germans were taken to Ogdensburg, held incommunicado and denied permission to telephone the German Consul in New York. After four hours the Immigration Board told them they had failed to meet the requirements for entry into the United States and were to be returned to Canada immediately.

The two men were bitterly disappointed. They were allowed to see reporters for a few minutes before being escorted back to Canada, and told them they could not understand why they were being returned while von Werra was still at liberty in the United States.

Later, in Washington, the Department of Justice, anticipating a protest from Germany, issued a statement explaining the difference between their case and that of von Werra. " The difference," the statement said, " was that Werra was not arrested until after he had entered the country, whereas the two officers supposedly applied for admission at the border, and after due consideration, were found to be unacceptable."

One sentence in the Department of Justice's statement was of very special significance to von Werra. It was that the Department was deliberating whether he should be " deported to Germany, *or to Canada.*"

This was the first official intimation that the possibility of handing him back to Canada was being seriously considered. It suggested that it was time for von Werra to get moving again.

CHAPTER XVIII

The Last Escape

FOR SEVERAL weeks nothing was heard of von Werra. Then, on 23 April, the news was out. " VON WERRA FLEES " screamed the headlines.

In Washington the Attorney General was quoted as saying that von Werra was in Peru, and was probably trying to reach Germany via the Pacific and the Trans-Siberian railway. He also said that von Werra's action " constituted a flagrant abuse of neutral hospitality which had been invoked on his behalf."

German officials blandly denied all knowledge of his whereabouts. " The last I heard of him ", said the German Consul General, " he was writing his memoirs in Westchester ". Bernhard Lippert, with whom von Werra had been staying told a reporter that the Baron had " gone south on a hunting trip ! "

In fact, he was back in Germany.

The $15,000 (then worth £3,750) bail paid for von Werra's provisional freedom was of course forfeited. There is no other instance in modern times of a government paying such a large sum for the liberty of one prisoner-of-war. What with legal and other expenses, the escape must have cost the German government well over £5,000, but, as the American Press pointed out, his training alone cost far more than that.

It is doubtful whether the Germans were primarily interested in von Werra's worth as a pilot. What they were most concerned about was his value as a source of military information. The cash involved was no real consideration ; they had to balance the value of von Werra's freedom against the deterioration of German-American relations which would result from his jumping bail. The fact that they chose to allow him to abscond shows the true value they placed on him. Governments are not in the habit of lavishing large sums of money and jeopardising international relations for the freedom of an individual prisoner-of-war.

Von Werra was the exception. The Germans knew his value as a source of information. And so did the British.

As a result of von Werra's escape, America's regulations governing escaped prisoners-of-war were at once tightened.

During the nine months that remained before America entered the war, several prisoners crossed the border from Canada, and penetrated deep in the States before surrendering or being arrested. None was allowed to remain.

The final judgment of responsible American opinion on von Werra's behaviour was given by the Attorney-General, in the course of a strongly-worded attack on German Consular officials. He had, he said, positive evidence that they had connived at the escape. " The airman's conduct was unlawful and ungracious . . . In marked contrast to the way he was treated here, American nationals have been seized in Germany without being informed of the charge against them, and detained in prison without right of counsel, communication or bail."

The American Press generally had assumed that von Werra left the United States by ship on 4 April. In fact, he left in the same way he had entered two months earlier—illegally, and on foot.

In America's refusal to give asylum to the two men who escaped from Canada on 22 March German officials saw the writing on the wall. Von Werra was told that as a result of certain new moves in the capital, it was likely that he would soon be handed back to Canada. He was to leave the country illegally at once.

He left New York the same day, 24 March. His departure provides a good example of German disingenuousness. All arrangements were made for him, he was given detailed instructions where to go, what to do and how to behave. But German Consular officials told him that, in view of their position, they were unable to provide him with the necessary cash. However, if he looked behind the cistern in the lavatory, he would find a present from someone who was interested in his case.

Von Werra did so and found $1,000 in notes and a slip of paper bearing a good luck message from " A friend ". He pocketed the money and asked no questions. The cash had not been handed to him directly, and later, Consular officials were able to protest with virtuous indignation that they had not aided von Werra to escape.

The journey to the railway station from the home of the German official where von Werra had been staying, was again in the best cloak-and-dagger tradition.

His two suitcases had been sent ahead to the station. A party of about half a dozen men left the house at night ; only two, von Werra and one other, reached the station, the other four having split off at various points on the journey to lay false trails. There were frequent changes of taxi, doubling back on tracks already laid, entering buildings by one entrance and leaving them by another. The purpose of these elaborate manœuvres was to shake off any F.B.I. or British agents. Apparently they succeeded.

Von Werra left New York alone by train. He travelled south, following a planned itinerary. He made a couple of overnight stops at cities en route, where he was met, taken care of and sent on his way the next morning. A few mornings later he reached El Paso, the largest city on the Rio Grande, at the extreme western tip of Texas. At El Paso there are two toll bridges across the Rio Grande —the Stanton Street Bridge and the Santa Fe Bridge. On the opposite side is the Mexican city of Ciudad Juarez.

Von Werra had been told that control by U.S. authorities of persons and vehicles leaving America across the two bridges was very strict. He also knew that, once past the American check-point, entry into Mexico presented no difficulty. In order to encourage tourists from America, and to enable tired business men to sample the fleshpots of the Mexican border cities without hindrance, entry into the country was unrestricted to a depth of 15 miles south of the border.

Von Werra arrived at El Paso by train at about 5 a.m. He left his two suitcases in the luggage office and made his way at once to one of the bridges crossing the Rio Grande.

He waited. At 6 a.m. Mexican labourers and peasants began to cross into the United States from Ciudad Juarez, on the far bank. They travelled by tram, bicycle and on foot. Some led carts piled with garden produce. They wore battered, sometimes split, broad-rimmed straw hats with high conical crowns, brightly coloured shirts, blue jeans and home-made sandals.

U.S. border police were out in force watching them enter the city. Now and again carts filled with manure trundled past. The bright spring sunshine caught the vapour rising off their loads. The police waved them on hurriedly, screwing up their noses. Von Werra noticed that the few people the police examined were usually those carrying bags or parcels.

He could not hope to get his two suitcases past the control point. He would have to leave them where they were in the station luggage office. It was a wrench, for they were filled with clothing and presents, including nylon stockings, which he had bought in New York for his fiancée and others. There was also a thick, leather-bound album of American press cuttings about his escape, which had been presented to him by a lady admirer in New York. The suitcases were never reclaimed from the luggage office. They may still be there.

Von Werra turned back into El Paso. He was wearing a new suit, a soft grey hat and carried a fawn gaberdine raincoat. After lunch, he found the bazaar district, where he bought a Mexican straw hat, a pair of jeans, a brightly coloured shirt and a pair of sandals. He went into a nearby public park, found some secluded bushes and changed into the clothes he had bought. To get rid of their obvious newness he screwed them up and rubbed them in the dust; the hat he stretched and bent out of shape. As he sauntered away, he wondered who would become the new owner of his Fifth Avenue turn-out.

With the straw hat well down over his eyes, his jacket draped over one shoulder and his new sandals squeaking, he made his way back along Alameda Avenue towards the international bridge.

It was quite like old times, but he felt so ridiculous in the straw hat that he could not keep his face straight. If anyone spoke to him in Spanish he would have to play deaf-and-dumb, as he'd only learned a few words from a phrase book in the train.

The workers started drifting back across the bridge to Ciudad Juarez shortly after 5 p.m. Half an hour later there was a steady stream. Von Werra stood at the edge of the pavement about fifty yards from the check-point, watching from under his broad-rimmed hat. To passers-by he was just another idle, rubber-necking Mexicano. He had an idea and waited his opportunity to put it into effect.

An empty manure cart approached. The carter walked at the

horse's head on the off-side, holding a rein in one hand and a stick in the other. A quick glance in the back. Just the job!

He stepped boldly off the pavement and trailed behind the cart. The smell was appalling. There was a shallow backboard, and on the floor, within reach, was a manure fork—the thing von Werra had been hoping for.

Ten yards to go. The wooden wheels rattled and creaked on the axle. Von Werra hung his jacket over the backboard, picked up the fork and slung it over his shoulder. He was hidden from the carter by the hindquarters of the horse.

At the check-point there was a group of border police standing watching the pedestrians. Von Werra passed within a couple of feet of them.

Once over the bridge he replaced the fork in the back of the cart, picked up his jacket and joined the crowd on the pavement. The driver went on his way ignorant of the fact that he had gained and lost a mate.

A little later von Werra squatted on his haunches, together with a crowd of other straw-hatted figures, on a platform of Ciudad Juarez railway station, waiting for a train to Mexico City, 1,300 miles away.

The train journey from Ciudad Juarez to Mexico City was the strangest von Werra had ever made. There was no glass in the windows of his third-class carriage, which struck him as rather a waste, as this time he had no need to dive out through one of them.

He was a little apprehensive until the train passed the Federal inspection point at Ysleta, twelve miles south of Ciudad Juarez; but, as he had been assured beforehand, the passport inspectors did not bother even to visit the third-class coaches. That was why, with the best part of $1,000 in his pocket, he was travelling so uncomfortably.

The carriage was packed with humanity, chickens and sucking pigs. Despite the ventilation, the smell was atrocious. Passengers changed from station to station, but not the smell.

But his fellow-travellers were childlike, gentle people and shared their food and wine with him as though he were one of the family. With the aid of pictures of himself and news items clipped from American papers, he tried to explain who he was and what he was doing in a third-class carriage.

No escaper ever had a less appreciative, a less comprehending,

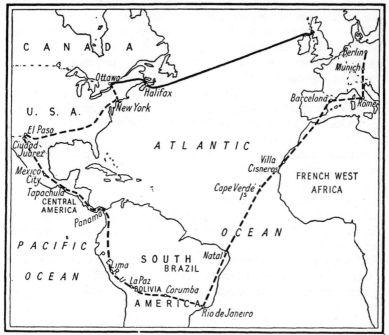

VON WERRA'S ROUND TRIP

audience. They seemed to think that Germany was part of Mexico or the United States; they thought of war in terms of Mexican revolutions. How would you explain escape if you could not explain a prisoner-of-war? If they identified him with the newspaper pictures at all, they probably thought he was a bank robber. They just beamed and passed him the wine jar from time to time.

The journey lasted two days and two nights. The train pulled into the terminus, Buenavista Station, Mexico City, late in the evening of 28 March. The German Embassy in Washington had warned the German Embassy in Mexico City to expect von Werra on that date.

Five minutes after the train arrived, an unwashed, unshaven, smelly little man wearing a crumpled shirt, jeans creased concertina fashion, a Mexican straw hat tilted back on his head and a jacket draped over one shoulder, detached himself from the crowd spilling out of the station. He looked along the rank of parked cars and taxis and suddenly grinned. He had spotted a gleaming Mercedes-Benz, bearing the letters " CD ". The uniformed chauffeur, obviously a German, scanned the crowd, chin in the air. He completely ignored the grubby little Mexicano.

" *Grüss Gott !* "

The chauffeur's head jerked. His mouth opened.

" Oberleutnant Franz von Werra. Any chance of a lift ? "

The chauffeur's face registered distrust, bewilderment, dawning comprehension, pleasure. He clicked his heels, grinned and opened the door quickly with a flourish.

" At the Herr Oberleutnant's service ! Will the Herr Oberleutnant permit me respectfully to welcome him to Mexico City ! "

Von Werra leaned back in the luxuriously upholstered rear seat. There was a faint smell of cigar smoke and perfume. The Mercedes bowled down the broad, straight Avenida de los Insurgentes and into the Paseo de la Reforma, with its wide dual carriage-ways, green trees, grass verges, flower beds and skyscrapers.

He felt a little sad. From now on he had only to obey orders and follow instructions. Everything would be taken care of. He had no further need of initiative.

His escaping days were over.

The next day Oberleutnant Franz von Werra temporarily assumed the identity of Dr. Bernd Natus. The German Embassy in Mexico issued him with a German diplomatic passport in that name, but bearing his own photograph and physical description.

The faked passport has been preserved. It seems to consist partly of faked pages and partly of pages from a genuine diplomatic passport issued in 1936 to a certain Bernd Natus, who returned to Germany from Mexico in 1938. The holder is described as " Student, at present clerical assistant " and as " Son of the Councillor of the German Legation in Mexico."

The transit visas needed by the bogus Bernd Natus for the next part of his journey home via South America, were issued in Mexico City on 29 March by the diplomatic representatives of the various republics concerned.

Von Werra spent one night at the German Embassy in Mexico City. The next morning he went shopping to renew his wardrobe, and in the afternoon he left by car for the ambassador's country house at Cuernavaca, fifty miles south of the city. He spent an enjoyable week-end there, sunbathing, dipping in the swimming pool from time to time, playing with the ambassador's two young children, shooting pigeons and taking the dogs for walks.

On 1 April von Werra left Mexico City by air. Ironically, he travelled by Pan American Airways. Halting that night at Tapachula, on the Mexican-Guatemalan frontier, he arrived at Panama early on 3 April. From Hotel Central, Panama, he wrote to his fiancée : "Everything is clammy with heat and the sunlight is so fierce that I can scarcely open my eyes. I am vexed because the connecting flight to Lima, Peru, has been cancelled for to-day. But to-morrow I shall be there. Another two thousand miles nearer . . . I have been snooping round the local shops trying to find nice things to buy for you. The snag is, I can carry so little luggage by air. I am making tremendous efforts to find the best things for you . . . If it were not for this terrible longing, my journey through the American continent from north to south would be perfect. It is like peeping through a keyhole at a fairyland. Sometimes it is intensely interesting, but the 'flying carpet' never stops and I have to make the most of a glimpse. I am wearing a blue linen suit with short sleeves, and as I can't continue my journey to-day I am dashing about all over the place; but every couple of hours I have to take a cold shower, or I should melt away completely. I have just been bargaining for some carved ivory animals, fifteen pieces in all—elephant, tiger, giraffe, crocodile, etc. I told the Indian I was a German, and as he doesn't like the British in the least, he gave me a special discount and said 'Heil Hitler!' The ivory animals I bought for myself, but at the same time I got you a wonderful cigarette holder . . . Mexico is wonderful. Sun, sand and gigantic cacti. I haven't been able to make out what the donkeys eat. One sees them everywhere. It can hardly be sand, but there seems to be nothing else available . . . Here in Panama I am strictly incognito. The people in Mexico were terribly kind to me, but it's good to be absolutely free again. I'm just going to take another shower. Then I must write a few lines to Mamma and to Moritz.[1] And to-morrow at 5 a m. off I go again."

Von Werra arrived in Lima, Peru, on 5 April. He stayed with

[1] Leutnant Heinrich Sanneman, von Werra's closest friend.

a German diplomat, Herr von Buch, for four days. His arrival in the Peruvian capital was later reported by one of the local papers together with the indignant comment that he had come " to organise subversive activities " and to "undermine the security of the legally constituted régime."

Endorsements in the passport show that von Werra reached La Paz, Bolivia, on 8 April. From there he flew on, via Corumba, in Brazil, to Rio de Janeiro, arriving there on 11 April.

Two days later he left Rio de Janeiro on a three-engined Savoia-Marchetti flying boat of the Italian Lati line. This was one of the last, if not the very last, Lati flight from South America before the service was suspended owing to the war situation.

The aircraft flew up the east coast of Brazil, alighted at Natal for refuelling, then headed out across the South Atlantic for the Cape Verde Islands. It reached Barcelona on 16 April and finally Rome on 17 April.

What happened to von Werra in Rome is recounted by Herr W. Müller-Clemm, formerly a Lieutenant-Colonel in the Luftwaffe, who at that time was Assistant to General Ritter von Pohl, German Air Attaché in Rome.

It should be remembered that Müller-Clemm is writing of events as they struck him at the time. He had no reason to doubt what von Werra told him and it is not unnatural that he should have been won over by von Werra's charm as so many others had been with less excuse.

In the middle of April 1941, he writes, the Air Attaché at the German Embassy in Rome received a radio signal in code from his opposite number in Madrid, informing him that a certain Doctor Bernd Natus would arrive at Ostia, Rome, that evening, on a commercial plane from Barcelona. It was requested that he be met and helped in every possible way.

Neither the Air Attaché, General Ritter von Pohl, nor any member of his staff had ever heard of Dr. Bernd Natus. The whole business was obscure and mystifying. As Assistant to the Air Attaché, I was instructed to meet the stranger at the airport. I had just enough time to get out to Ostia, the seaplane base, before the plane was due to arrive. After a wait of about five minutes we saw the aircraft coming in to alight on the water.

The passengers were shepherded into a building to attend to the customary landing formalities.

As one invariably does under such circumstances, I had formed a mental picture of the appearance of the mysterious doctor, but none of the passengers who disembarked from the seaplane bore any resemblance to my preconceived notions. However, I noticed a young man looking closely at me and my uniform as he came out of the aircraft, and I gathered that he was the man for whom I was waiting. Sure enough, when he came out of the building after completing the passport and luggage examination, he walked straight towards me.

" Have I the honour of addressing Doctor Bernd Natus ? " I inquired.

The stranger smiled and said, " Yes, sir, I am——"

I introduced myself. Hardly were the words out of my mouth when the young man jumped to attention.

" Herr Oberstleutnant," he said, " I am Oberleutnant von Werra ! "

These few words were at once a report, a fanfare and a cry of triumph. They kindled a flame of the greatest, purest joy.

" *Werra !* " I cried. Never will I forget that handshake !

After his unique, modern Odyssey, this young man had reached allied territory and was safe.

His escape had succeeded !

We drove straight to the Embassy. Nothing von Werra could have asked us to do for him would have been too difficult, if it gave him pleasure. His first wish—" A German passport made out *in my own name* ! " Away with false papers ! He wanted at long last to be himself again. Well, that was easy enough to arrange.[1]

On our arrival I had immediately got through on the house phone to the Ambassador, von Mackensen, who was still busy in his office despite the lateness of the hour. Mackensen, who before he joined the diplomatic service had been an officer of the First Regiment of Guards, at Potsdam, interrupted an important conference in order personally to extend the heartiest

---

[1] In fact, for security reasons, von Werra's identity was concealed even from German passport officials and, to his disgust, he arrived at Munich airport, and later, Tempelhof airport, Berlin, as Bernd Natus.

welcome to the young officer who had returned crowned with so much glory.

Meanwhile, I arranged for all the necessary papers to be completed to enable him to continue his journey without let or hindrance. His arrival in Rome had been signalled Top Secret to Luftwaffe Headquarters in Berlin.

I hardly need say that I insisted on his staying with me as my guest. Many were the wondrous tales he told. All attempts to persuade him to rest awhile in Rome after the last and doubtless tiring lap (from Rio de Janeiro) of his flight from captivity, failed to turn him from his overwhelming urge to fulfil two duties : to rejoin his unit, and to see his mother, who was living in Cologne. These were reasons we had to respect, and dearly though we should have loved to have him stay with us and to spoil him a little longer, we saw it was impossible to make him change his mind.

Von Werra radiated a charm such as one is seldom privileged to meet with, of the kind that one remembers with a sense of wonder. Open and unassuming, endowed with the sunniest of natures, he made even the most fantastic of his adventures sound quite ordinary by the simple, matter-of-fact way in which he related it ; and he himself never noticed that it was precisely this way of relating a story that evoked the deepest feelings of friendship and respect for him in his hearers. It was late indeed before we could bear to part with him for the night.

The next morning, von Werra wanted to be away on the final stage of his journey by the very first plane on which I could wangle him a seat. He longed to be home at last. After I had completed the arrangements for his journey, we had one final, festive little meal together. There were no guests to do him honour. Such was his wish.

On Guidonia Aerodrome we met General Ritter von Pohl, the Air Attaché, who was to fly in the same aircraft as von Werra. I presented von Werra and requested the General to be good enough to smooth out any possible unforeseen difficulty that might arise when the plane arrived in Germany, if von Werra's papers were found to be not quite in order. Very disappointed that the General agreed to this request shortly, coldly, without the slightest show of enthusiasm, I felt obliged to make some apology to von Werra and to beg his indulgence. He dismissed the incident with a gesture. He understood these prosaic, phlegmatic brass hats, and had had to deal with them before. In any case, what did it matter now? The propeller of the aircraft turned. The last, the very last, little lap of his flight from captivity to freedom, over the lagoons of Venice and over the Alps to Germany, was about to begin. Radiantly happy and excited, he shook my hand.

A special signal had been received from Luftwaffe Operations Staff to the effect that no hint of Oberleutnant von Werra's safe and successful return to Germany was to be given to the Press, or made public in any way. Thus there was no crowd of admirers and well-wishers at the airport to see him off. The passengers entered the plane and took their seats. I waved once more towards it as it taxied away. A few seconds later it was airborne.

One of the great, modest and faithful sons of the Fatherland was returning home. It seemed as though he were being borne by his own wings.

Von Werra reached Berlin on 18 April. Five days later Colonel Hubert Stetham, Director of Internment Operations in Canada, announced that warships had been ordered to intercept the ship on which he had escaped.

On 29 April, when von Werra had been home nearly a fortnight, a Canadian cruiser halted the U.S. liner *President Garfield* bound for Japan from San Francisco.

A boarding party found no trace of von Werra. But they took off four German civil airline pilots on their way home to Germany. They were taken back to Canada and interned. What they thought of von Werra is not recorded.

CHAPTER XIX

Return of a Hero

VON WERRA's reception in Germany was an anti-climax. There were no reporters, no photographers, no flowers, no toasts, no autograph books to sign, no hero worship. The red carpet of which he had dreamed did not materialise.

The reason was simple. For security reasons the Germans took elaborate precautions to keep his return a secret.

He arrived in Berlin, not as Oberleutnant Franz von Werra, acclaimed as a hero of the Third Reich, but as Dr. Bernd Natus, ignored as a nonentity—and a bogus nonentity at that. His return was not mentioned by the German Press or radio. He was not allowed to see or communicate with any but his relatives and closest friends, and even they were ordered to tell no one of his return.

Even when, a few weeks later, this secrecy was relaxed, and von Werra began to reap some of the pleasures of fame—receptions, parties, flowers and adulation—the ban on Press publicity remained in force. The German public as a whole was kept in ignorance of his return.

A few weeks after he got back, von Werra went to the Reich Chancellery to receive from Hitler's hands the Knight's Cross awarded him for his attack he claimed to have made on a British airfield.

Hitler congratulated him on his escape and on the brilliant exploit which had earned him his decoration. It had shown his ability, said Hitler, " to turn a tactically unfavourable situation to his own advantage."

In the midst of so many official engagements, von Werra did not forget his fiancée. He bought a large second-hand sports car and, as soon as he could get some leave, took her on a brief holiday to Poland. It was not only for pleasure.

Hitler had promised that after the war, warriors who had been awarded the Oak Leaves to the Knight's Cross of the Iron Cross and higher honours would be given estates in conquered countries. Von Werra had not yet won the Leaves to his Knight's Cross, but he was supremely confident that he would do so. He thought he would see what Poland had to offer in the way of estates.

Describing the trip, his fiancée wrote :

" It was a mixture of the ghastly and the amusing. All the places we saw were in a terrible state of disrepair—it was impossible that they could have been reduced to that state by military occupation. We drove around but could not make up our minds whether we wanted to breed cattle or fish. I wanted a lake and streams with fish and also a house that had a tower. He wanted land and facilities for breeding horses . . ."

Von Werra also found time to pay a two-day visit to his old squadron, which was once more stationed in the Pas de Calais.

Von Werra's escape had consequences out of all proportion to its significance as an individual feat of daring.

Within a few days of his return to Berlin he was attached to the Intelligence Branch of G.A.F. Operations Staff. The next few weeks he spent writing reports and answering questions.

In May the Intelligence Branch published a twelve-page booklet dealing with his experiences as a prisoner-of-war. It was an amplification, and a permanent record for everyday official use, of the reports he had prepared in America, and became the Luftwaffe's standard guide to aircrew and P.O.W. security. It was still in use, with only minor modifications, in July 1944.

Until von Werra's escape, German propaganda alleging that Nazi prisoners were ill-treated had played right into the hands of British interrogators. The opening sentence of von Werra's report gave the lie to stories of British brutality :

" Generally speaking, British treatment of German war prisoners is unexceptionable. Such isolated instances of maltreatment as have occurred have resulted from wrong behaviour on the part of the prisoners concerned in the first, decisive moments of captivity."

The information he took back to Berlin was not confined to matters of interest to the Luftwaffe. For instance, as a result of his talks with captive U-boat officers he was able to give the German Navy valuable details about how certain U-boats were sunk—destroyer manœuvres prior to attacks, depth-charge patterns and intervals, and certain facts about Asdic, the Royal Navy's underwater listening apparatus.

He reported that British interrogators showed an extraordinary interest in prisoners' Field Post numbers, often taking great pains to get this apparently harmless and useless scrap of information. When the Germans looked into the matter they realised that the British could deduce a prisoner's unit and its location from his Field Post number. The system of numbering was changed forthwith.

All arms of the Wehrmacht, the intelligence agencies and other departments connected with the German war effort were anxious to obtain information from von Werra. He was kept extremely busy.

Reich Marshal Goering sent for him and ordered him to visit all R.A.F. prisoner-of-war camps in Germany. He was to compare conditions with those in British camps, and instruct German camp commandants on the anti-escape measures used by the British.

Goering promoted von Werra to Hauptmann (Flight Lieutenant) in recognition of his escape. The Reich Marshal was apparently surprised and tickled to find that von Werra was so small, but jokingly remarked that it did not matter—he was now famous and could marry any rich and beautiful German woman he liked.

Several books about British escapes from German prison camps mention von Werra's tour. He is reported to have commiserated with R.A.F. prisoners at Barth camp, he was seen at Sagan, and P. R. Reid mentions his visit to Colditz Castle in *The Colditz Story*. Many British P.O.W. bear witness to the introduction of additional security measures following a visit from von Werra. Judging by the continuing rate of escapes, they do not appear to have been much of a deterrent.

However, his visit to the German Air Interrogation Centre had far-reaching consequences which lasted throughout the war. This was the notorious Dulag Luft—transit camp for aircrew at Oberursel, near Frankfurt-on-Main. Dulag Luft was to Allied airmen what the British Air Interrogation Centre at Cockfosters had been to von Werra and other German aircrew captured during the Battle of Britain.

Although Dulag Luft had already been placed under command of the Luftwaffe's Operational Intelligence Branch by the time of von Werra's visit, the Germans had not yet appreciated the immense importance of interrogation as a source of military information. Owing to the small scale of air operations over Germany and the occupied countries up to that time, relatively few R.A.F. men had been taken prisoner, and their interrogation at Dulag Luft was of a superficial, almost farcical, nature.

Von Werra " sat in " at these interrogations. " I would rather be interrogated by half a dozen German inquisitors than by one R.A.F. expert," he reported to Reich Marshal Goering.

As a result of his visit, Dulag Luft was remodelled and both British organisation and methods of interrogation were adopted.

Writing of conditions generally in German prisoner-of-war camps, von Werra made it clear in his report to Goering that he would rather be interned in Britain than in Germany. He made a number of recommendations for improving the lot of British prisoners. One copy of these recommendations is said to have been returned to him with Goering's signed comment " *Wird gemacht* " —" will be carried out," scrawled on the first page.

Deutscher Verlag, the German publishers, had taken up von Werra's offer, made by cable from New York, for the rights of his autobiography. He was now under contract to them, and had drawn substantial advance royalties.

Von Werra had an interview with Goebbels—whom he had already met at his investiture by Hitler—at which plans for exploiting his career and escape for propaganda purposes were discussed. Goebbels agreed that a working script of the autobiography should be finished and submitted for consideration and approval. The Propaganda Ministry would then be in a better position to decide the best ways of exploiting the story. Goebbels was thinking especially of the cinema and radio.

The " autobiography ", was not, in fact, written by von Werra but by a German journalist named Joachim Bartsch, whom von Werra hired as a ghost-writer.

The book was compiled in a tearing hurry under the most hectic conditions. Von Werra was caught up in a vortex of official and social engagements. He was in great demand and everybody wanted to see him at once.

Bartsch followed von Werra round for weeks, taking down the story during hurried meals in Wilhelmstrasse canteens, in trains, in passenger aircraft, at parties, and late at night over the telephone. Later, when von Werra was posted to the Russian front, he pulled strings to get Bartsch temporarily assigned to his unit, and there he continued dictating—at night, during moves from one part of the front to another, and between sorties.

Von Werra had few notes and had to rely almost entirely on his memory. Bartsch himself knew none of the places or people involved in the story. It is hardly surprising that the resultant manuscript was a formless hotch-potch, full of platitudes and loose ends, replete with every kind of inaccuracy and larded with Luftwaffe slang. But von Werra had in mind the reading public of wartime Nazi Germany, a public whose faith in Hitler and victory was as yet unshaken by any serious military reverse.

This, for example, is how he describes what happened in the Adjutant's office at Hucknall after he had surrendered and revealed his identity :

Nobody moved. Behind me the rapid breathing of the group of officers. In front of me the bloodless face of Boniface. He looked as though he'd had a stroke.

I looked round to the officers, bowed and said :

" That's all ! "

Boniface raised himself by gripping the edge of the desk, straightened himself and came towards me. He put his arms round me in a wordless embrace. Then he slapped me madly on the back. All the other officers cheered, as though at a football match.

" Three cheers ! " they cried, and " Clever boy ! . . ."

Boniface suddenly became quiet. The reaction had set in. He suddenly realised the danger in which he had placed himself as Station Adjutant. He fell back into the swivel chair at the desk.

" Good gracious ! " he gasped. " If I had got there a couple of minutes later . . . It doesn't bear thinking about."

" Well," I said, " you *would* send a vehicle specially to fetch me . . ."

" Good gracious ! "

" Never mind," I added. " It was I who was caught."

Then everybody started shouting at once :

—" Don't take it too hard ! "

—" We'll come and see you at the camp ! "

—" You were splendid ! "

—" We'll bring you some whisky, too ! . . ."

Meanwhile, Boniface . . . was trying to get through to the War Office. . . .

" *I found him sitting in a bloody Hurricane !* " he cried at one point. He removed the receiver from his ear so that we could hear quite distinctly the " Oooh ! " of the man at the other end of the line.

Roars of laughter. Exactly the same thing happened when he rang up the Intelligence Service (sic) . . .

Again, when he rang up the police, his story was greeted with a long " Oooh ! " and we all laughed again.

More and more people came into the room to see me . . . There was a constant coming and going—like a film star's reception.

Even in the title of the book, von Werra could not resist improving on reality. He called it *Meine Flucht aus England—My Escape From England*, though he escaped from Canada ; as it happened, no German prisoner succeeded in escaping from England during the war.

But in one important and refreshing way the von Werra manuscript is unique : for a book written by a member of the German Armed Forces during World War II, and especially at that early stage, it is not steeped in anti-British sentiment nor cluttered up with ideological clichés and claptrap. Its tone throughout is surprisingly friendly and appreciative of the British. When one considers the *post-war* books by ex-Luftwaffe men such as Werner Baumbach, Heinz Knoke, General Ramcke and Hans Rudel, one is impressed by von Werra's fairness and absence of political bigotry.

Its fairness was in fact one of the reasons why the Propaganda Ministry banned its publication. It was considered pro-British.

Eugen Hadamowsky, chief programme director of the Nazi radio and one of Goebbels's aides, who had been deputed to look after the von Werra story, said that the entire book would have to be rewritten from a positively anti-British standpoint. For instance, where von Werra had described how he was given a cup of tea by a policeman after his recapture in the Lake District, Hadamowsky wanted to have him beaten up by " Jewish police."

Publication was, in fact, prohibited on security grounds. Even a year later, when the manuscript was resubmitted, the German High Command was unwilling to let it be known how much information von Werra had brought back with him, and publication was forbidden for the duration of the war. After the war the manuscript remained hidden in the loft of a house in Kitzbühel until the authors of this book asked Frau von Werra to let them see it.

Preliminary plans were made for the production of two films about von Werra's escape, one a full-length feature film, the other a documentary designed to be shown to German military personnel. Von Werra stipulated that his fiancée should play a leading role in the feature film.

A correspondence file dealing with these preliminary plans shows that the Ufa film company wanted Sacha Guitry, whose film *Le roman d'un tricheur* had just had a great success in Germany, to write the scenario and commentary for the feature film ; but there is no evidence that he accepted the commission or that he was formally approached.

But the ban on publication of von Werra's own story of his exploits did not prevent accounts of his prowess in the air appearing, with a variety of embellishments, in collections of war stories, popular works on the Luftwaffe, boys' annuals, etc.

In the middle of June von Werra flew a Messerschmitt again for the first time. Intelligence Branch of G.A.F. Operations Staff had given him permission to make practice flights at Werneuchen Fighter School " whenever his duties elsewhere allow."

A week later, on 22 June 1941, Germany invaded Russia. Von Werra remained in Berlin, answering questions, writing reports, giving lectures. The conquest of Russia was regarded as a foregone conclusion—a matter only of weeks. Luftwaffe pilots, especially fighter pilots, approached the campaign as though it were money for old rope. Von Werra read of the tremendous scores fighter pilots on the Eastern Front were knocking up, and fumed with frustration.

At the time he was shot down over England, he had been in

the top ten with thirteen accredited victories. Now the top aces had about sixty, while pilots he had never heard of were up in the forties. He had been left hopelessly behind. At the end of a fortnight's persistent wire-pulling, he finally had his way. He was posted to the Russian front as Commanding Officer of the First *Gruppe* of No. 53 Fighter *Geschwader*—famous as the " Ace of Spades " *Geschwader*.

At that early stage of the campaign the front was fluid and von Werra's unit was constantly on the move. Squadrons were pressed forward with tremendous speed in order to give the advancing ground forces maximum and continuous support.

In August von Werra's *Geschwader* was withdrawn from Russia to be re-equipped with a new Mark of Me. 109, the F-4. During his few weeks at the front, von Werra had been officially credited with eight more air victories—bringing his supposed total to twenty-one.

From Mannheim he went on leave. It was to be the last leave of his life. It was also his honeymoon. He was married at Beuron, the little village in Southern Germany where he had been brought up. The honeymoon was spent in Italy.

In September von Werra's *Gruppe* was moved to the coast of Holland, and his wife went with him. They rented a converted fisherman's cottage by the sea. Here, Frau von Werra and her husband—in his off duty time—worked on the revision of his book.

The role of von Werra's *Gruppe* was purely coastal defence. Von Werra was in any case forbidden to take part in operations against Britain lest he should once more fall into British hands.

After taking off from Katwijk on patrol, von Werra would fly over the cottage, dipping his brand new Me. 109 in greeting to his wife.

On the morning of 25 October, leading a patrol of three fighters, he dipped over the cottage as usual and turned out to sea. Twenty miles out, his engine developed a fault. Before the other two pilots realised there was anything wrong, his aircraft tipped forward and dropped like a stone into the sea.

Although air-sea rescue launches, seaplanes and salvage vessels ordered out by Reich Marshal Goering had sped to the scene, no trace was found of von Werra or the aircraft.

Von Werra's death was not reported in the Press. Only a few

days before, General Ernst Udet, fighter ace of World War I, and Colonel Werner Mölders, top fighter ace of World War II, had been reported killed. Perhaps it was felt that the announcement of the death of a third air ace and national favourite within so short a time might prove too severe a blow for German morale. When the announcement was made, nearly a month later, it was stated that von Werra had been killed in action—in Russia, according to some newspapers, leading his *Gruppe* in attack after attack until he met a hero's death.

In contrast to this was the report of the Court of Inquiry set up by the German Air Safety Branch to investigate the loss of von Werra's aircraft ; it said that the accident was due to engine failure and the pilot's carelessness.

Either way, the result was the same: this time there was no escape.

THE END

APPENDIX I

In the Archives of the Nobility in Vienna there is a file marked " Von Werra ". It contains a document, deposed in 1806 by Ferdinand von Werra, of Leuk (Loèche), in the Republic of Wallis (Valais),[1] petitioning for recognition of his noble quality and antecedents by the conferment on him of an Imperial title. The petitioner mentions that his family's records and deeds had been lost in the course of the many wars and disturbances to which the province had been subjected. The document is witnessed by the Lord Lieutenant of the Republic, who testified that the von Werras (formerly Werren) had from time immemorial been regarded as hereditary nobility, had always held high office, indeed a position of supreme honour in the Republic of Wallis, and had never married beneath them. Ferdinand von Werra was stated to be married to the Baroness von Storkalper, to hold the offices of Right Honourable Lord Steward and Chief Justice of the Worthy Council of Leuk, and to be the legitimate son of the Hereditary Junker Josef von Werra, Standard Bearer to the said Council.[2] In response to this petition the Emperor Franz was graciously pleased to raise Ferdinand von Werra to the rank of Imperial Freiherr.

Franz von Werra (christened François Gustave de Werra) was born in Leuk in 1914, and was the eighth child and fourth son of Léo de Werra, who, in spite of the honour bestowed on his ancestor, had fallen on evil days. A short time after the birth of François, Léo de Werra was financially ruined.

As a result of the *débâcle*, François and the next youngest child, a girl, were adopted by an old friend of the family, Baroness Luisa von Haber, and went to live with her at Beuron, Kreis Sigmaringen, in Southern Germany. Her husband was Major Oswald Carl, a cavalry officer. They had no children of their own. François became Franz and the " de " was translated to " von ". He and his sister grew up looking upon Baroness von Haber as their mother. As far as Franz was concerned, the break with his own family was complete and final.

From an early age Franz displayed the tremendous vitality and

[1] Formerly part of the German Empire. Bonaparte declared Valais an independent republic in 1802, but later incorporated it with France. It was freed by the Austrians in 1813 and became a full member of the Swiss Confederation two years later.
[2] The population of Leuk in 1935 was 2,000.

restlessness that were to remain two of his most marked characteristics throughout his life. But the Baroness was as severe and exacting as he was wilful and exuberant. His childhood was abnormal and not always happy; relations between the Baroness and her husband were strained and she eventually divorced him.

When Franz was in his early teens, he ran away from home, possibly as a result of a domestic crisis. He went to Hamburg where he spent several days, hungry and destitute, trying to find a shipping company in need of a cabin-boy. He was taken on by the Hamburg-Amerika Line. Just before he sailed he wrote giving the news to his foster-mother.

When the ship docked in New Orleans, a representative of the shipping company's local agents came on board and handed him frantic cables from his foster-parents. The agent had himself received cabled instructions from Hamburg to take Franz off the ship and look after him until he could be put on the first vessel bound for Germany. Thus began one of the happiest holidays in Franz von Werra's life.

There can be no doubt that the trip to New Orleans played an important part in the development of his character. It gave him self-assurance and tended to confirm his belief that he was rather special; it encouraged him to think that no matter what he did, somehow or another he would always land on his feet. Above all, it whetted his appetite for adventure, and fortified his ambition to achieve great things with his life.

The time came for Franz to board a ship for Germany. If his return home brought forth tears and reproaches, he was welcomed back to school as a hero. He was called upon to give a lecture on his experiences and impressions before the whole school. It was his first taste of fame and popularity.

He was more than ever confident now that he would make his mark in the world. But he was to find disillusion. He left school shortly before the Nazis seized control of Germany. There was mass unemployment. The country seethed with industrial and political unrest. In order to live (he had now left home for good) he had to take whatever casual work he could find. For some time he was a jobbing gardener, and then he took regular work as a locksmith's mate. He remained in this trade for about two years. It was a far cry from the life of action, excitement and adventure for which he craved, the more since his trip to America.

Then Hitler and the Nazi Party came into power. In 1934 conscription was introduced in Germany. The following year Hitler and Goering announced the formation of the Luftwaffe which they had already been building up under cover. To the youth of Germany, who had known only hunger, hardship and frustration, the picture of life in the German Air Force painted by official propaganda was like a dazzling vision.

Franz volunteered as a private. After two years' basic training he was selected as an officer candidate for flying duties. His vitality, dare-devilry and individualism made him an obvious choice for further training as a fighter pilot. He was commissioned as Leutnant in September 1938 and given his first operational posting—to No. 3 Fighter *Geschwader*, then in process of formation.

Von Werra soon got the measure of the Luftwaffe and realised that it was useless to wait patiently for merit to be recognised and expect virtue to bring its own reward. The thing that impressed was dash and aggressiveness, plus a touch of dare-devilry. In peacetime there were relatively few opportunities for exhibiting these qualities, and one had to do the best one could with air exercises, mock battles, target practice and official and unofficial races. Then there were various strictly pro-hibited sports, such as diving under bridges, treating one's girl-friend to a free display of aerobatics over her home, or careering across an airfield in a galvanised bath towed by a wealthy fellow-pilot in a sports car. *The important thing was to get oneself talked about.*

He built up a picture of what the Luftwaffe wanted its fighter pilots to be and did his best to personify the type. Judging by the comments of his fellow pilots, he took to the part well.

It was to aid him in this role that von Werra called in his noble antecedents. Leutnant Franz von Werra became Leutnant Baron Franz von Werra.

Although Hitler had an aversion to aristocratic titles and planned to replace the old German nobility by a new *élite* of National Socialist warrior knights and deserving Party men, the ancient ranks had lost none of their glamour and snob value. In the officer caste of the German Armed Forces, National Socialism notwithstanding, it was still useful to have a handle to one's name.

Neither the German High command nor the Press ever accorded von Werra his title. This was not due to any general ruling; hundreds of Luftwaffe officers genuinely entitled to use the title *Freiherr* were accorded it in official communiqués.

To do von Werra justice, he had been encouraged by his foster-mother to believe in his noble birth and to be proud of it. A coronet was embroidered above his initials on his linen and personal possessions, and was engraved on his visiting card. But he must have known that his use of the title *Freiherr*, bestowed more than a century before by a defunct monarchy on a citizen of a democratic republic (Switzerland has no noble titles)—was, to say the least, highly questionable: the more so as it was claimed by a descendant who had become an adopted citizen of National Socialist Germany.

Years of political indoctrination, the absorbing of false ideals and values, now helped still further to warp von Werra's imagination. Superficially, the militarists may have "licked him into shape", they may have "made a man of him", but they fostered rather than cured his adolescent romanticism and conceit. He saw himself as an exceptional human being, a highly romantic figure destined to play a highly romantic role in life. To him, it was not only natural that such a figure should possess a noble title, it was indispensable.

It is interesting to see how his various commanding officers reacted to his personality. One wrote: "Werra has a mature personality with a degree of self-assurance that is quite remarkable. He is somewhat inclined to be arrogant and to have grandiose ideas, and therefore needs to be held in close check." But another wrote: "He is the 'Fighter Type': extremely dashing, good-looking and humorous. Absolutely reliable. Some of his pranks misfire, but it is impossible to be mad with him. He would cut off his arm for his commanding officer."

One of the "pranks" misfired so badly that it might well have had fatal consequences. In June 1939, von Werra, stunting as usual, crash-landed on his unit's airfield at Koenigsberg. The nose of the Me. 109 was buried in the ground but luckily did not catch fire. Unable to move, von Werra was lifted from the wreckage and taken to hospital, where he was found to be suffering from spinal injuries. It looked as if that was to be the end of his career in the Luftwaffe. He lay on his back for several weeks, fretting his heart out.

Periodically he was visited by his commanding officer, Oberleutnant Wilhelm Balthasar. Though barely his senior in years, Balthasar had already achieved all that von Werra longed for; he was a national hero as a result of a record-breaking flight round Africa and dazzling exploits as a fighter ace with the Condor Legion in the Spanish Civil War. Glad as von Werra always was to hear news of the squadron and of his friends, he found it hard to stomach the reproach implicit in the two Franco decorations and the Spanish Cross in gold with diamonds which decorated Balthasar's chest.

On one of his visits Balthasar brought along a companion—a girl whom he had met at a party, and who he thought might lift von Werra out of his depression. Von Werra fell in love with her at first sight. She was to become his wife.

With a new interest in life, an added reason to overcome his injuries, von Werra made rapid progress. He passed a medical board just in time to take part in the Polish campaign which opened at the end of August.

By the time of the Battle of Britain, von Werra had become fairly typical of German fighter pilots of the period. Up till then the Luftwaffe had gone from victory to victory, and had had things almost all its own way. The back of the Polish Air Force had been broken in one day's operations; the small Norwegian Air Force had been destroyed virtually in one raid ; the Dutch, Belgian and French Air Forces had been smashed and the Royal Air Force driven from the Continent in a matter of weeks. Mesmerised by their easy successes, German pilots went into the Battle of Britain feeling certain of their invincibility and sure that final victory in the West was but a hand's stretch away. Time was getting short. In a few weeks the whole show would be over. There was a sense of urgency abroad, which produced a scrambling for honours before it was too late.

To von Werra it seemed that there were only a few weeks left in which he could realise his ambitions and become Baron von Werra, the fighter ace.

APPENDIX II

THE FOLLOWING report by War Correspondent Harry Gehm appeared in the *Berliner Zeitung* on Wednesday, 4 September 1940, under the heading " German Fighter Pilot's Daring Exploit Over England " :

An audacious single-handed attack on an enemy airfield was carried out on 28 August 1940 by Oberleutnant von W.

After shooting down one enemy fighter during an air battle over the Thames estuary, he lost contact with his formation and then found he was flying near an enemy fighter base. Boldly resolute but coolly calculating, Oberleutnant von W. attacked three aircraft that were going in to land, after making it appear that he also was about to touch down. Two of the three aircraft crashed. He then proceeded to destroy five more aircraft and a petrol tanker on the airfield. Alone, and using his last reserves of petrol, Oberleutnant von W. then broke through the curtain of anti-aircraft fire over the aerodrome and through the ring of attacking enemy fighters and finally landed unhurt on the forward airfield on which his unit is based.

Nearly an hour overdue

Once again the fighter *Geschwader* had been ordered to carry out an offensive patrol over Britain. Most of the aircraft taking part had already returned from their mission. There had been a fierce air battle with Spitfires, eight of them having been reported shot down by pilots of the *Geschwader*. But three of the pilots had not yet returned, one of them being the Adjutant of the Second *Gruppe*, the debonair Oberleutnant von W., the favourite of officers and men alike.

A report is received from the air-sea rescue service : one of the missing pilots has been picked up in the Channel and another has made an emergency landing on the coast. Neither of these pilots is Oberleutnant von W.

It is now more than half an hour since the last of the other aircraft returned. Another call is put through to the air-sea rescue service. They have nothing further to report. None of the other pilots noticed anything in the course of the sweep over England that would shed any light on what happened to their missing comrade. There has been no reply to the calls made to him over the radio.

Everybody is thoroughly depressed. The fact that the destruction of eight enemy aircraft has been confirmed gives cold comfort. Even Simba, the lion cub mascot of the *Gruppe*, seems to sense that his master is overdue and slinks snarling under the H.Q. staff car.

Hours have passed since the aircraft took off on their mission. By now, the last drop of petrol must have been used up. All hope for the return of the Adjutant of the Second *Gruppe* must be abandoned. Officially he will be listed as " Missing ". An air of depression prevails. But radio watch is to be maintained, just in case . . .

Transmitter put out of action

Suddenly a Messerschmitt 109 roars over the airfield waggling its wings. Everybody dashes out of the tents and huts and stares upwards. To many of them it seems like a miracle . . .

" It's him ! It's him !—and he's made a kill ! "

The word spreads over the airfield and everybody who has a moment to spare hurries over to the H.Q. hut—the *Kommandeur*, pilots and ground crew in their black denim blouses.

The aircraft touches down and taxies across the wide airfield. Everyone expected that the faithful Me. 109 would be riddled with holes, but only three can be found in the wings. However, a radio mechanic makes a discovery : the aircraft's transmitter has been hit and put out of action. So that's why contact could not be made with the pilot!

Meanwhile, Oberleutnant von W. has climbed out of the cockpit and is surrounded by his comrades. He comes to attention before the *Gruppenkommandeur*.

" Oberleutnant von W. reporting his return from operations over enemy territory. Three enemy aircraft shot down, five definitely destroyed on the ground and others probably destroyed by fire."

The pleasure this astounding success causes can scarcely be imagined. Here stands a man who only a few moments ago was believed to be dead. One expected to hear that he had been hard put to it to evade a superior enemy force and had only just managed to limp home. But he reports having shot down three enemy planes and having destroyed five more on the ground! Astonishment increases as Oberleutnant von W., still standing in the middle of a group by his aircraft, begins to describe his experiences in his racy, south German manner.

Looped in cloud

" First there was a frenzied scrap over the Thames estuary. Up till then we had kept in formation. Suddenly a Spitfire got on to my tail. I nearly came to a sticky end, but as luck would have it, just at that moment the fellow's guns jammed. I immediately put the nose of my aircraft down and went into a steep dive. The Englishman followed me down. Into the clouds! I looped the loop in the clouds in such a way that at the end of the manœuvre my adversary was just ahead of me. I gave him a long burst of machine-gun fire. All at once he caught fire and went hurtling to the ground! "

That was Oberleutnant von W.'s first combat of the day. It was sheer luck that his opponent's guns jammed just at the crucial moment, but then, where would any flyer be without luck ? After replying to several routine questions the Oberleutnant continued his account as follows :

Six Hurricanes below me

" Meanwhile, I had come down to about 500 metres and was circling around on my own. It was hopeless to try to rejoin my formation ; and in view of the Spitfires stooging about in the clouds above me, not only hopeless but suicidal. So I went down to well below cloud base. Suddenly I noticed a formation of six aircraft just below me. They were flying slowly and had their ' feet ' (undercarriages) down as though they were about to land.

" ' Watch your step ! ' I said to myself, ' those are Hurricanes and if you're not careful, you've had it !'

" Then I saw other aircraft taxi-ing or parked on the ground below and I realised I was over an enemy fighter base. In order to make myself as inconspicuous as possible, I too lowered my wheels and flew close behind the six Hurricanes as though I were part of the formation and about to land. As we circled low over the aerodrome waiting for permission to land I was able to get a good view of the lay-out below, and I particularly noted the direction in which other aircraft taxied and disappeared after landing.

" We turned in for the final approach. After the third of the six aircraft in front of me touched down, I suddenly retracted my undercarriage, opened the throttle and attacked the remaining three airborne aircraft. The first crashed immediately and the second went down after a short squirt from close range. Unfortunately, the third Hurricane had already touched down before I could attack it, so although I destroyed it, I cannot claim to have shot it down.

Single-handed attack on airfield

" I roared over the aerodrome at zero feet in the direction taken by aircraft that had landed previously.

" I saw a large petrol tanker ahead of me. I flew straight at it, pressing the gun button. The tanker blew up. Several aircraft were lined up behind it. I blazed away at them with my guns. Then I noticed a huge green tent. There must be something interesting under that, I thought, so I gave it the works, too.

" After I had accomplished all that I was curious to see the effect of my attacks. I flew in a wide sweep over the airfield and took a good look at the mess below. It was a sight worth seeing! Petrol was pouring out of the tanker I had shot up and all around was a sea of flames. Two aircraft behind it were already ablaze and those nearby were about to catch fire at any moment. The tent was already alight.

" In the meantime, conditions over the airfield were beginning to get unhealthy. Light anti-aircraft guns were firing at me rather pointedly. It was high time to get going. I ran the gauntlet of the defences to the Thames estuary and then crossed the Channel only a few feet above sea level. I arrived back here using the drops of juice in my tank."

The foregoing account (taken down at the time by the war correspondent who happened to be on the spot) does not really do justice to the greatness and audacity of the exploit of this young Luftwaffe officer, whose previous five air victories had already earned him the Iron Cross, Class I and Class II. He was on his own over enemy territory more than 100 kilometres from his home base; his radio transmitter had been put out of action and he had to depend entirely on his own skill and courage. Yet he attacked a greatly superior enemy force over its own lair, shot down three British fighters, destroyed others on the ground and shot up airfield installations. And he did all that after he himself had narrowly escaped being shot down ! That takes nerve ! That is an exploit that deserves to be recorded.

The German Press announced the award of the Knight's Cross of the Iron Cross to von Werra at the beginning of January 1941. The following citation appeared in the *Völkischer Beobachter* of 8 January 1941 :

The Führer and Supreme Commander of the German Armed Forces has authorised the award of the *Ritterkreuz* to a number of gallant airmen. The heroic deeds for which they have been decorated are described below :

Oberleutnant von Werra. In the course of 47 operational flights von Werra has shot down 8 enemy aircraft and destroyed 5 more on the ground. On one occasion, flying along over England, he turned

a tactically unfavourable situation to his own advantage, and successfully attacked a formation of Hawker Hurricane fighters going in to
land on an airfield. He then made four low-level attacks on the airfield
itself, destroying aircraft and a petrol tanker on the ground and firing
into groups of enemy personnel. This attack is unique in the annals
of fighter aviation in this war. Oberleutnant von Werra had proved
himself to be an outstanding and courageous fighter pilot, worthy of
the high honour bestowed on him.

The Knight's Cross was awarded to von Werra at a time when it was
still a highly coveted honour. He was only the 164th member of the Luftwaffe to receive it. It was claimed that the rules governing the award
of the *Ritterkreuz* were inflexibly strict and foolproof; it was inconceivable
that it could be awarded to any man who did not fully deserve it. In
the case of fighter pilots, it was not normally awarded for less than twenty
confirmed air victories, each of which had to be individually confirmed by
at least one eye-witness, by the finding of wreckage, or in certain
circumstances, by admissions in enemy communiqués or broadcasts.
A pilot might also qualify for the award by a single feat of outstanding
daring and bravery. But this would have to be of so desperate and
hazardous a nature, probably in defiance of orders, that the man's
chances of surviving it were negligible; and if he did survive, he
would probably be court-martialled for disobeying orders. Usually the
facts of any such feat were incontrovertible. Such, at least, was the
theory.

An essential feature of von Werra's alleged exploit was that there
were no eye-witnesses. Harry Gehm, at least, had to rely entirely on
von Werra's word.

Von Werra's story could not be checked, much less confirmed. It is
unlikely that the Germans would send out a reconnaissance plane for
the sake of checking one fighter pilot's success story. There were three
or four fighter airfields in the area in which he claimed to have made
the attack. He was unable to give the exact location of the one he
attacked, and even suggested it might be a new one.

Von Werra was by no means the first, and certainly not the last, of
the Luftwaffe line-shooters.

That Goering himself suspected that many claims were spurious is
suggested by a scene described by Adolf Galland in his book *The First
and the Last*. The A.O.C. German Fighter Command describes how in
one acrimonious argument, the Reich Marshal in a fit of temper " hurled
reproaches and accusations at us, to the effect that . . . Fighter Command
had been a failure as early as the Battle of Britain, and that many pilots

with the highest decorations had faked their reports to get Knight's Crosses over England."

A German pilot of a later crop, Willi Heilmann, who did not begin his flying career until long after the Battle of Britain, refers in his book, *Alarm in Westen*, to " the wild and often vainglorious claims made by some pilots in the early years of the war," and describes the stringent precautions adopted later to " ensure that no claim founded on fantasy would be dished up."

Reference to the fact that R.A.F. records contain no trace of any incident resembling von Werra's claimed exploit is made by J. M. Spaight, C.B., C.B.E., former Principal Secretary of the Air Ministry, in his book *The Battle of Britain* 1940. He states that after von Werra was taken prisoner he was interrogated about his exploits as claimed in his broadcast —" exploits which could not be reconciled with any incidents of the air fighting known to the Royal Air Force."

In 1953 it was disclosed that a complete set of records concerning the award of the *Ritterkreuz* had " come to light ". They had been concealed from the Allies after the war and now formed part of a German military documents centre recently set up in the old Benedictine monastery of Kornelimünster, near Aachen. The German Press at the time rejoiced that it would be now possible publicly to expose bogus claimants to the *Ritterkreuz*. There is, of course, no question that von Werra was awarded the *Ritterkreuz*, but in any such collection of records one might expect to find some papers bearing on the award such, for instance, as the recommendation forwarded by the C.O. of his unit. With this hope, a request was made to the Kornelimünster Documents Centre to make available any such information. There has been no reply.